THE
DISCOVERY
OF THE
HEBRIDES

THE DISCOVERY OF THE

HEBRIDES

VOYAGERS TO THE WESTERN ISLES 1745-1883

ELIZABETH BRAY

COLLINS
LONDON AND GLASGOW

AUTHOR'S ACKNOWLEDGEMENTS

My thanks are due to my shipmates on *Fingal* who shared my voyages over many a summer in the Hebrides; to the kindly peoples of the Isles who made us welcome wherever we dropped anchor; and to the librarians who in the winter months patiently supplied me with books, especially Miss Bannister of Helensburgh Library.

I would also like to thank the following for granting me permission to quote passages from the cited works. Full details are given in the References and Bibliography on pp. 262-5. Dr J.L. Campbell, for the extracts from *Hebridean Folksongs* (ed. J.L. Campbell and F. Collinson; Oxford University Press); the Trustees of the Late Alexander Carmichael, for the extracts from his *Carmina Gadelica* (Scottish Academic Press); the Clyde Cruising Club, for the extract from their *Sailing Directions*; Donald A. Fergusson, for the extracts from his *From the Farthest Hebrides* (Macmillan of Canada); Valda Grieve, for the extracts from Hugh MacDiarmid's *Complete Poems 1920–1976* (ed. M. Grieve and W.R. Aitken; Martin Brian & O'Keeffe); the Controller of Her Majesty's Stationery Office and the Hydrographer of the Navy for the extract from the *West Coast of Scotland Pilot* (HMSO); the W.L. Lorimer Memorial Trust Fund, trustees for the late George Hay (Deòrsa Caimbeul Hay) for the extract from his translation of 'Donald Gorm's Lullaby'; Margaret Fay Shaw, for the extracts from her *Folksongs and Folklore of South Uist* (Oxford University Press).

First published 1986

© 1986 Elizabeth Bray

ISBN 0 00 435661 6

Designed by John Laing
Maps by Gordon Barr and John Laing
Typeset by Bookmag, Inverness
Photographic reproduction by Arneg, Glasgow
Printed in Great Britain by Collins, Glasgow

Frontispiece: Fingal's Cave, Staffa. Engraving after William Turner.
Endpapers: The Western Isles of Scotland, From Joan Blaeu's *Atlas Scotia* (1662 edition).

Contents

PREFACE

THE HEBRIDES: remote and beautiful – the Isles (according to the ancients) on the Edge of the World. It was sailing that brought me to these isles and these seas. These are challenging waters: tide race, winding kyles, hidden skerry, pinnacle rock. Here you must navigate in poor weather, make landfall by good chart-work, beat into an anchorage between breaking seas that mark off-lying rocks. At least in retrospect there is the thrill of danger: the gybe in the fierce squalls that scream down from the high peaked Cuillins of Skye; the rocks in Iona sound which loomed threateningly and unexpectedly when a sudden sea mist had closed in; the despair of making headway as we pitched about in the Minches, with the white combs of breakers streaming out in spindrift; the urgency of dragging anchor in a rock-girt bay, with a Force 9 gale in the black heart of the night.

There is also the glory of blue skies and white sails; the sunlight scattered and glancing from wavelets; the croon of flocks of shearwater; the friendly visitations of porpoise or whale. Where else can you sail past such majestic peaks, deep blue against a paler sky, and see deer roam the hills which purple with heather in the late summer? There is in the Hebrides an austere and remote beauty – rock and mountain, crag, corrie and sheep-bitten turf, lonely isles and wind-swept braes, the isolation of great waters and tremendous skies.

Where better to drop anchor than in a snug pool between bird-haunted crags, or alongside a sturdy little fishing vessel moored close by a castle, or safe within the encircling bay with white shell-sand beach backed with flower-fragrant machair? The tern cries and from some distant skerry comes the unearthly music of the seal. The skirl of pipes and dancing feet and the ancient modes of Hebridean song steal invitingly across starlit waters, for in the village they are gathering for a ceilidh.

The Highlands and Islands are one of the last great wilderness areas of Britain. Ruled until the mid-thirteenth century by Norse kings, inhabited by Gaelic speakers, they were never fully incorporated within the Kingdom of Scotland. Though the Stuart monarchs eventually destroyed the power base of the Lords of the Isles, the anachronistic clan society of the Hebrides survived almost intact well into the eighteenth century. Within Scotland, religious uncertainties, abortive conspiracies, economic backwardness and political ineptitude all delayed the integration of the Hebrides.

Thus it was with astonishment that, in 1745, King George II and his counsellors learned that the son and heir to the Stuart pretender to the throne had landed in the remote, unchartered Hebrides.

The isolation of the Hebrides was shattered. This book is the story of the resulting exploration, and exploitation, of the Isles. For English speakers – both the English and indeed the Lowland Scots – the Hebrides were an eighteenth-century discovery, and their exploration continued well into the nineteenth. For the peoples of the Isles, the Gaelic-speaking communities, those centuries were to be a period of traumatic adjustment.

The records of the voyages of these early explorers still lie on the shelves of our great libraries: musty leatherbound volumes that are in fact an intriguing account of the meeting of two worlds. Open the pages, and you can read of manhunts for Bonnie Prince Charlie and of the charting of the seas, essential if the Hanoverian government were to control the seditious Scots. You may join in the early scientific expeditions of Sir Joseph Banks, who revealed the wonders of Fingal's Cave, and his contemporary, Thomas Pennant, naturalist and travel writer. You may follow in the wake of the great Dr Samuel Johnson himself, who, with his faithful biographer, James Boswell, was nearly drowned off Ardnamurchan. The books that they wrote describing their voyages were to tempt many more to explore the Western Isles: romantics and adventurers, artists and poets, scientists and evangelists, sportsmen and yachtsmen.

It is the tale of this period – of discovery and yet continuing ignorance of the deep undercurrents of Gaelic life – that I tell in this book. I have choosen to tell it through contemporary witnesses, through the record of those voyagers and the poems of Gaelic song makers. I have used their own words because these have an interest and immediacy peculiar to first-hand records. It is for this reason that I have retained each author's quirks of spelling and punctuation.

I first became fascinated by this tale of discovery because it was a record of sea voyages through the ancient seaways of the clans. The

accounts of these voyages stirred my imagination, for these were
seas and lochs and kyles I know from my own voyages, but on ships
the like of which I will never sail. But as I read on – and as I grew to
love the Hebrides – I also found in the story insights into the past –
and the present – of the island communities.

The islands of
Rhum and Eigg.
Aquatint by John
Schekty (1848).

9

1

Antient Customs: The Hebrides Before The '45

Martin Martin

STANDING IN THE GREAT STONE CIRCLE at Callanish, under the windswept skies of the Isle of Lewis, you are aware of a shadowy past. Four thousand years ago the megalith builders raised these silent sentinels. Their priests must have approached, through a long avenue of monolithic standing stones, the central cairn. What rites and sacrifices they celebrated we do not know. Was this a celestial calendar? The north-south axis of the avenue (experts tell us) would have been perfectly aligned with the rising point of Capella in 1800 BC. Other standing stones mark astronomical alignments: to the west, the setting point of the equinoctial sun; eastwards, the rising point of Altair in 1800 BC; southwards, the meridian of the sun.

When Callanish was raised, man was a relative newcomer to the Hebrides. Only as the last of the ice ages had receded had stone-age men penetrated thus far north. They were to be followed by the workers in bronze and then iron, and within historic times the Gaelic-speaking Celts, talented metal workers. At about the time of the Roman empire, the Celts – Galatians, Gauls, Gaels – were moving westward along the northern fringes of the empire. They were tall handsome tribesmen, blue or grey eyed, many with red hair, a cultured people. They spread from Gaul (France) across to the British Isles, then were driven by the Anglo-Saxon invaders into mountain fastnesses of Wales, and the Cornish peninsula, and across the seas to Ireland. From there one tribe, the Scots, took to their coracles and sailed for the Western Isles and the western coast of what is now called Scotland, but was then known as Albany or (by the Romans) Caledonia. By then the Roman empire was already on the point of collapsing – its hold on central Scotland had been tenuous enough. The Scots possessed the land, absorbing the Picts (another Celtic race), and gave their name and language to the country.

Among the late migrants from Ireland was St Columba (521-597). Princely born, a leader of men, scholar and saint, preacher and pastor, he left an abiding mark on the spirit and culture of the Gaelic-speaking Islanders. He built his abbey on Iona, sacred and secure. From here his monks could sail north, south, east and west, to bring about the conversion of the Isles to Christianity. His success owed much to his tough-mindedness, his great courage, his seamanship and practicality, and also to the affection he inspired through his tenderness and gaiety.

Barely a century later the monks lay massacred on the white sands of Iona's beaches. Ruthless warriors from Norway had sailed their dragon-prowed longships west over the sea by way of the Orkneys and Cape Wrath. These Vikings came to fight and to plunder, to extract homage, to capture women and slaves. An unquiet pagan people, a contemporary chronicler called them.

For six centuries Norse kings were overlords of the Hebrides. Each summer piratical crews arrived to extract tribute and homage, and in the autumn sailed for home. Although small groups settled, they assimilated rather than changed the Islanders' language, culture and religious practices. Today the Norse influence only survives in certain place names. Viking rule was not unchallenged. On mainland Scotland the nation was gradually welded together to fight the raiders. The Islanders grew restive, and began to build ships to outsail their conquerors. In 1156 a local chieftain, Somerled – of mixed Celtic and Norse extraction – won a notable sea battle against Godred, the Norse King of Man. They divided the Hebrides between them, and Somerled's descendants became the Lords of the Isles. Yet the overrule of Norse kings continued. Eventually in 1263 the aging King Haakon of Norway made a fatal last expedition, and was defeated at Largs more by the weather and ill health than the forces of the Scottish king, Alexander III.

Nominally, the Hebrides came under the rule of the Scottish crown, but as a semi-independent territory. Under Viking rule the cultural divide between the Gaelic speakers of the western seaboard and the Lowlanders had widened. The Scottish court now spoke Gaelic seldom. The new tongue was Scots, an Anglo-Saxon dialect akin to English, derived from the invaders – Angles and Saxons –

A Norse
chesspiece
from Lewis.

who had occupied much of eastern and lowland Scotland (as well as most of England), while the Norse had been ruling the Isles. Norman blood now ran in the veins of Scotland's royal house, her peers and her prelates, for since 1066 Anglo-Norman adventurers from south of the border had insinuated themselves into positions of authority. Powerful noblemen built up a medieval feudal society in which the clan was an anachronism. Prelates headed a church in Scotland which followed the Roman calendar and rites, while the Celtic church of St Columba stemmed from traditions that had survived on the fringes of Europe during the dark ages when barbarians had occupied Rome.

For the next few centuries the ill-fated House of Stuart held only intermittent sway over the 'wild heilandmen'. The power of the Lords of the Isles remained largely unbroken until 1493, when James IV succeeded in abolishing the Lordship. The long minorities of the Stuart kings led to feuds and political ineptitude. The geographical, cultural and linguistic isolation of the Hebrides and the economic backwardness of Scotland delayed integration. The Isles were bypassed by the Renaissance, and the Reformation penetrated only slowly and incompletely. In 1604 the Union of the Crowns under James VI of Scotland and I of England yet further distanced the Hebrides from the centres of power and prosperity, as Edinburgh was superseded by London.

The period that followed the Union of the Crowns was for Scotland a time of conspiracies and religious rivalries, civil wars and the rise of the new mercantile classes. The Hebrides gained little from the gradually improving economy. Remote and backward, they attracted little attention, except when local chiefs sided with losing factions in mainland politics. In the Civil War, for example, they suffered under the iron-fisted rule of Cromwell's navy. In peace no one visited them, no one wrote about them. The *Mariners' Mirror* (the standard seventeenth-century 'rutter' or route-finder for seamen) warns briefly of these 'dangerous islands', urging sailors to sail well clear of these rock-bound coasts and to avoid their barbarous inhabitants.

Foreigners, sailing thro the Western Isles, have been tempted, from the sight of so many wild Hills, that seem to be cover'd all over with Heath, and fac'd with high Rocks, to imagin the Inhabitants, as well as the Places of their Residence, are barbarous; and to this opinion, their Habit [the kilted plaid], as well as

12

their Language [Gaelic], have contributed. The like is suppos'd by many that live in the South of Scotland, who know no more of the Western Isles than the Natives of Italy. . .[1]

Thus wrote Martin Martin, a native of the Isle of Skye, in his *Description of the Western Isles of Scotland* (1703). His was the first book on the Hebrides ever to appear in print. What is more, it was an insider's view of the Hebrides, based on a series of voyages the author had made in the Islands in the 1680s and 1690s. Nearly a century would elapse before other travellers would start exploring these isles.

Some seventy years after Martin's *Description* appeared, Dr Samuel Johnson wrote in his *Journey to the Western Isles* (1775) this scathing dismissal of Martin:

Martin was not a man illiterate: he was an inhabitant of Sky, and. . .without great difficulty might have visited the places he undertakes to describe; yet with all his opportunities, he often suffered himself to be deceived. He lived in the last century, when the chiefs of the clans had lost little of their original influence. The mountains were yet unpenetrated, no inlet was opened to foreign novelties, and the feudal institutions operated upon life with their full force. He might therefore have displayed a series of subordination and a form of government, which, in more luminous and improved regions, have long been forgotten, and have delighted his readers with many uncouth customs that are now disused, and wild opinions that prevail no longer. But he probably had not the knowledge of the world sufficient to qualify him for judging what would deserve and gain the attention of mankind. . .
What he has neglected cannot now be performed. . .[2]

While Johnson believed his own *Journey to the Western Isles* was vastly superior, it is Martin's curious book that provides the earliest first-hand record of the Hebrides. His *Description of the Western Isles* in its second edition (1716) consists of nearly four hundred packed pages covering every topic which caught the author's attention: an eccentric catalogue of superstitions and antiquities, unnatural births, herbal remedies, instances of second sight, clan customs and folklore, local produce and agriculture, fisheries, bird life and ancient legislation, banshees, sea monsters, mermaids and tall stories. Despite Johnson's criticisms, the impression given to the educated reader in the eighteenth century was of an exotic and archaic society, remote from the coffee houses of literary London and the dignified Georgian mansions and prosperous farms of the landed gentry in southern England.

Little in what Martin wrote prepared early voyagers for the physical impact of the Hebrides: the remoteness of the islands, their craggy peaks and deep sea lochs, the dangerous crossings of stormy seas and peat-bog moors, the wild glens and heathery bens, the ancient castles and crumbling splendours of the chiefs, the crude dwellings of their subjects, and the backwardness of agriculture. Martin Martin was ill equipped to depict the scenery and physical setting of life in the Hebrides, which was to produce such a striking impression on later travellers. The painting of landscapes and seascapes – either in words or on canvas – was an art unknown in the Hebrides and relatively little practised in either England or Scotland at the time when Martin wrote. He was unable to recognize the unique and unusual beauty of his birthplace – an unfashionable beauty which would have had little appeal to his first readers.

Nor did Martin Martin's *Description* give much guidance to the would-be traveller on the conditions he would meet by sea and by land. Martin Martin was more widely travelled in the Hebrides than any of his successors for many generations. He built on a lifetime of experience, and in addition made at least five separate voyages, across the length and breadth of the Hebrides. He must have stayed with local chiefs and the principal tenants, the tacksmen (his own social class). He would have sailed across the dangerous seas by a variety of craft, ridden on horseback across the rough moors, or traversed them on foot. He had, however, pretensions as a man of science, and a contributor to learned journals. So he effaces himself. He withdraws the narrative thread – the story of his voyages and travels, his hosts and his personal experiences – leaving his observations strewn, like unthreaded beads, across his pages. With no coherent development, no line of argument or ordering of subject matter, his offering is whimsically disjointed.

Naïve, garrulous, disorganized, credulous, Martin is nevertheless an engaging author. Despite its many deficiencies, Martin's *Description of the Western Islands of Scotland* gives us many vivid insights into how people really lived in his native isles. For Martin Martin had an advantage over almost every subsequent explorer: he was an islander, a Hebridean. Gaelic was his mother tongue. As he explains, modestly using the third person,

14

Reconstruction of Martin Martin's probable voyages in the Hebrides. He also visited St Kilda, Orkney and Shetland, and had therefore travelled more widely in the Hebrides than most of the other voyagers featured in this book.

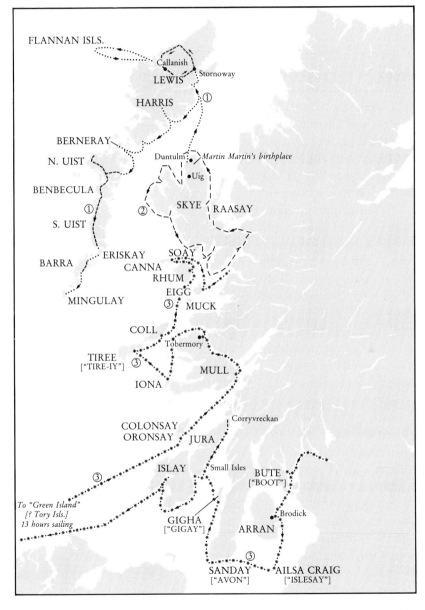

1 Outer Hebrides
Sea ·············
Land ----------

2
Circumnavigation
of Skye -- -- --

3 Clyde-Skye via
Inner Hebrides
Sea ✳·✳·✳·✳·✳
Land ----------

FLANNAN ISLS.

Callanish
LEWIS · Stornoway

HARRIS ①

BERNERAY

N. UIST

Duntulm ·› *Martin Martin's birthplace*

·Uig

BENBECULA

① ② SKYE RAASAY

S. UIST

ERISKAY SOAY

BARRA CANNA
RHUM

MINGULAY EIGG
③ MUCK

COLL

Tobermory

TIREE
["TIRE-IY"] ③ MULL

IONA

COLONSAY
ORONSAY JURA

Corryvreckan

ISLAY Small Isles BUTE
["BOOT"]

③

To "Green Island"
[? Tory Isls.]
13 hours sailing

GIGHA
["GIGAY"] ARRAN · Brodick

③
SANDAY ·✳·✳ AILSA CRAIG
["AVON"] ["ISLESAY"]

He himself was born in one of the most spacious and fertile Isles in the West of Scotland [Skye]; and besides his liberal Education at the University [of Edinburgh], had the advantage of seeing foreign places, and the honour of conversing with some of the Royal Society, who rais'd his natural curiosity to survey the Isles of Scotland more exactly than any other; in prosecution of which Design he has already brought along with him several curious productions of Nature, both rare and beautiful.[3]

Martin, writing towards the end of the seventeenth century, knew, as his successors could never know, a clan society still close to its ancestral roots. He had served under chieftains who led their followers into battle, or captained the Island galleys across the narrow kyles to raid a neighbouring clan for cattle. He had hunted the stag with his youthful chief on the high crags of Trotternish and in the shadow of the Cuillins. He had feasted in castles at the table of both Macdonald and MacLeod chiefs, listening as the whisky circulated to the bards who celebrated clan loyalty and linked the living to the heroic past of the legendary Fingal.

Yet Martin Martin was also a member of a new generation of chiefs and gentlemen whose fathers had been forced by the Statutes of Iona (1609) to educate them in the English-speaking Lowlands. These same Statutes had shorn the chiefs of many of their powers. While Martin was a youth, the Hebrides had emerged shaken from the repressive regime of Cromwell. Ambitious young men like Martin Martin left the Hebrides and sought to make their way in the world. Many (to quote Martin) 'travelled young into foreign Countries' and returned home 'loaded with superficial Knowledge; as the bare Names of famous Libraries, stately Edifices, fine Statues, curious Paintings, late Fashions, new Dishes, new Tunes, new Dances, painted Beauties, and the like'. Martin himself seems to have used his time more productively. After studying at Edinburgh University, he became 'governor' (tutor) first to the heir to the Macdonalds of Skye, and then to the future chief of the MacLeods. Under the influence of Sir Robert Sibbald, a noted scientist, he investigated medical lore and the use of herbs in the Islands. Later he sought patronage in London, and seems to have been taken up by eminent scientists, including the President of the Royal Society, as something of a curiosity. He eventually studied medicine in the University of Leyden, in the Netherlands. Uniquely, Martin Martin interested himself too in his native isles, made a number of voyages to explore them, and, at the behest of his scientific patrons, seems to have read papers to learned gatherings.

His audience seem to have pressed him to publish an account of his voyages. Martin hesitated briefly. He was aware that his English – not his mother tongue – still showed some gaucheries. He confessed his incapability of giving 'the politest turns of phrase' to what he calls his 'Stile'. Yet he is convinced that 'the intelligent and philosophick part of Mankind would value the Truth of such Accounts'. Successive writers about the Hebrides have ransacked his treasure trove of information.

Of particular interest, both to eighteenth-century readers like Dr Johnson and to ourselves, is a long section he devoted to the 'Antient and Modern Customs of the Inhabitants of the Western Islands of Scotland'. Here he describes the ancient clan system, and in particular the traditional role of the chief, who was hereditary head of his clan. To him every clansman owed loyal and unquestioning service. His word was law, his officers were judge and jury in every case, and could pronounce sentence, including the death sentence. Such power was maintained by the chief's own prowess and his ability to protect his followers, to which proof had to be given on his accession:

> Every Heir, or young Chieftain of a Tribe, was oblig'd in Honour to give a publick Specimen of his Valour, before he was declar'd Governor and Leader of his People, who obey'd and follow'd him upon all Occasions.
>
> This Chieftain was usually attended by a Retinue of young Men of Quality, who had not beforehand given any Proof of their Valour, and were ambitious of such an Opportunity to signalize themselves.
>
> It was usual for the Captain to lead them, to make a desperate Incursion upon some Neighbour or other that they were in Feud with; and they were oblig'd to bring by open force the Cattel they found in the Lands they attack'd, or die in the Attempt.[4]

As the next-door clan's chief reciprocated the raid it was 'not reput'd Robbery'. This custom Martin believed to be almost extinct. But the tradition was moribund rather than dead.

On the return of the victorious chieftain, friends and followers and clansmen swore fealty to him. Then the Chief Druid (or Orator)

pronounc'd a Rhetorical Panegyrick, setting forth the antient

A weaver's cottage on Islay. Engraving after Moses Griffith, from Pennant's *Voyage to the Hebrides, 1772* (1773).

Pedigree, Valour, and Liberality of the Family, as Incentives to the young Chieftain, and fit for his imitation.[5]

The chieftain's retinue had traditionally included certain officers, often hereditary. Martin cites the case of the household of Sir Donald Macdonald of Sleat (his former pupil). These officers included a standard bearer, quartermaster, and a 'constant Centinel on the top of their Houses call'd Gockmin, or, in English Tongue, Cockman, who was oblig'd to watch Day and Night'. There was also a 'bold Armour-Bearer. . .call'd Galloglach', who was given double rations. There were two stewards or 'marischalls', who were well versed in etiquette. Among the chieftain's 'numerous retinue' were also

> a competent number of young Gentlemen call'd Luchktaeh, or guard de Corps, who always attended the Chieftain at Home and Abroad. They were well train'd in managing the Sword and Target [the round shield of the Celts], in Wrestling, Swimming, Jumping, Dancing, Shooting with bows and Arrows, and were stout Seamen. . .[6]

The fealty of the chief's retinue was all important. When, in 1745, the young Stuart Prince won over some of the island chiefs, he won for himself the loyalty of the whole clan, including an officer class well versed in the arts of war, and their followers who had sworn allegiance to the death. They would fight for his cause long after it was lost. They would shelter his escape at the cost of their lives and liberty.

When the troops went in to battle, the Chief Druid would 'harangue' the army. He

> address'd them all. . .putting them in mind of what great things were perform'd by the Valour of their Ancestors, and rais'd their Hopes with the noble Rewards of Honour and Victory, and dispell'd their Fears. . .After this Harangue, the Army gave a general Shout, and then charg'd the Enemy stoutly.[7]

These charging tartan-clad troops, with their savage war cries, were to lead initially to rapid victories for Prince Charles. As Martin says, these troops were hardy, loyal, used to exploits calling for great physical endurance. The kilt they wore was ideal for guerrilla campaigns; Martin describes the length of tartan plaid, home woven from homespun wool, wrapped around the body, and belted at the waist so that it fell in pleats to the knee, with the free ends secured on the shoulder with a brooch, thus forming a cloak too. At night it could be used as a blanket (it was some ten yards in length); as travel wear it was, Martin Martin reports, 'found much easier and lighter than Breeches, or Trowis [trousers]'.

But, says Martin, 'The Lion is not so fierce as he is paint'd. . .The Inhabitants have Humanity, and use Strangers hospitably and kindly.' That too Prince Charles would discover, as would the many voyagers who explored the Hebrides peaceably. The hospitality of the Highlanders and Islanders is legendary.

Martin Martin was at pains to commend the many other good qualities of his fellow countrymen:

> They are generally a very sagacious People, quick of Apprehension [the ability to grasp ideas], and even the Vulgar exceed all those of their Rank, and Education, I ever yet saw in any other Country. They have a Genius for Musick and Mechanicks. . .Several of both Sexes have a quick Vein of Poesy, and in their Language (which is very Emphatick) they compose Rhyme and Verse both which powerfully affect the Fancy. . .with as great a Force as that of any ancient or modern Poet. . .They have very retentive Memories, they see things at a great distance.
>
> The unhappiness of their Education, and their want of Converse with foreign Nations, deprives them of the opportunity to cultivate and beautify their Genius, which seems to have been form'd for great Attainments. . .On the other hand. . .they are

Rent-day in the Wilderness. Landseer's painting depicts the scene as the rents are collected on behalf of the Mackenzie chief exiled after the '15.

to this day happily ignorant of many of the Vices that are practis'd in the learned and polite World: I could mention several, for which they have not as yet got a Name, nor so much as a Notion of them.[8]

Along with this innocence went pagan superstitions that Martin – man of science, educated, Protestant – found antiquated but disturbing, for he was unable to dismiss all the strange but deeply held beliefs of his forefathers. He stood in the great stone circle at Callanish, and, inquiring of the local inhabitants, learned that it had been used by the druids. It was, they believed, a Teampull na Greine (a temple of the sun). He reported persisting evidence of sun worship: the Beltane feast, and the sun-wise magical circle used by seamen when setting out on a voyage and by midwives when the child sets forth in life. He may describe with patronizing humour the lingering worship of pre-Christian gods, particularly the sea god, Shony, to whom annual sacrifices had been made in Lewis within living memory, but he is respectful about strange apparitions like the mischief-making 'Browny', which was well known in certain glens: this spirit, Martin tells us, 'always appears in the shape of a Tall Man'. He clearly believed in second sight – the power to foresee future events and prognosticate by means of dreams and the casting of omens. He instances many examples of men, women and

20

even little children foretelling events, usually dire, which indeed came to pass. Even today there are many in the Highlands and Islands who are believed to have the 'gift'.

No second sight protected the Isles from the future that awaited them. As the clan system fell into disrepair, chiefs and educated men like Martin drifted southwards, and neglect of the needs of the Islanders grew greater with each generation.

Martin dedicated both editions of his *Description of the Western Islands* in fulsome terms to Prince George of Denmark, consort to Queen Anne. Neither the Queen nor her Hanoverian successors visited or interested themselves in the distant, irrelevant Hebrides. Martin's pleas for understanding, and for economic and legislative support for the impoverished islands, fell on deaf ears.

Martin Martin's *Description* closes with strongly worded arguments for support for the fishing industry, which could have brought some prosperity to the Isles. Though powerful and far-sighted, his pleading went unheeded. There was no 'concurrence' from the government, no 'encouragement' of those in power. In vain he argued:

> If the Dutch in their Publick Edicts call their Fishery a Golden Mine, and at the same time affirm that it yields them more Profit than the Indies do to Spain; we have very great Reason to begin to work upon those rich Mines, not only of the Isles, but on all our Coast in general. We have Multitudes of Hands to be employ'd at a very easy Rate; we have a healthful Climate, and our Fish, especially the Herrings, come to our coast in April and May, and into the Bays in prodigious Shoals in July and August. . .[and] I have known the Herring-Fishing to continue in some Bays from September till the end of January.[9]

This plentitude, followed by the great number of foreign ships attracted by the great shoals,

> ought to excite the People of Scotland to a speedy Improvement of that profitable Trade, which they may carry on with more Ease and Profit in their own Seas, than any Foreigners whatever.[10]

The sombre truth was that the early eighteenth century was a lean period for Scotland. There were a series of poor harvests, and famine stalked the land. The controversial Union of Parliaments in 1707 with England did little to improve weak Scotland's economic

John Campbell, 2nd Duke of Argyll and Greenwich (1678-1743), author of the Act of Union of 1707 and commander of the Hanoverian troops in 1715. Portrait by William Aikman.

plight, and the removal from Scotland of political and economic decision-making drained Scotland of enterprise.

An enlarged second edition of Martin Martin's *Description* had been rushed out in 1716. January 1716 had seen the failure of the '15 and the decisive rout of the Old Pretender. The abortive attempt of James III (as he called himself) to recover the throne for the Stuart dynasty had ended in ignominy. Of this, Martin (a staunch Hanoverian) makes no mention. It had taken place entirely on the mainland, but many clansmen had rallied to the cause, and Martin was aware of Jacobite sympathies in the Hebrides.

It was not perhaps an auspicious date for pleading for economic support for the Hebrides. By 1716, all that was needed, London argued, was a firm hand. General Wade was dispatched north to plant fortresses connected with all-weather roads throughout the Highlands. If there was any recurrence of Jacobitism, government troops could act swiftly and decisively to quell a rising. The House of Hanover could rest secure. Any concern about the economic well-being of this remote corner of the kingdom was unnecessary. The Hebrides were forgotten for a generation.

Martin Martin died in obscurity about the time that the morose and unsuccessful Pretender, James Edward Stuart, fathered a child he christened Charles Edward – the Bonnie Prince Charlie of history.

2
OVER THE SEA TO SKYE

Bonnie Prince Charlie

O N THE EVENING OF 21 JULY 1745, Captain Durbé of *Le du Teillay*, a light frigate with eighteen guns and a crew of 67, ordered soundings to be made. It was a clear, calm evening, but far to the north, discernible in the long twilight, was a low bank of cloud which rested on the horizon. To the Captain's experienced eye, it suggested land. The line was heaved overboard, and fathom after fathom paid out. At 108 fathoms – over 600 feet – they struck bottom.

Close watch was kept through the short northern night. When day dawned the island of Berneray was just visible. As they sailed slowly, under the lightest of breezes, the island gradually took shape. By late afternoon they were sailing past the towering cliffs of this, the most southerly of the long chain of islands known as the Outer Hebrides, or Long Island. Barra Head, the 600-foot high bastion-like cliffs on Berneray, the most southerly of the Barra group of isles, is still a forsaken spot.

Throughout the late afternoon and the short night, the little French vessel coasted along. She had slipped through the British naval cordon in the Channel. She had circumnavigated Ireland. Now, as she came under the lee of Berneray, out of the huge Atlantic swell, a young prince came up on deck. This was his first sight of the kingdom he had come to claim for his father: James III of England and Wales, and the eighth Stuart monarch of that name to lay claim to the Scottish crown.

As the isles were silhouetted against the setting sun, the young man must have wondered at their wild appearance. Huge breakers crashed against the fortress cliffs of the western headlands. On the east, beaches of pure white sand were backed by dunes. Peat smoke drifted up from the low thatched 'black houses' of the tiny villages. Women worked the patchwork run-rig in-field, the communally held arable land, on which allotments were allocated each spring by lot. Herd boys could be seen on the hills, tending flocks of thin sheep and sturdy little black kine. Groups of men launched their primitive boats across the surf of the exposed beaches. One such vessel offered to pilot *Le du Teillay* to Castle Bay, Barra. The men were MacNeill clansmen.

What were the islands called? asked the Prince. Mingulay, Pabbay, Sandray, Vatersay, they said: musical names older than either English or French, that come not from the Gaelic of the natives, but the Norse of their erstwhile Viking rulers.

Expertly piloted, *Le du Teillay* threaded her way between the reefs that bar the Sound of Vatersay to drop anchor on 22 July in the lee of Kiessimul Castle, the island home of MacNeill of Barra, which dominates the safe haven of Castle Bay. MacNeill, a known Jacobite, was away. So again the French captain put to sea. Guided by a canny MacNeill fisherman, they sailed up the east coast of Barra – that graveyard of ships, renowned for its off-lying rocks. They put into the spacious anchorage of An-t-Acairseid Mhór, which lies between Barra and the islets of Gighay, Fuday and Hellisay. Here the green sea runs shallow over white sands. Seals sport below the surface, playing hide-and-seek between the seaweed patches streaming out like purple embroidery. The sea, so green over the shallows, deepens through every shade of amethyst and sapphire, turquoise and emerald, to an ultramarine of exquisite purity on the horizon.

This was, however, no time for contemplation. A white sail had been spotted afar off. An English man-o'-war? Hurriedly, the Prince and his party – half a dozen retainers – disembarked on the white curving strand of Eriskay. Bonnie Prince Charlie had set foot on Scottish soil – and one of the most foolhardy, ill-fated and romantic adventures in British history had begun.

The '45 – the Jacobite uprising – was for the Hebrides a cataclysmic event. Until this date, the life of the Islanders had been encapsulated within the clan system, with its own language, culture, economy and traditions, but now they were about to make history.

Soon the clans were on the move. Marching swiftly along the very roads constructed by General Wade, speaking their barbaric language, led by the skirl of pipes, they poured down from the glens of Scotland. Edinburgh was captured almost without resistance. The Highlanders' mountain-warfare tactics defeated the loyalist forces at Prestonpans. Carlisle fell before the tartan army. Soon they were at Derby.

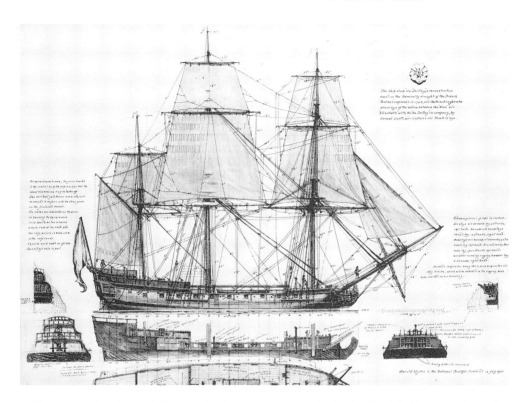

Le du Teillay, the ship on which Bonnie Prince Charlie was carried to Scotland from France in 1745.

But while the Bonnie Prince had captivated the Gaels, he had little appeal for the English. The rising failed, and the defeated Pretender was forced ever further north, until his forces were broken on Culloden field. It was April 1746.

Whither could the defeated Prince flee? Only the Hebrides seemed to offer some refuge from 'Butcher' Cumberland's forces. Only among the loyal islanders could the fugitive hope for concealment. With a price of £30,000 on his head – worth over a million today – the hunted man would need luck and good friends if he was to be rescued by one of the half dozen small French vessels that were occasionally known to break the British naval cordon and swoop down on the Isles. His priority was to make contact with friends, and, if possible, escape from mainland Scotland.

Although the escape of the Prince has been romanticized, the tale is still a moving account of the courage, fidelity and endurance of the clansmen who pinned so many hopes on the young heir to the House of Stuart. One such was 68-year-old Donald MacLeod, a Gaelic speaker famed throughout the Hebrides as a skilful pilot.

What follows is his own account, dictated (through an interpreter) in 1747 to Bishop Robert Forbes, a Jacobite sympathizer who himself had spent some time in prison for his political sympathies.

Donald MacLeod recounted to Robert Forbes how the Prince had sought him out when a fugitive after Culloden. Prince Charles Edward was quite alone when on 20 or 21 April he met the old seaman on the shore of Arisaig. 'You see, Donald,' said the Prince,

> 'I am in distress. I therefore throw myself upon your bosom, and let you do with me what you like. I hear you are an honest man, and fit to be trusted.'

When Donald gave Forbes this part of the narrative, 'he grate [wept] sare, the tears running down his cheeks [noted Forbes] and he said, "Wha deel could not help greeting when speaking on sic a sad subject?" '[11]

The Prince's first request was that Donald carry letters to Sir Alexander MacDonald of Sleat and the Laird of MacLeod, of Dunvegan. What, cried Donald, do you not know these men have already 'played rogue to you'?

The Prince then proposed that Donald should transport him to the Outer Hebrides:

> Donald answered he would do anything in the world for him; he would run any risque. . .For this purpose Donald procured a stout eight oar'd boat, the property of John MacDonald [who] . . .was either killed at the battle of Culloden or butchered next day in cold blood (which was the fate of many), for he had never been heard of since that time. Donald took care to buy a pot for boyling pottage or the like when they should happen to come to land, and a poor firlot of meal [small measure of oatmeal] was all the provision he could make out to take with them.
>
> April 26th. They go on board in the twilight of the evening in Lochnannua [Loch nan Uamh, Arisaig], at Boradale, being the very spot where the Prince landed at first on the continent . . .There were in the boat the Prince, Captain O'Sullivan, Captain O'Neil, Allan MacDonald. . .and a clergyman of the Church of Rome; and Donald MacLeod for pilot managing the helm, and betwixt whose feet the Prince took his seat.[12]

With fatherly pride, Donald told Forbes how one of the eight oarsmen was his own son, Murdoch MacLeod, then a lad of only 15, and, said his father,

> a scholar in the Grammar School of Inverness. When he heard of

the appearance of a battle, having got himself provided in a claymore, durk [dirk], and pistol, he ran off from the school, and took his chance in the field of Culloden battle. After the defeat he found means to trace out the road the Prince had taken, and followed him from place to place; 'and this was the way,' said Donald, 'that I met wi' my poor boy.'

. . .The Prince and his small retinue were thinking of going on board the eight oar'd boat, Donald MacLeod begged the Prince not to set out that night, for that it would certainly be a storm, and he could not think of his exposing himself. The Prince asked how Donald came to think it would be a storm. 'Why, sir,' said Donald, 'I see it coming already.' However, the Prince, anxious to be out of the continent [mainland] where parties were then dispersed in search of him, was positive to set out directly without loss of time. They had not rowed far from shore till a most violent tempest arose, greater than any Donald MacLeod had ever been trysted with before, though all his lifetime a seafaring man, upon the coast of Scotland. To all this they had the additional distress of thunder and lightening and a heavy down-pour of rain, which continued all the time they were at sea.

When the Prince saw the storm increasing still more and more he wanted much to be at land again, and desired Donald to steer directly for the rock, which runs no less than three miles along one side of the loch. 'For,' said the Prince, 'I had rather face canons and muskets than be in such a storm as this.'

But Donald would not hear of that proposal at all, assuring the Prince that it was impossible for them to return to land again because the squall was against them, and that if they should steer for the rock the boat would undoubtedly stave to pieces and all of them behoved to be drowned, for there was no possibility of saving any one life amongst them upon such a dangerous rock, where the sea was dashing with the utmost violence. The Prince then asked Donald what he had in mind to do. 'Why,' replied Donald, 'since we are here we have nothing for it, but, under God, to set out to sea directly. Is it not as good for us to be drown'd in clean water as to be dashed in pieces upon a rock and be drown'd too?'

After this all was hush and silence; not one word more amongst them, expecting every moment to be overwhelmed with the violence of the waves, and sink to the bottom. To make the case still worse they had neither pump nor compass nor lantern with them, and the night turned so pitch dark that they knew not where they were for the most of the course. This made them

The arrival and escape of Prince Charles Edward Stuart, 1745-46.

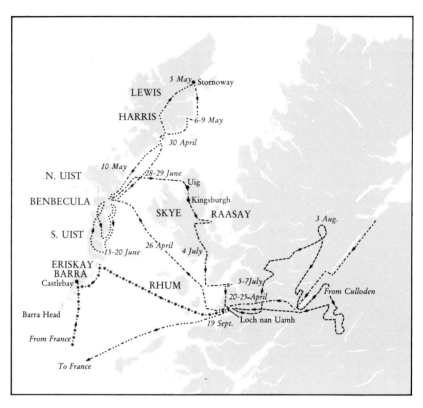

··*·*·*   The arrival of the Prince, 1745.

The escape of the Prince, 1746.

------- *20 April- 27 April* *

·········· *29 April- 13 May*

············· *13 May- 27 June*

------- *28 June- 10 July*
         (with Flora MacDonald)*

--------- overland
         (*"Skulking in the heather"*)

········· *19 Sept.*, final escape

*main events in Chapter 2

afraid of being tossed upon some coast (such as the Isle of Skye) where the militia were in arms to prevent the Prince's escape. 'But,' to use Donald's words, 'as God would have it, by peep of day we discovered ourselves to be on the coast of the Long Isle, and we made directly to the nearest land, which was Rushness in the Island Benbecula. With great difficulty we got on shore, and saved the boat, hawling her up to dry land, in the morning of April 27th.'

At this point, notes the Bishop, he

asked how long the course might be that they made in the violent storm. Donald declared that they had run at least thirty two leagues in eight hours. About this Malcolm MacDonald made some doubt, alleging the course not to be so long, and they reasoned the matter betwixt them. After some debate Malcolm acknowledged that Donald was in the right.

(Thirty-two leagues – sixty-four miles – is a good approximation, and a remarkable distance for a 25-foot open boat.) Forbes continued,

Let this piece of history be cooly and impartially considered only from April 16th to September 20th [i.e. from the Battle of Culloden until the date of the Prince's escape from Scotland on *L'Herieux*, a French privateer], and I dare venture to say one will not find a parallel for it in any history whatsoever. For a Prince to be skulking five long months exposed to the hardships of hunger and cold, thirst and nakedness, and surrounded on all sides by a numerous army of blood-thirsty men, both by sea and land, eagerly hunting after the price of blood, and yet that they should miss the coveted aim, is an event in life far surpassing the power of words to print. [13]

For two long months the redcoats scoured the Outer Hebrides, but the Prince, attended by two or three friends, eluded them. For much of the time they were piloted by the staunch old Donald MacLeod, but the heroine of the romantic escape from Benbecula is Flora MacDonald.

By late June the net was closing. An attempt to stow away on a ship in Stornoway had failed. The Prince was back on the Uists. General Campbell and his Gaelic-speaking troops had landed at Barra, and were making their way nothwards. The desperate game of hide and seek among the bens and glens, the isles and skerries, was doomed unless the Prince could break through the cordon of

British warships patrolling the Minches, and rendezvous with a
French privateer somewhere, somehow.

> The Almighty only knows, and the Divine dispenser of human
> providence allennarly [alone] knows, what inexpressible perplex-
> ity of mind and anguish of soul and body his royal highness and
> his small retinue laboured under when taking it into their serious
> consideration that they were now encompassed by no less than
> three or four thousand bloody hounds [the redcoats], by sea and
> land, thirsting for the captivity and noble blood of their Prince,
> the apparent heir of Great Britain, France, and Ireland, and that
> none of the many thousands that should be in readiness to relieve
> him at the expense of their lives were then about him, but only
> one O'Sulliven, one O'Neille, and twelve MacDonalds.

Thus wrote Captain Alastair MacDonald. In desperation (Mac-
Donald continues) the Prince's few remaining advisers pitched

> upon the strategem of getting Miss MacDonald. . .At first the
> young woman was surprized, but then when spoke to sincerely
> did condescend to go with his royal highness through the vast
> world if it should contribute in the least to his safety. She goes off
> to Benbecula where the lady Clanranald was desired to have
> suitable cloaths [clothes] for Bettie Burk who was engaged in the
> station of a servant with Flora MacDonald to go with her to the
> Isle of Skye.[14]

It was in the disguise of a serving wench that they hoped to smuggle
out the fugitive Prince.

They took great risks. General Campbell, the feared commander
of the Argylls, had billetted himself on the Clanranald household.
Flora had already spent a night under arrest. Yet somehow the
pretty young woman prevailed on her stepfather, Hugh MacDonald
of Armadale, to provide her with a passport to cross the Minches
with her Irish 'serving maid, Betty Burk, an excellent spinner'.
(Quite what Hugh MacDonald's role in this was we cannot be sure:
he was serving on the government side, but with a marked lack of
effectiveness.)

Despite the dangers, the two women set about providing 'all the
necessaries for getting Mrs Burk cled suitable to her new servile
station'. Garments had to be hastily sewn for the tall young Prince –
under the nose of the government forces stationed in the Clanranald
house. Nevertheless, the clothes were soon ready:

> The Lady Clanranald [Alexander MacDonald recounted to

30

The entry of
Prince Charles
Edward Stuart
into Edinburgh,
1745. Painting by
Thomas Duncan.

Forbes] begged of his royal highness to try on his new female apparel, and after mutually passing some jocose drollery concerning the sute of cloaths, and the lady shedding some tears for the occasion, the said lady dresses up his royal highness in his new habit. It was on purpose provided coarse as it was to be brooked by a gentlewoman's servant. The gown was of caligo, a light coloured quilted pettitcoat, a mantle of dun camlet [a tough waterproof cloth] made after the Irish fashion with a cap to cover his royal highness whole head and face, with a suitable head-dress, shoes, stockings, etc.[15]

Flora MacDonald had vivid and amusing memories of the Prince donning his disguise. Here is her tale, as recorded by Bishop Forbes a year later (he was able to meet Flora on her way to the Tower of London after her capture):

When the Prince put on women's cloaths [she recalled] he proposed carrying a pistol under one of his pettitcoats for making a small defence in case of attack. But Miss [Flora] declared against it, alleging that if any person should happen to search them, the pistol would only serve to make a discovery. To which the Prince replied merrily: 'Indeed, Miss, if we shall happen to meet with any that will go so narrowly to work in searching as what you mean will certainly discover me at any rate.' But Miss would not

31

Prince Charles
Edward Stuart in
1732. Portrait by
Antonio David.

hear of any arms at all, and therefore the Prince was obliged to
content himself with only a short heavy cudgel, with which he
design'd to do his best to knock down any single person that
should attack him.[16]

Thus clad, they made their way to the rocky, heathery shores of
Benbecula, taking cover when four wherries carrying armed redcoats passed within a few hundred yards. About eight in the evening
the coast seemed clear, and the party boarded the tiny open boat in
which they hoped to make their way across the Minches: a four-
oared ketch, with a waterline of only fifteen feet. At the helm was
John MacDonald (a nephew of Captain Alexander MacDonald).
Most of the crew – four oarsmen – were relations. Flora herself was
his cousin. All were Gaelic speakers – even the Prince by now had a
smattering of uncouth Galeic (this is why 'she' was described as an
'Irish' serving wench, to account for 'her' strange accent.) Their one
chance of escape was their insignificance: a boatload of elderly,
Gaelic-speaking fishermen with two female relations, one young
and pretty, the other a gawky servant.

Once out of the lee of the island, calm airs gave way to tempes-
tuous seas. 'Hard gales and squally weather,' was the entry made in
the log book by the captain of the naval sloop, the *Raven*, one of the
many government ships patrolling the Minches nearby. Her orders
were to capture the Prince, dead or alive. She had a crew of 110 men,
a dozen six-pounder guns, and was a massive 270 tons, compared
with the cockleshell boat bobbing about in the heavy seas. Squally
rain fell. Flora, says Bishop Forbes,

> us'd to tell us that in their passage to the Isle of Skye a heavy rain
> fell upon them, which with former fatigues distressed her much.
> To divert her the Prince sung several pretty songs. She fell asleep,
> and to keep her so, the Prince still continued to sing. Happening
> to awake with some little bustle in the boat she found the Prince
> leaning over her with his hands spread about her head. She asked
> what was the matter? The Prince told her that one of the rowers
> being obliged to do somewhat about the sail behoved to step over
> her body (the boat was so small), and lest he should have done her
> hurt either by stumbling or trampling upon her in the dark (for it
> was night) he had been doing his best to preserve his guardian
> from harm.[17]

By midday the next day – after seventeen hours at sea – they were
becalmed and blanketed by a thick sea fog. Uncertain of their course

– they had no compass – they dared not approach the coast of Skye too close. Government troops were on the lookout. The MacLeods, traditional enemies of the MacDonalds, were possessors of the northern parts of Skye, and to fall into their hands would be disaster.

Supposing that they had rounded MacLeod territory, they took shelter under the lee of a peninsula to gain some protection from a wind that had sprung up. Suddenly a group of soldiers, 'about a musket-shot distant', spied them. About fifty armed men rushed out of a guard house, 'crying vehemently to land at their peril'. The fugitives changed course slightly, and did not pull harder on their oars lest they roused suspicion. Prince Charles 'rubbed up their courage not to fear the villains'.

So they rounded the 'tedious point' of Vaternish, leaving Mac-Leod country behind them. They took refuge in a cleft in the rocks to rest the men. They saw a number of men-o'-war not too distant; in the log of one an officer recorded a small unidentified boat near the coast.

In broad daylight the little vessel made her slow progress across the twelve weary miles from the Vaternish peninsula across Loch Snizort. It was windless; so they rowed, while the men-o'-war lay motionless on the glassy sea.

At last the exhausted boatmen drew the ketch up on the beach at Monkstadt, near Flora MacDonald's kinswoman's house. It was Sunday about midday and they had been at sea for nearly three days and three nights. The militia men, who should have been on the lookout, were in church.

The Prince – or rather, the Irish maid, Betty Burk – stepped ashore and hid awkwardly, while Miss Flora MacDonald went boldly up to her kinswoman's house. But Lady Margaret Mac-Donald was not alone: there were government troops billeted on her household, and her husband was a Hanoverian loyalist. The two women made a rapid arrangement for the Irish maid to be taken by Flora MacDonald and MacDonald of Kingsburgh by foot across the neck of the Trotternish peninsular.

So Flora and MacDonald of Kingsburgh set off followed by the strange serving wench, and the ever faithful Neil MacKechan. A strange sight they must have been, for the maid had the greatest difficulty with her hood, and persisted in lifting her skirts when leaping over burns in the most unfeminine fashion.

Flora MacDonald. Portrait by an unknown artist after Allan Ramsay.

33

After a weary tramp, they arrived at Kingsburgh. One day it would be Flora's home (she was destined to marry MacDonald of Kingsburgh's son). It was late at night. Too late, said the mistress of the house (who was not in on the secret) for her to rise to greet her young kinswoman and her strange servant woman. But one of the MacDonald children woke and caught sight of the strange woman. She ran to her mother, and told her in suprise,

'O mother, my father has brought in a very odd, muckle, ill-shaken-up wife as ever I saw! I never saw the like of her, and he has gone into the hall with her.'[18]

At her husband's insistence, the goodwife got up and came down. But she was so taken aback by the 'muckle woman', that she would not come forward. For, as she later explained to Flora (and Flora recounted her words to Bishop Forbes), 'I saw such an odd muckle trallup [trollop, or long lanky person] of a carlin [old woman, witch] making lang wide steps.'

The wife demanded of her husband who the 'lang, odd hussie' was. Worse was to come. The Prince, unshaven after three days at sea, gave her a kiss. This was no woman! 'My dear,' said her husband, 'it is the Prince. You have the honour of him in your house.'

'The Prince,' cried she, 'O Lord, we are a' ruin'd and undone for ever! We will a' be hang'd now!'

'Hout, goodwife,' says the honest stout soul, 'we will die but ance; and if we are hanged for this, I am sure we will die in a good cause.'[19]

So supper was served, and the Prince, still in his maidservant's garb, called for a dram, and (to use the words of Mistress MacDonald), 'the deel a drap did he want in 's weam'.

Many of those who were involved in the escape did suffer severely. The boatmen were beaten senseless, tortured until they confessed, then imprisoned. Flora herself was a prisoner on board one of the warships for many a long month (but was allowed visitors, among whom was Bishop Forbes). She spent time in the Tower of London before her release.

Prince Charles Edward did finally make his escape with the help of a French privateer. Many of those who aided him were captured. Some were beheaded or hanged for their part in the uprising. Many prisoners died in the appalling squalor of the hulks in the Thames, or in prisons. Forbes records their 'deplorable state of misery, their cloaths wearing off them so that many of them had not a single rag to cover their nakedness'.

It is extraordinary the loyalty inspired by the magnetic personality of the handsome young Prince, so full of charm, gaiety, high spirits in the face of adversity, and great personal courage. The long debauchery of his later years cannot totally tarnish his nobility and fortitude. Why did none of the hundreds of Islanders who knew his whereabouts betray him? Here is how Donald MacLeod, the Prince's pilot, answered the question when it was put to him after he was captured by the ruthless General Campbell:

> 'Do you know,' said the General, 'what money was upon that man's head? no less a sum than *thirty thousand pounds sterling* which would have made you and all your children after you happy for ever.'
>
> Donald's answer to this [comments Forbes] is so very good that the beauty of it would be quite spoil'd if I did not give it in his own words, which are these.
>
> 'What then? *thirty thousand pounds!* Though I had gotten't I could not have enjoyed it eight and forty hours. Conscience would have gotten up upon me. That money could not have kept it down. And tho' I could have gotten all England and Scotland for my pains I would not allow a hair of his body to be touch'd if I could help it.'
>
> Here Donald desired me particularly to remark for the honour of General Campbell, and to do him justice, that he spoke these words, 'I will not say you are in the wrong.'[20]

Among those most deeply affected by the stirring events of the '45 was another of Bishop Forbes' informants, Captain Alexander MacDonald (an extract of whose account of the crossing with Flora MacDonald – his cousin – has already been quoted). Pasted inside the back board of one volume of Bishop Forbes' manuscript, the *Lyon In Mourning*, are fragile slivers of wood, 'pieces of that identical eight oar'd boat', in which the Prince escaped from mainland Scotland to Benbecula after Culloden. The hand that brought this relic to the Bishop was that of Alexander MacDonald. It is to this enigmatic man that we now turn.

3

THE BIRLINN OF CLANRANALD

Alasdair MacMaighstir Alasdair

T HE ESCAPE OF THE PRINCE is one of the great romantic stories of history. It also signalled the collapse of a bid for Gaelic autonomy. No one felt this more bitterly than Alexander MacDonald, whose account of the Prince's escape over the sea to Skye has already been quoted. To Alexander MacDonald the person of his 'dear Prince' and the cause of Gaeldom were inseparably connected. For he was a passionate man who fought with unswerving loyalty throughout the Jacobite rebellion as an officer in Clanranald's regiment (his account of the campaign survives), and his writings, both Gaelic and English, are an expression of his fervour and dedication.

For Captain MacDonald was none other than Alasdair Mac-Mhaighstir Alasdair, the great eighteenth-century Gaelic poet: a defiant writer of Jacobite songs, a great nature poet, the author of one of the tenderest love poems, *In praise of Morag*, and above all the writer of the thundering *Birlinn of Clanranald* (Clanranald's galley or warship). This poem, probably the greatest sea poem written in the British Isles, is little known, for it is singularly difficult to translate from the Gaelic the hard, terse language, the clean rhythm of the lines, the controlled excitement of a sea voyage through the cold, clean salt water and violent winds of the Hebrides.

The *Birlinn* is, at first sight, a straightforward description of a voyage from South Uist to Carrickfergus, in Belfast Lough, in Ireland; but it takes on a new meaning when we realize that it is a defiant restatement of Gaeldom, a celebration of the old values of clan and culture, a proclamation of nationhood, and a reassertion of the power of the Gaelic language.

Its author was a turbulent, impulsively reckless man. He was a man of considerable courage: he risked everything for his Prince's cause, fought in the thick of battle from Prestonpans to Culloden, lived dangerously in hiding, and then dared to publish, in the only printed edition of his poems to appear in his lifetime, seditious verses that brought down the wrath of the authorities and resulted in the burning of almost all the copies. In some ways he was a very physical, sensual man, whose youthful indiscretion led to an early and none too happy marriage, cutting short a promising university career. He indulged in at least one long passionate love affair in his middle age. In his cups, among boon companions, he would compose bawdy verse which is even more outrageous, apparently, than that of his contemporary, Robert Burns (examples of which do not often find their way into the latter's collected poems). Mac-Donald was unreliable as a schoolmaster – the only job he could get as a result of his early departure from Glasgow University – and was in frequent trouble with his employer, the Society for the Propagation of Christian Knowledge.

Yet at the same time he was a sensitive nature poet with an eye for tiny details, a close and accurate observer, a lover of beauty. To his friends and, above all, his chief, he was a loyal and popular companion. In spite of his poverty – his schoolmastering bought him an annual income little more than the meanest servant, eked out with a small holding – he was a gentleman and an officer. And this mattered in the clan hierarchy. He was moreover surprisingly well read. There are a wealth of classical allusions, and echoes of English-speaking writers, in his poems. Above all, he was a Gaelic scholar. Captain Alexander MacDonald, wrote Bishop Forbes in his journal after a meeting,

> is a very smart, acute man, remarkably well skilled in Earse [Gaelic], for he can read and write the Irish language in its original character, a piece of knowledge almost quite lost in the Highlands of Scotland, there being exceedingly few that have any skill at all that way. For the Captain told me that he did not know another person (Old Clanranald only excepted) that knew anything of the first language in its original character; but that the natives of Ireland (particularly in the higher parts of the country) do still retain some knowledge of it. Several of the Captain's acquaintances have informed me that he is by far the best Earse poet in all Scotland, and that he has written many songs in pure Irish.[21]

The hazardous adventure of the '45 was the climax of his life. It offered an escape from the tedium of schoolmastering for a pittance, from a soured marriage which had lasted probably quarter of a

Mingary Castle, on the Ardnamurchan peninsula. Alexander MacDonald was born nearby in about 1700, and for many years was a schoolmaster in Ardnamurchan. Aquatint by William Daniell, from his *Voyage round the Coast of Great Britain* (c. 1818–21).

century, from an existence which seemed to have little point beyond some squalid quarrels with the authorities. From the moment he met the young Prince, young enough to be his son, he was captivated. There survives, in the papers of Lockhart of Carnworth, a long, detailed description of the campaign, which undoubtedly comes from the pen of Captain Alexander MacDonald, from the time of the Prince's landing to the grim battle field of Culloden. Also among the Lockhart papers is MacDonald's description of the Prince's escape (quoted in the previous chapter). The stirring events had seared themselves on to Alasdair MacDonald's consciousness. Despite the terrible sufferings of two winters skulking in the glens and mountains with his wife (who, to quote Bishop Forbes, 'fell with child' and gave birth to a baby girl while in hiding) and with his younger children, Alexander MacDonald continued to hope for and plot a new uprising. Riskily, he composed seditious Jacobite poems, which he had the audacity to publish in 1751.

As hope receded he became more and more irascible and embittered. The gall of the defeat of the Jacobite cause bit deeper and deeper into his soul. So terrible a man was he at one period — before, perhaps, old age dimmed his powers — that it is said that his ill-tempered ghost still haunts Old Clanranald's Glenuig estate on the Uists. Alasdair died, at a great age, some time after 1770.

The Birlinn of Clanranald is, in a sense, the poignant 'last post' sounding for the lost world of the Gaels. It was said to have been composed in the bitterness of defeat: partly on the Isle of Canna, where Alasdair was baillie (1749-1751), and from whence he sent Bishop Forbes a catalogue of the appalling atrocities of Cumberland's troops; and partly on Uist, where he spent a short unhappy period at Eignaig, on the Glenuig estate of Clanranald, as tacksman (tenant farmer). Some blazing indiscretion of Alasdair's soon resulted in his removal to Knoydart, on the Glengarry estate; he was incapable of concealing his hatred of the Hanoverian authorities who administered the forfeited estates, and whose Disarming Act of 1746 and subsequent legislation was aimed at destroying the feudal powers of the clan chiefs and the social bonds of the clan. Defiantly, Alasdair was composing a glorification of Clanranald.

Ever a traditionalist, Alasdair composed his poetry in the time-honoured way described in 1703 by Martin Martin in his *Description of the Western Islands of Scotland*. (Martin would have been in his mid-forties at the time of Alasdair's birth, which is usually put at about 1700, though no records survive). According to Martin, his fellow countrymen had a 'genius for Poesy':

Contemporary engraving of the execution of Jacobite lords in London after the failure of the '45.

I must not omit to relate their way of Study, which is very singular: They shut their Doors and Windows for a day's time, and lie on their backs, with a Stone upon their Belly, and Plads [plaids] about their Heads, and their Eyes being cover'd, they pump their Brains for Rhetorical Encomium or Panegyrick; and indeed they furnish such a Stile from this dark Cell as is understood by very few: and if they purchase a couple of Horses as the Reward of their Meditation, they think they have done a great matter.[22]

One wonders how Clanranald rewarded Alasdair for the *Birlinn*.

The *Birlinn* was composed orally, and stored in the bard's retentive memory, to be recited on great occasions. One such (tradition claims) was a visit in the company of Old Clanranald — Alasdair's chief and patron. The MacDonalds of Clanranald had crossed McNair's ford to North Uist to see Iain McCodrum, the celebrated bard of Sir James MacDonald of the Isles. The gentlemen of North Uist met at Tigheary and entertained the two bards. Both sang and recited many of their own songs, some of the best and some of the worst. Alasdair is described as a good singer, tall, broad-chested, fair and good looking. The entertainment ended with the poet reciting the *Birlinn Chlann-raghnaill* from beginning to end. It is in such a setting that we must imagine the recitation of the *Birlinn*: the Highlanders defiantly kilted, despite the outlawing of the national dress; the peat fire in the midst of the hall lighting up the ruddy faces and greying hair of these survivors of Celtic feudalism; the whisky flowing freely, and the sound of the wind without drowned by the good cheer of the company within. And the two bards, the carriers and renewers of Gaelic culture, sparring with words, striving to outdo the other in wit, in audacity, in satire, in bawdry, until Alasdair's *tour de force* – for the *Birlinn* is the longest poem in the Gaelic language – triumphantly recreated for those assembled the heroic exploits of their youth, half a century ago: a golden age before the defeat of the Stuarts.

The poem opens with the clansmen gathered reverently round their vessel on the foreshore at the head of Loch Eynort, repeating together under the stars the ancient ship blessing that had come down from the days of St Columba. As they board the ship the pace quickens and there comes the incitement to row the heavy *birlinn*. These ships were descended from the Norse longship, with carved prows and high stern posts, low freeboard and graceful lines. Each was rigged with a single square-cut sail slung from the mast. The design had changed little in five centuries. Such a ship cannot tack or manoeuvre easily – and so the crew bent to the task of rowing to the 'sailing point': four miles down the dark, winding, narrow, rock-girt loch, to the tidal race where the twisting treacherous waters sluice out through a cleft in the cliffs. Once through this rock-strewn kyle, they ship oars; they have come to the point where the sail can be raised to pick up the southwesterlies, while still under the lee of South Uist.

Now the crew are given their duties by the Chief himself, Clanranald, then (perhaps in 1730) in his youthful prime, newly come to his title and (possibly) yet to prove his worth. Each thumbnail sketch of the crew members must have prompted guffaws from the audience, for each is a recognizable local character. One is certainly the poet himself – but which?

As dawn breaks they begin on their perilous voyage: nearly two hundred miles, in an open boat, across some of the most exposed, most treacherous seas in the Hebrides. This route is exposed to every wind from the Atlantic, and the swell breaks in huge waves over the wild rocks. It is across this dangerous area, where the shallow bottom produces mountainous seas, and the jagged rocks threaten destruction, that Clanranald's galley sailed, in gale-force winds, bound for the Sound of Islay. In storms such as the poet describes, wind and water consort to make the air thick with spindrift, and the churned-up waters hold a strange flotsam of deep-sea creatures, grotesque monsters pounded lifeless by the fury of the waters dashed against the reef.

Finally, the galley runs down the Sound of Islay, on the ebbing tide, to make her stately way through the noble Sound of Jura, to the safe harbour of Carrickfergus, in Gaelic-speaking Ireland. Then there is feasting, and song, and drink unstinted. For Clanranald has proved himself a chief indeed, and his clansmen have demonstrated their fealty, their manhood, and their seamanship.

Here then, somewhat abridged, is the poem Alasdair recited, his rousing *Birlinn Chlann-Raghnaill*. The translation I have chosen is that by Hugh MacDiarmid, perhaps the greatest of Scotland's twentieth-century poets. Though not a completely literal translation, it catches the sea rhythms of the Gaelic, the taut writing, the almost overwhelming power of the imagery, and the way the fury of wind and wave echo through the description of the tempest.

The conjectured route of the birlinn (galley) of Clanranald.

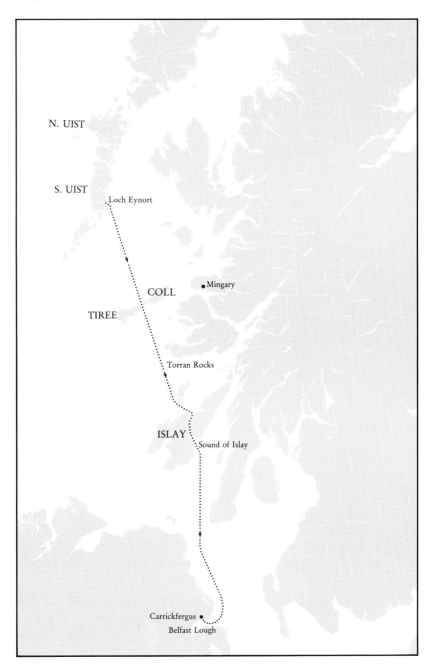

BIRLINN CHLANN-RAGHNAILL

The Birlinn of Clanranald

Being a ship-blessing, together with a sea-incitement made for the crew of the Birlinn of the Lord of Clanranald

God bless the craft of Clanranald
When brangled first with the brine,
Himself and his heroes hurling;
The pick of the human line!

The blessing of holy Triune
On the fury of the air;
The sea's ruggedness smoothed away
Ease us to our haven there!

Father who fashioned the ocean
And winds that from all points roll,
Bless our lean ship and her heroes,
Keep her and her whole crew whole!

Your grace, O Son, on our anchor,
Our rudder, sails, and all graith
And tackle to her masts attached,
And guard us as we have faith!

. . .

Holy Ghost, be you our helmsman
To steer the course that is right.
You know every port under Heaven.
We cast ourselves on your sleight!

The Blessing of the Arms

God's blessing be on our claymores
And flexible grey toledos
And heavy coats of mail-harness
Through which no dull blade can bleed us.

Bless our shoulder-belts and gorgets
And our well-made bossy targes,
Bless each and all of our weapons,
And the man who with it charges.

43

Bless our gleaming bows of yew-wood
Good to bend in battle-melee,
And birchen arrows, not to splinter
In the surly badger's belly.

Bless every dirk, every pistol,
Every kilt of noble pleating,
Every martial apparatus
With us under this ship's sheeting.

. . .

Incitement for Rowing to Sailing-Place

To put the black well-fashioned yewship
   To the sailing-place
Thrust you out flexible oarbanks
   Dressed to sheer grace;
Oars smooth-shafted and shapely,
   Grateful for gripping,
Made for lusty resolute rowing,
   Palm-fast, foam-whipping;
Knocking sparks out of the water
   Towards Heaven
Like the fire-flush from a smithy
   Updriven,
Under the great measured onstrokes
   Of the oar-lunges
That confound the indrawn billows
   With their plunges,
While the shrewd blades of the white woods
   Go cleaving
The tops of the valleyed blue-hills
   Shaggily heaving.

. . .

A Herculean planked on the fore-oar
   Roaring: "Up, on with her!"
Makes all the thick shoulder muscles
   Glide better together,
Thrusting the birlinn with snorting
   Through each chill sea-glen;
The hard curved prow through the tide-lumps
   Drives inveighing,

On all hands sending up mountains
  Round her insistence.

. . .

They are the choice set of fellows
  To hold an oarage
Outmanoeuvring the dark swirlings
  With skill and courage,
Without a point lost or tiring,
  Timely throughout,
Despite all the dire devilment
  Of the waterspout!

> (Then after the sixteen men had sat at the
> oars to row her against the wind to a sailing-
> place, Calum Garbh, son of Ranald of the
> Seas, who was on the fore-oar, recited an
> iorram (or rowing song) for her, as follows:)

. . .

Oar's sawdust on the rowlocks,
Hands run with sores like golochs,
Waves' armpits like any mollusc
        Screw the oars.

Cheeks be lit all blazing red,
Palms of skin all casing shed,
While sweat off every face and head
        Thumping pours.

Stretch you, pull you, and bend you
The blades the pine-trees lend you,
Ascend, descend, and wend you
        Through the sea.

Banks of oars on either side
Set your labour to her tide
And spray on ocean's thorter-pride
        Throw freely.

. . .

Let her oak go skelping through
Big-bellied troughs of swingeing blue;
In their two thighs pounding too
        Each spasm down.

45

Though the hoary heaving ocean
Swell with even more commotion,
Toppling waves with drowning notion
      Roar and frown,

And incessant wash pour in
O'er her shoulders and the din
Groan all round and sob to win
      Through her keel,

Stretch you, pull you, and bend you.
The red-backed sleek shafts tend you.
With the pith strong arms lend you
      Victory feel.

Put that headland past your prow
Where you strain with sweat-drenched brow
And lift the sails upon her now
      From Uist of the sheldrakes!

(Then they rowed to a sailing-place. They
took in the sixteen oars which were swiftly
pruned down against her thigh to avoid sheet-
ropes. Clanranald ordered his gentlemen to
see to the disposition in the places for which
they were qualified of men who would not be
daunted by any spectre from the deep nor

The Sound of
Islay, through
which the Birlinn
of Clanranald
sailed on its epic
journey to
Carrickfergus.
Aquatint from
John Schekty's
*Sketches and
Notes of a Cruise
in Scottish Waters*
(1848).

any chaos in which the ocean might involve
them. After the selection every man was
ordered to take up his appointed place, and
accordingly the steersman was summoned to
sit at the rudder in these words:)

Set at the rudder a brawny
  Grand fellow,
Top nor trough of sea can unhorse,
  Coarse skelp nor bellow;
Broad-beamed, well-set, full of vigour
  Wary withal;
Who hearing the shaggy surges
  Come roaring
Her prow expertly to the rollers
  Keeps shoring;. . .
Yielding no thumb-long deviation
  Of her true course
Despite the bounding wave-summits'
  Opposing force;. . .

  . . .

Who no rope strains tackwindwarding
  But easily
Lets run and tacks under full canvas
  None so meetly
And her tacking on each wavetop
  Binds so featly,
Straight harbourwards under spray-showers
  Running so sweetly!

  (There was appointed a shrouds-man.)

Set another stalwart fellow
  For shrouds-grasping;
With finger-vices, great hand-span,
  For such clasping;
Sage, quick; to help with the yard's end
  When that's needed,
With masts and gear, leave no neighbour
  Task unheeded;
Wind-wise, and aptly adjusting
  With shrouds-manning
The sheet's-man's slacking—and t'assist
  In all ways scanning.

(A sheet's-man was set apart.)

Set too on the thwart a sheet's-man
  With great arms ending
In horny compulsive fingers
  For the sheet-tending;
Pull in, let out, as is wanted,
  With strength of grabbing;
Draw in when beating to windward,
  The blast crabbing;
And release when the gust again
  Ceases rending.

(There was ordered out a tacksman.)

. . .

(There was ordered to the prow a pilot.)

. . .

(There was set apart a halyard-man.)

Take place at the main halyard
  A clear-headed
Athletic fellow, with vigour
  And care wedded,
An able fellow without flurry,
  Grim and alert,
To take from her and give to her
  Just and expert,
To lie with hand of due power
  There on the halyard,
The weight of his grasp decisive
  Rive oakwoodward;
Not tie the halyard about the clear
  Tight beyond use
But fix it firmly, cunningly,
  With running noose;

. . .

(There was set apart a teller-of-the-waters,
since the sea was becoming too rough, and
the steersman said to him:)

I'll have at my ear a teller
  Of the waters;
Let him keep close watch windward

A page from the
Book of Kells.
Many scholars
believe that the
monks of Iona
were responsible
for this magnifi-
cent volume.

48

An Incident in the Rebellion of 1745,
by David Morier (generally taken
to be the Battle of Culloden).
Morier used Jacobite prisoners in
London as models for the Highlanders
in this vivid painting.

The persecution of the clansmen after Culloden was to capture the imagination of later generations. Shown here is John Pettie's *Hunted Down* (1877).

On these matters;
A man somewhat timid, cautious,
  Not altogether
A coward however!—Keeping
  Stock of the weather. . .

. . .

Clamorous at the least threat of danger
  This man must be,
And not fear to give the steersman
  Any hint of hazard.
– But let him be the one teller
  Of the waters heard,
And not the whole of you bawling
  Advices mixed,
A distraught steersman not knowing
  Who to heed next!

   (There was ordered out a baler, since the sea
   was rushing over them fore and aft:)

Let attend on the baling space
  A hardy hero
Not to be cramped or benumbed
  By cold at zero,
Raw brine or stinging hail dashing
  In thrashing showers
Round his chest and neck – but armoured
  In dogged powers,
A thick round wooden baling-can
  In his swarthy hands,
Throwing out the sea forever
  As soon as it lands;
Never straightening his lithe backbone
  Till his task's o'er,
Not one drop left in her bottom
  – Or keelson-floor!

   (Two men were appointed for hauling the
   peak-downhauls, since it appeared that the
   sails would be torn from them by the
   exceeding boisterousness of the weather:)

Put a pair of hefty fellows
  Thick-boned, strong-thewed,

A highland chieftain, painted by Michael Wright around 1660. It is interesting to compare this picture of a clan chief with Raeburn's portrait of Macdonnell of Glengarry (p.217), painted 150 years later.

To take charge of her peak-downhauls
  With force and aptitude;
With the power of great fore-arms
  In till of need
To haul them in or let then run,
  But always lead
When wayward back to the middle;
  For this two men
Of the Canna men, Donnchadh Mac Chomaig
  And Iain Mac Iain,
Were chosen—deft and definite fellows
  In brawn and brain.

(Six men were chosen to man the ship's floor
as a precaution against the failing of any of
those mentioned, or lest the raging of the sea
might pluck one overboard, one of these six
might take his place:)

. . .

(Now that every convenience pertaining to
sailing had been put in good order and every
brave dependable fellow had taken up the
duty assigned to him, they hoisted the sails
about sunrise on St Bride's Day, beginning
their course from the mouth of Loch Ainort
in South Uist.)

The Voyage

The sun bursting golden-yellow
  Out of his husk,
The sky grew wild and hot-breathing,
  Unsheathing a fell tusk,
Then turned wave-blue, thick, dun-bellied,
  Fierce and forbidding,
Every hue that would be in a plaid
  In it kneading;
. . .

Now they hoisted the speckled sails
  Peaked and close-wrought,
And stretched out the stubborn shrouds
  Tough and taut
To the long resin-red shafts

Of the mast.
With adroit and firm-drawn knotting
  These were made fast
Through the eyes of the hooks and rings;
  Swiftly and expertly
Each rope put right of the rigging;
  And orderly
The men took up their set stations
  And were ready.

Then opened the windows of the sky
  Pied, grey-blue,
To the lowering wind's blowing,
  A morose brew,
The sea pulled on his grim rugging
  Slashed with sore rents,
That rough-napped mantle, a weaving
  Of loathsome torrents.
The shape-ever-changing surges
  Swelled up in hills
And soared down into valleys
  In appalling spills.
The water yawned in great craters,
  Slavering mouths agape
Snatching and snarling at each other
  In rabid shape.

. . .

When we would rise on these rollers
  Soundly, compactly,
It was imperative to shorten sail
  Swiftly, exactly.
When we would fall with no swallowing
  Down into the glens
Every topsail she had would be off.
  —No light task the men's!

The great hooked big-buttocked ones
  Long before
They came at all near us were heard
  Loudly aroar
Scourging all the lesser waves level
  As on they tore . . .

A birlinn (galley) similar to that featured in *The Birlinn of Clanranald*. Derived from the Norse longboat, the design changed little for five centuries. Detail from the grave of Alexander Crotach at Rodel, Harris, carved in 1528.

The sea churning and lashing itself
  In maniacal states,
Seals and other great beasts were even
  In direr straits,
The wild swelth and the pounding waves
  And the ship's nose
Scattering their white brains callous
  Through the billows. . .
Small fish that were in the waters,
  Murderously churned,
Floated on the top without number
  White bellies upturned. . .
The whole sea was a foul porridge
  Full of red scum
With the blood and ordure of the beasts,
  Ruddy, glum,
While screaming with their gill-less mouths,
  Their jaws agape,
Even the air's abyss was full of fiends
  That had no shape.

What then with the ocean's turmoil
  Pounding the ship,
The clamour of the prow flenching whales
  With slime-foiled grip,. . .
We were blinded by the sea-spray
  Ever going over us;
With, beyond that, like another ocean,
  Thunders and lightnings to cover us,
The thunderbolts sometimes singeing
  Our rigging till the smoke
And stench of the reefs smouldering
  Made us utterly choke.
Between the upper and lower torments
  Thus were we braised,
Water, fire, and wind simultaneously
  Against us raised.

–But when it was beyond the sea's power
  To make us yield
She took pity with a faint smile
  And truce was sealed,
Though by that time no mast was unbent,
  No sail untorn,

Yard unsevered, mast-ring unflawed,
  Oar not shag-shorn,. . .
Her gunwale and bottom-boards
  Were confounded;
Not a helm left unsplit,
  A rudder unwounded.
Every timber creaked, moaned, and warped.
  Not a tree-nail
Was unpulled, no plank had failed
  To give in the gale.

  . . .

The sea proclaimed peace with us
  At the fork of Islay Sound
And the hostile barking wind
  Was ordered off the ground.
It went to the upper places of the air
  And became a quiet
Glossy-white surface to us there
  After all its riot.
And to God we made thanksgiving
  That good Clanranald
Was spared the brutal death for which
  The elements had wrangled.

Then we pulled down the speckled canvas
  And lowered
The sleek red masts and along her bottom
  Safely stored,
And put out the slender well-wrought oars
  Coloured, and smooth to the hand,
Made of the pine cut by Mac Bharais
  In Finnan's Island,
And set up the right-royal, rocking, rowing,
  Deft and timeous,
And made good harbour there at the top
  Of Carrick-Fergus.
We threw out anchors peacefully
  In that roadstead.
We took food and drink unstinting
  And there we stayed.[23]

4

The Charting of the Seas

Murdoch Mackenzie

IT WAS DURING THE PERIOD that MacDonald was composing his great description of a sea voyage in the Hebrides, the *Birlinn of Clanranald*, that another, very different, description was being pieced together. For ten years – 1748-1757 – Murdoch Mackenzie, Hydrographer to the Admiralty, painstakingly surveyed the entire west coast of Scotland, producing the earliest systematic survey of the British coast, and his outstanding sailing directions, *A Nautical Description*.[24]

Why did the Admiralty commission the first such survey ever to be undertaken in Britain, and why were the Hebrides chosen as a starting point? These isles were remote from major shipping lanes, and economically unimportant.

The reason was the humiliating failure of the Hanoverian forces to capture the Young Pretender, the Bonnie Prince. His arrival in 1745, on the remote and unlikely island of Eriskay, was bad enough – though luck came into it. The French privateer, *Le du Teillay*, had slipped out of a Channel port, escaped from the pursuing English navy (then at war with France) and succeeded in landing the daring young Prince and a mere handful of gentlemen. In 1746 the government should have been more successful in capturing the defeated fugitive, but five weary months of patrolling the Minches failed to net the prize.

The Hanoverian navy was operating in dangerous waters. The captains of the vessels were hampered by lack of information. Few of the local populace would inform on the Prince, except under torture. Local pilots were difficult to obtain, and the commanders had no local knowledge of winds, tides, safe havens, or hazards, for these waters were unexplored and uncharted.

Twenty-three ships of the Royal Navy were, at one time or another, engaged in the hunt in these northern waters. The largest were battleships like the *Lyon* and the *Exeter*, with 58 guns; the smallest were ketches which could manoeuvre with great effect in the confined waters of West Highland lochs. The pride of the British navy was ranged against the fugitive pretender to the throne.

The story of the frustrating patrolling of the Minches, and the audacious attempts – no less than six in number – of French vessels to pluck out the Prince and escape with him from this difficult area, with its myriad isles, mountainous terrain and stormy seas, is well told in Gibson's *Ships of the '45*. I will not repeat the tale. One conclusion was inescapable for the authorities: maps and charts they must have. The advantage had all lain with the insurgents, familiar with their native glens, with every little anchorage, with the tides and winds. Without local pilots the French vessels would never have been able to creep through the British defences and whisk away their prize. The Hanoverian forces, on the other hand, were without local knowledge for much of the time. The need for charts was obvious.

In 1745 maps of the northern portion of George II's kingdom were few, expensive, and inaccurate. Blaeu, the famous Amsterdam publishing house, had published a magnificent *Atlas Scotia* in 1655, with a second edition in 1662. The Dutch were the foremost shipping nation and fished extensively in Hebridean waters. But the information for the *Atlas* came principally from a Scotsman, Timothy Pont, who, in the late sixteenth century, travelled far and wide. His hand-drawn maps were updated for Blaeu by Gordon of Straloch. John Adair, who was paid to survey Scotland by the Scottish Parliament in the late seventeenth century, never succeeded in publishing most of his surveys of the coast. His manuscript charts were later lost in a fire after his death, and his map of Scotland published in 1688 merely reproduced that published a hundred years earlier by Nicolay D'Affreville, which was based on a circumnavigation of Scotland by James V in 1540.

These were the most up-to-date printed maps, but even they were unobtainable by the Hanoverian forces in the '45. Small wonder General Hawley, on his way to assume command of the King's troops in Scotland, wrote querulously to the Duke of Newcastle in late 1745,

> I am going in the dark: For Mareschal Wade won't let me have his map: He say, his majesty has the only one to fellow it. I could wish it was either copied, or printed, or that his majesty would please lend it me: 'Tis for service, or I would not be so bold.[25]

This map seems to have been a hand-drawn map, belonging to

The title page of *The Mariner's Mirror* (1588). Frequently reprinted, it was the only 'rutter' (route finder for seamen) which covered the entire British coast. It devotes only one page to the distant and dangerous isles of northwest Scotland, and was useless to the Hanoverian navy.

General Wade. It was hastily published in 1746 – too late for the campaign – by Thomas Wellday. Wade's map had been drafted to aid his construction of military roads throughout the Highlands after the uprising in 1715. Ironically, these roads had allowed Prince Charles to mobilize the clans swiftly, and march on the Lowlands with such rapidity. But no maps were available for the campaign, or the naval searches which followed.

The Duke of Cumberland determined that a complete survey of the Highlands and Islands should be put in hand. The Board of Ordnance (the army engineers) were responsible for the land survey. The resulting maps were the first Ordnance Survey Maps. The

60

Admiralty naturally turned to Murdoch Mackenzie, who had already made a marine survey of the Orkneys for the Admiralty. Murdoch Mackenzie's charts of the western coasts of the British Isles were the outcome of the next twenty years' surveying of these difficult coastal waters (1748-1769).

The choice of Murdoch Mackenzie was a fortunate one. A gifted mathematician, he was also a man of great energy and practical ability. He had been born in Orkney in 1712, the grandson, it is said, of a former Bishop of Orkney. In 1742 he was recommended to the Admiralty by Professor Colin Maclaurin, as qualified to make a 'geometrical survey'. At the time of the '45 he was engaged in making a 'geographic and hydrographic survey' of the Orkneys. With his local connections and knowledge, this was a good place to start his career. The dangerous Pentland Firth, with its racing tides, was a hazard to all westbound shipping from Scotland's east-coast ports, as well as to shipping from the Baltic.

But for the '45, Mackenzie would, no doubt, have proceeded southwards along the east coast of Scotland, and then down the eastern coasts of England. But instead we find him, in 1748, surveying Lewis. Funds were forthcoming from the Admiralty for a survey of these baffling seas, and Mackenzie was to devote the rest of his working life to surveying Britain's western seaboard.

Mackenzie seems to have had little interest in politics, or, if he had views, he kept them to himself. As a Mackenzie, and perhaps an Episcopalian, he may have had Jacobite sympathies; but other Mackenzies (a widespread clan throughout Ross-shire, with a branch on Lewis) did not come 'out' for the Jacobite cause in 1745. He probably knew some Gaelic, although Orcadians spoke English or a Scandanavian dialect (the Orkneys were only ceded to Scotland in 1485).

Of Mackenzie's personal life we know virtually nothing. In twenty years he surveyed thousands of miles of ragged coastline; seafaring was not a life which encouraged domesticity, and as far as we know he never married. His nephew, who bears the same name, worked as his assistant in his later years. The evidence suggests that increasingly Mackenzie tended to work throughout the winter in London, no doubt so that he could be close to the Admiralty. At any rate, it was to London that he retired, probably in about 1770. In 1775 and 1776 he oversaw the publication of a magnificent series of charts, covering the whole of the west coast of Britain, from the

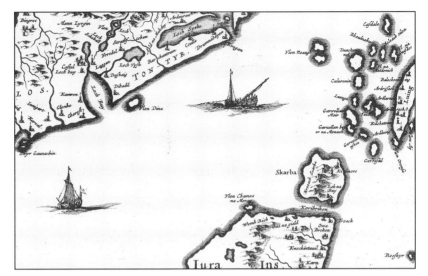

A detail showing part of Jura and the Corryvreckan from Blaeu's *Atlas Scotia* (1662 edition). This was the most up-to-date printed chart available to the Royal Navy at the time of the '45.

Orkneys to the Bristol Channel, and including the entire coast of Ireland, on the scale of one inch to a mile. It was a phenomenal undertaking, but inevitably much of the survey is unsatisfactory by modern standards.

The year 1776 also saw the publication of his precise and beautifully organized sailing directions, or *Nautical Descriptions*. These show a lucid, workman-like approach, and a real understanding of the needs of seamen. Compared with earlier 'pilots' ('rutters' as they were often called), his *Nautical Descriptions* are superb. They are far superior to the early Admiralty *Pilots* of the area, which began to appear in 1867-71 – a century later.

Above all, Mackenzie was a professional: a cartographer who, by the standards of his time, was highly scientific, and who communicated his surveys to mariners in his well-produced charts; and a writer of sailing directions who understood the requirements of seamen, the need for clarity, and the importance of detail. The responsibilities on the cartographer are heavy. On dry land, if you misplace a hill or misdraw a river, the consequences may not be very serious. At sea, lives depend on the accuracy of a chart.

To anyone who has sailed in Highland waters, the crudity and inaccuracy of Mackenzie's charts is all too apparent. It is only when they are compared with those of his predecessors that the advance is obvious.

Moreover, Mackenzie was working within great limitations. The

62

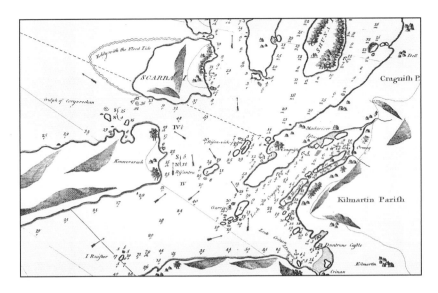

Murdoch Mackenzie's chart of the Dorus Mor and the Corryvreckan (published c. 1770).

professional surveyor today has a vast number of resources: satellite pictures, giving a map-like outline, and capable of massive enlargement; sophisticated navigational aids, like LORAN-NAVSAG, which, when linked to a computer, can position any spot on the globe, giving both longitude and latitude to within a couple of metres; electronic devices, such as echo sounders, which can give a detailed, three-dimensional model of the sea bed which can be analysed by computers. But what did Mackenzie have at his disposal?

Fortunately, in his old age, he wrote a *Treatise on Maratim Surveying*.[26] It was to remain a standard work for many years, and, along with his charts, earned him a well-merited Fellowship of the Royal Society. This work gives us many insights into the surveyor's craft and his equipment, enabling us to reconstruct the kind of life he must have lived as, year after year, he pursued his task.

He wintered in London, where he would make final drafts of his previous year's charts, negotiate pay with his Admiralty masters, and supervise the refitting of his survey ship. In early spring he would set sail for the north. His home for the next nine months would be a strongly built seaworthy vessel, of about 120 tons. He describes her as 'pretty broad in the beam, and full in the bows; of such a mould as to draw little water, and to take ground easily'. Such a ship would roll uncomfortably in heavy seas, but come to no harm; moreover she could be sailed through shallows and among

A merchant captain holding a Hadley quadrant, an essential navigational instrument. Painting by R. Willoughby, c. 1746.

reefs with relative safety, and be beached for repairs. A smaller vessel, he observed, 'cannot keep Sea well, nor carry Provisions sufficient for a Season'.

On board would be his crew, many of whom had sailed with him on similar expeditions. They were often tough old salts, men with years of sea-going experience, much of it in the chill northerly waters for which he was heading. There was the ship's master, the purser to manage the funds and stores for the eight-month voyage, a mate, a midshipman, a carpenter and a sail-maker to make running repairs, a boatswain, a cook and fourteen able seamen who slept in the dark fo'c'sle before the mast in hammocks. A local pilot would make up the ship's complement.

The heavily laden vessel, with supplies to see her through the long summer, would head down the Channel, round the Lizard, and up the Irish Sea, bound for the Hebrides. In his cabin, the surveyor would be making his preparations for the months ahead. It was a spacious cabin, measuring (according to Mackenzie) twelve foot by twelve, and well lit by windows with glass panes to give the maximum light. In the centre was a massive table, with beautifully fitted drawers on either side. There were wide, shallow drawers for the reams of white paper, and carefully fitted compartments with his goose-quill pens, his expensive graphite pencils, indian inks and sand for blotting, and drawing instruments such as compasses, rulers and protractors. His gleaming navigational instruments – sextants and quadrants, telescopes, theodolites and bearing compasses — with their polished brass scales and ivory or bone handles, were carefully packed in padded boxes. Overhead swung brass lanterns to give illumination for evening work. On the wall was a somewhat unreliable ship's clock, wound everyday by the surveyor, and reset as necessary.

The modern navigator would be surprised by the absence of a chronometer – the highly reliable, sea-going timepiece that is essential for estimating a ship's longitude (your easting and westing). But the chronometer had not yet been perfected, and for Mackenzie there was no alternative but elaborate observations of occasional eclipses of Jupiter's tiny moons (forecast in complicated almanacs) to get a time check. (An accurate time check of the exact second when the sun, at midday, reaches its greatest height is essential if you are to estimate your longitude by comparing local time with Greenwich Mean Time.) Also absent was any instrument for recording barometric pressure. Advanced warning of storms must have come from observation of cloud formations.

On reaching the Hebrides, Mackenzie would take up his systematic survey where he had left off the previous year. The survey was based on a network of triangles Mackenzie had thrown across the seas of the Hebrides from mountain peak to mountain peak. At the beginning of his survey Mackenzie had painstakingly measured a three-mile base line for his triangulation across the sands in the Outer Hebrides, where the booming Atlantic surf breaks ceaselessly on the long, empty white sweep of one of the most perfect beaches in the British Isles. Westward stretches the seemingly boundless ocean. The nearest land is America. On the landward side are the rolling dunes, wind-sculpted and shifting. Behind lie the machairs – flower-fragrant pastures enriched by the lime of the shell sand. In spring time they are aglow with thousands of primroses, nodding cowslips, and the bluebells of Scotland. In summer, the sweet grass is spangled with daisies and buttercups, while above the larks trill ceaselessly. Out to sea, the gannets can be seen, making their death-defying plunges from great heights into the shoals of fish. They were probably scarcely noticed by the men as they plodded across the sands, with their rods and heavy chains, with which the base line was so carefully measured.

The next step had been to build up a series of triangles on the base. Small parties of natives would have been dispatched up prominent peaks, the old sea marks whose Norse names told of earlier conquests. Cairns were built on each peak. Mackenzie himself must have toiled up the key bens, for these were the triangulation points in the net of triangles which he threw across the seas of the Hebrides. On each wind-swept peak he would take a reading of the other triangulation points, reading off the angle on his sextant. From this eminence, too, he would sketch by eye the lie of the coastline, taking bearings on headlands, islets, rocks, and other features.

With the land-based triangulation points fixed, the surveyor would return to his base-ship. The triangulation method of surveying was quite new in British waters, although it had been adopted by the French some time before. At the same time, the surveyors of the ordnance were mapping the bens and glens of the Scottish mainland. Like Mackenzie, they were employed by the nervous Hanoverian government to safeguard the kingdom. Surely

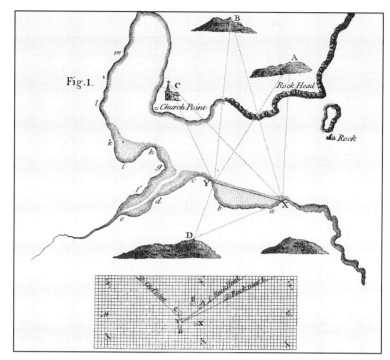

A diagram from Mackenzie's *Treatise on Maratim Surveying* (1774), showing his method of surveying from the baseline X–Y.

Murdoch Mackenzie must have met William Roy, his land-based counterpart, like him pioneering the use of triangulation to survey the difficult terrain of Scotland, and Paul Sandby, his talented assistant.

Triangulation was used to establish the seamarks – the mountainous peaks of islands. But surveying at sea is more difficult than surveying on lands. If you trace the soundings that zig-zag across Mackenzie's charts you are following the course of his stout survey ship. At each sounding a seaman swung overboard the long line with the weight at the end, and a hollow tube with a core of tallow to pick up specimens from the seabed. Down plunged the line until at last it rested on the bottom. The depth was carefully noted, and the nature of the seabed – sand, mud, pebbles, rock or weed – a useful guide to fog-bound vessels. The survey ship wove her way between the dangerous skerries and isolated pinnacle rocks which rise almost vertically from the depths, among the Torran Rocks, and the Skerryvore reefs, and the below-water rocks that lie off Barra's western shores, up to three miles out to sea. Those who sail in the Hebrides will know these to be exposed waters, and the graveyard of many fine ships. When Mackenzie found a below-water rock far off a headland, he would make fixes, using a sextant, on his triangulation points, and these would sometimes be supplemented with compass bearings. Additionally, he carefully noted leading lines.

Each day, the soundings and triangles would be marked up on his drafts in pencil. Bit by bit he would put together the puzzle of the coast and the isles. No one should underestimate the difficulty of mapping an area virtually for the first time. At sea, perspectives are deceptive, especially so where there are no clues as to the size of objects. Seen from the sea, a bay gives few indications of its shape. Deep inlets are foreshortened, a spit of land pointing out from the shore may look like just a rocky mass on the beach. In the gloaming, or in fog, drizzle, rain or sleet, it is impossible to tell whether the dimly seen land ahead is a distant range of mountains, or a low-lying hillocky island not half a mile away.

Maps and views of Castle Tioram (in Moidart) and Duart Castle (on Mull). Paul Sandby made these surveys and views in 1748 to enable the Hanoverian army to identify and if necessary storm Jacobite strongholds.

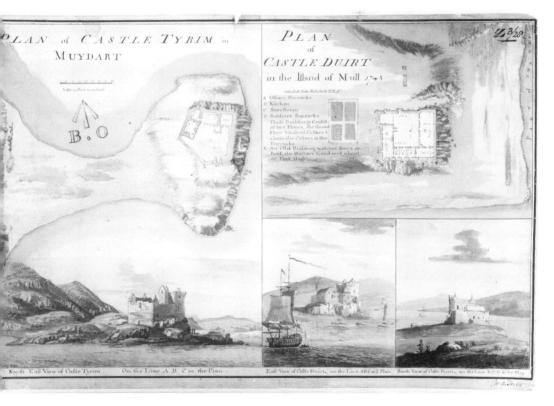

Yet it was clearly impossible for Mackenzie, harried by an Admiralty anxious to produce the charts, to investigate every bay and anchorage, plot every kyle and islet, or sound off every headland for rocks. He had to rely on his eye to map out the coastline between his triangulated fixes, and must often have consulted his local pilot to get an approximation of the correct shape of creeks and bays into which he had no time to venture.

A feature of his charts that looks unusual to the modern eye are the quaint little hills, viewed from every angle, which he sketched in on the terra firma. Contemporary sources show that this feature was of particular value to seamen making landfall in unfamiliar waters.

The invention of the chronometer, first used extensively by that prince of surveyors, Captain Cook (Mackenzie's junior by a mere sixteen years) soon exposed Mackenzie's charts to criticism. Yet they were just as fiercely defended by ships' masters and pilots who knew how infinitely superior they were to the miserable sketches that had preceded them. 'With the assistance of Mr M'Kenzie's Draughts', wrote the master of the *Lady's Adventurer*, 'and nothing else but God's blessing, we went clear of every danger'.[27] Similar testimonials poured in when Mackenzie's cartography came under attack in the press in the 1780s.

It is extraordinary that this one man should, in a lifetime, chart the previously almost uncharted western seaboard of the British Isles. It was the first systematic survey of the British coastline and, whatever its inaccuracies, a monumental work. Yet, not content with this, Mackenzie went on to produce in retirement his superb *Nautical Descriptions*. Their elegance and clarity is a model when we consider the paucity of information then available. They are well organized, crisply printed and beautifully laid out. Yet these directions were printed in 1776; Mackenzie was then about 65, and he was working over notes he must have made some twenty to thirty years earlier. Clearly, he must have been a painstakingly methodical man, who kept systematic notes and had a prodigious memory.

An experienced yachtsman reading Mackenzie's directions for the Corryvreckan today would be aghast at the man's temerity. This is the gulf against which even the sober *West Coast of Scotland Pilot* of 1974 gives solemn warnings. 'Navigation', it sternly reminds the reader, 'is at times very dangerous and no vessel should attempt this passage without local knowledge.' It goes on to give warnings in no uncertain terms:

There are no harbours anywhere on the bleak and rugged coast. . . Streams in the Gulf of Corryvreckan [run] at rates of up to 8½ knots at springs. . .There is also very violent turbulence especially with strong W winds during the W-going stream, and eddies form on both sides of the main stream. . .With strong W winds during the W-going stream the gulf breaks right across and heavy overfalls extend as much as 3 miles to sea-ward from the W-entrance. . .The eddy meets the main stream over the in-equalities of the bottom off Camas nam Bairneach where there is very violent and dangerous turbulence.[28]

Yet here is Mackenzie, in a six-oared boat, venturing out with his sextant to take bearings and his lines to take soundings. His graphic description deserves to be read in full. But even a short extract gives some indication of his intrepid professionalism:

Corryvreckan is a violent breaking sea, and whirlpool, formed between the Islands Jura and Scarba, which will wash over any ship's deck, and be apt to sink her if the hatches are open. . . The stream is so excessively rapid, and the sea swells and breaks so violently, even in the calmest weather, that it is impossible to measure the greatest celerity of the stream; but it does not seem to be less than twelve or fourteen miles an hour. . .The counter-stream seemed to run about five or six miles an hour; for a boat with six oars, in a calm day, could not stem it. . .

To manage a vessel over Corryvreckan. . .the most prudent way seems to be, to secure the hatches, and everything that is loose on deck, and to endeavour, by sails and helm, to steer the vessel right through the middle of the Sound so as the tide may carry her between the most violent breakers, which lie on each side.[29]

What a superb seaman, what a professional at his craft! Here was a man who could combine mathematical problem-solving with prac-tical surveying, meticulous draftsmanship with courageous lead-ership at sea.

Mackenzie's contributions to science well merited his election to a Fellowship of the Royal Society and he has rightfully been called the founder of British cartography. Among those who nominated him for his FRS were two notable scientists, Thomas Pennant and Joseph (later Sir Joseph) Banks. Armed with Mackenzie's charts these two gentlemen made their separate ways to the Hebrides, on voyages of exploration which were to attract the attention of the scientific and literary world, not only of Britain, but of Europe.

5

A Voyage to the Hebrides

Thomas Pennant

A T ABOUT ONE O'CLOCK in the morning of 30 June 1772, the cutter the *Lady Frederick Campbell* nosed her way into the anchorage known as the Small Isles of Jura. There is a long spit across the entrance, and the vessel touched bottom.

On board was Thomas Pennant, Fellow of the Royal Society, traveller and zoologist. He had been encouraged to set out on this voyage by his fellow scientist, Murdoch Mackenzie, surveyor of the seas of the Hebrides. Equipped with Mackenzie's newly published charts of these hitherto unknown waters, Pennant had set out on a voyage of exploration.

Thomas Pennant's *Voyage to the Hebrides, 1772* is deservedly famous. Even the great Dr Johnson recognized Pennant as 'the best travel writer' of the time. Pennant's eight-week voyage on the *Lady Frederick Campbell* began on the Clyde, and took him round the Mull of Kintyre, up the Sounds of Gigha, Jura and Islay, to Iona and thence to Canna, and then on, via Rhum, to Kyle Rhea and Kyle Akin (the narrows which separate Skye from the mainland), and then, after an exploration of Skye, on northwards till he reached Loch Broom. He then turned southwards again, returning via the Inner Sound, past the great headland of Ardnamurchan, and through the Sound of Mull. From Seil Island (south of the Sound of Mull) he returned overland to Edinburgh.

Not only was the *Voyage* a most extensive exploration of this almost unknown coast, it was also a detailed documentation of every aspect of life.

Thomas Pennant was born in 1726, so he was in his late forties on this, his second tour of Scotland. He came from an old family, and was born in Downing, near Holywell, Flintshire. As the eldest son, he was heir to the family estate, and was brought up as a country squire. However, he was also a naturalist of distinction. He seems to have been briefly an undergraduate at Oxford, but left without a degree (not unusual in those days), though later Oxford gave him a doctorate. By the time he was in his thirties he was well known in the scientific world. He corresponded with Linnæus, whose distinguished classifications of living species laid the foundations of modern biology. He himself was then working on his massive *British Zoology*, begun in 1761, and published in several parts from 1766. This work, when completed, had 132 plates. By then he had succeeded his father at Downing, and was wealthy enough to endow a school with the profits made from his *Zoology*, and to travel extensively on the continent, where he stayed with Buffon (the great zoologist), and Voltaire, whom Pennant found 'very entertaining'.

In 1767 Pennant was elected a Fellow of the Royal Society, of which Joseph Banks (see the following chapter) was already a fellow. Pennant had arrived in the world of science, but he had further ambitions.

Two years later he had, as he puts it, 'the hardihood to venture on a journey to the remotest part of North Britain'. This was his historic first tour of Scotland. Luckily for posterity, he kept an elaborate journal. This was a reform on his part: in his early twenties he had toured Ireland and kept a most imperfect journal, 'such,' as he remarked, 'was the conviviality of the country'.

This first *Tour of Scotland* proved so successful that three years later, on 18 May 1772, Pennant again set off northwards, accompanied as before by a groom and a couple of servants, including Moses Griffith, a 'worthy servant' of modest artistic talent, whom Pennant had trained as an illustrator of his works. An artist was as necessary to the scientific traveller of the time as a camera is today. Griffith had no great eye for the picturesque, and was a naive draughtsman, preferring to tidy up ruins and flatten 'horrid' mountains in his drawings from which the engraver prepared plates. The results are rather mechanical, but they were based on detailed on-the-spot sketches done under Pennant's personal supervision, and designed to give as accurate a pictorial record as possible. So they provide a valuable supplement to Pennant's text. They are the earliest views we have of the remoter parts of Scotland.

Horace Walpole, a contemporary man-of-letters, sneered at Pennant for his travelogues and the omniverous appetite Pennant displays for information of every kind. Walpole had a poor view of the smattering of local history and antiquarian tittle tattle – 'he picks up his knowledge as he rides'. (He did not find Pennant's observa-

Thomas Pennant.
Portrait after
Thomas
Gainsborough.

tions as a naturalist open to such objections, however.) Walpole found Pennant 'full of corporeal spirits, too lively and impetuous', though 'a very honest and good natured man'. But Pennant was in fact a clever questioner and a good listener, who could elicit a vast amount of information from those whom he met. He subsequently followed up this information with research: for example he quotes from manuscripts kept in the library of the Advocates in Edinburgh; he quarried extensively from works by classical authors, such as the geographers Strabo, Mela, Pliny and Ptolemy, from the venerable Bede and Adamnanus the biographer of Columba, from the Scottish historians Camden, Buchanan and Boece, from Holinshed's Chronicles, from the Dean of the Isles' manuscript description dating from the mid-sixteenth century, as well as contemporary scientists like Linnæus, 'that skilful pilot, Mr MacKenzie', and the journals of Sir Joseph Banks, FRS. He corresponded extensively with informants in his endeavour to give the most accurate and up-to-date account.

The basis of his record, however, was his own journal, which he filled in daily with all his numerous observations. This is the backbone of his book, *A Tour of Scotland and Voyage to the Hebrides, 1772.* And it is this – his daily log of his voyage – that is so fascinating.

He had set off from Helensburgh – Ardencapel, as it was then called – on 17 June 1772. His vessel was the *Lady Frederick Campbell.* She appears – becalmed – in one of Moses Griffith's drawings, with the standard cutter rig: a gaff mainsail, somewhat concealed in the illustration by the topsail hanging from the square yard above the lower topsail, which is cut away to allow the jib freedom. The long bowsprit allows not only the two triangular sails shown in the engraving, but also a staysail or flying jib on the forestay. A third square-rigged sail could also be raised on the horizontal yard halfway up the mast. It is a good choice of vessel – fast, seaworthy, and serviceable. It was not for nothing that the navy used cutters as auxilliaries to its great fleets, or the excise men to prevent smuggling. But the accommodation would not have been very luxurious, and the chancy weather of the Hebrides was to test her handling in difficult situations, under the skilled master, Mr Thompson.

They proceeded in a leisurely fashion down the noble Firth of Clyde, with ample time for Pennant to explore the islands of Bute

Thomas Pennant's voyage to the Hebrides, 1772.

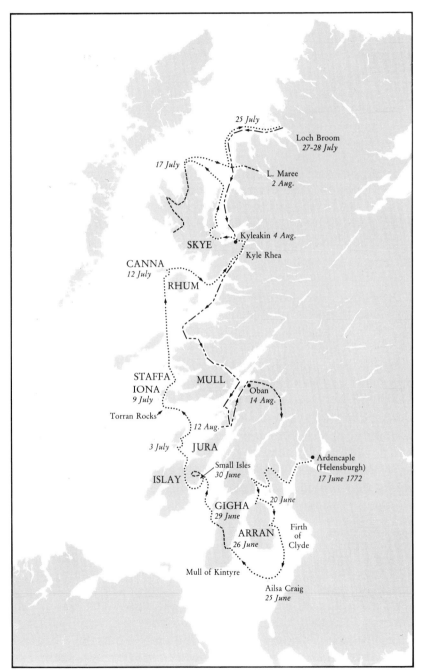

Outward bound ············

Homeward bound ‒‒‒‒‒

Expeditions on foot ---------

25 July

Loch Broom
27-28 July

17 July

L. Maree
2 Aug.

Kyleakin 4 Aug.

SKYE

Kyle Rhea

CANNA
12 July

RHUM

STAFFA
IONA
9 July

MULL

Oban
14 Aug.

Torran Rocks

12 Aug.

3 July

JURA

Small Isles
30 June

Ardencaple
(Helensburgh)
17 June 1772

ISLAY

GIGHA
29 June

20 June

ARRAN
26 June

Firth
of
Clyde

Mull of Kintyre

Ailsa Craig
25 June

and Arran. Fearful of the heavy seas around the notorious Mull of Kintyre, he crossed the Kintyre peninsula on horseback, and rejoined ship at Gigha.

By 29 June they were motionless in the Sound of Jura. The scenery was magnificent, but the lack of wind frustrating:

> Attempt to steer for the island of Ilay [Islay], but in vain. Am entertained with the variety and greatness of the views that bound the channel, the great sound of Jura; to the East the mountains of Arran over-top the far extending shores of Cantyre [Kintyre]; to the West lies Jura, mountainous and rugged; four hills, naked and distinct, aspire above the rest, two of them known to the seamen by the name of the Paps, useful in navigation : far to the North, just appears a chain of small isles; and to the South, the island of Rathry [Rathlin], the supposed Ricnea, or Ricina, of Pliny, on the coast of Ireland, which stretches far beyond to the West.[30]

'The leisure of a calm gave ample time,' Pennant continues, 'for reflections on the history and great events of the islands now in view.'

Pennant's 'brief history of the Hebrides' covers some fifteen pages, and is the first printed history of Scotland's Atlantic seaboard and the Isles. For Pennant's first readers, and for us, it goes a long way to explaining why the Hebrides are so different from the rest of Britain in culture, language, and tradition. For, as he shows, the Hebrides have been heirs to a different legacy: separated from the rest of Britain not only by their geographical remoteness but by accidents of history and climate and language that make the Highland line – the division between the Gaelic-speaking Highlands and Islands, and the Sassenachs (the 'Saxon' or English-speaking Lowlands and south Britain) – a border of as great significance as the border between Scotland and England.

After surveying the long, troubled history of the islands, he sums up the events of his own century thus:

> The turbulent spirit of old times continued even to the present age. The heads of clans were by the divisions, and a false policy that predominated in Scotland during the reign of William III, flattered with an unreal importance: instead of being treated as bad subjects, they were courted as desirable allies; instead of feeling the hand of power, money was allowed to bribe them into the loyalty of the times. They would have accepted the subsidies, notwithstanding they detested the prince that offered them [i.e.

William]. They were taught to believe themselves of such consequence that in these days turned to their destruction. Two
recent rebellions [1715 and 1745] gave legislature a late experience
of the folly of permitting the feudal system to exist in any part of
its dominions. The act of 1748 [the act for abolishing heritable
jurisdiction, etc.] at once deprived the chieftains of all power of
injuring the public by their commotions. Many of these *Reguli*
[chieftains] second this effort of legislature, and neglect no
opportunity of rendering themselves hateful to their unhappy
vassals. . .The *Halcyon* days are near at hand: oppression will
beget depopulation; and depopulation will give us a dear-bought
tranquillity.[31]

His 'brief history' of the Hebrides completed, Pennant resumes
his narrative. His historical survey was inserted in his description of
the ship's passage to the Small Isles of Jura. There they anchored for
the night of the 29/30 June. The next day Pennant rose early. With
his customary energy, he began to explore Jura. It was, he said, 'the
most rugged of the Hebrides. . .composed chiefly of vast mountains, naked and without the possibility of cultivation'. The zoologist observed that the island was alive with wildlife — a hundred stags,
and wild cats, otters, stoats, rats and seals (he noted) – but the
condition of many of the inhabitants (here, and throughout the
Hebrides) was wretched. Pennant was himself a country squire, so
he looked with a practised eye at the rural scene, and was horrified
to observe women and children collecting 'their daily wretched fare,
limpets and perriwinkles' on the shore. By midsummer, with the
harvest still a couple of months away, there was little else to eat.
Many, he reported, were

> worn down with poverty: their habitations scenes of misery,
> made of loose stones; without chimnies, without doors, except-
> ing the faggot opposed to the wind at one or other of the
> apertures, permitting the smoke to escape through the other, in
> order to prevent the pains of suffocation.

Their cottages were wretched, even compared with the rural poor of
England and Wales:

> A pothook hangs from the middle of the roof, with a pot pendent
> over a grateless fire, filled with fare that may rather be called
> permission to exist, than a support of vigorous life: the inmates,
> as may be expected, lean, withered, dusky and smoke-dried.[32]

The primitive agriculture was semi-nomadic, semi-pastoral. In

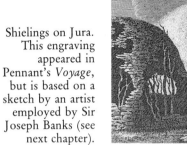

Shielings on Jura. This engraving appeared in Pennant's *Voyage*, but is based on a sketch by an artist employed by Sir Joseph Banks (see next chapter).

early summer, although some islanders remained in the village to tend their crops of oats, barley and potatoes, others would drive their flocks to upland pastures, where they made cheeses and butter of the milk – food to be consumed in the lean winter months. While away from home they lived in temporary huts, into which Pennant peered, before instructing his servant, Moses Griffith, to sketch them:

> Land on a bank covered with sheelins, the habitations of some peasants who attend the herds of milch cows. These formed a group; some were oblong, many conical, and so low that entrance is forbidden, without creeping through the little opening . . . They are constructed of branches of trees, covered with sods; the furniture a bed of heath, placed on a bank of sod; two blankets and a rug; some dairy vessels, and above, certain pendent shelves made of basket work, to hold the cheese, the produce of the Summer. In one of these little conic huts, I spied a little infant asleep, under the protection of a faithful dog.[35]

Pennant enjoyed excellent health for over seventy years of his long life, due mainly, so he believed, to temperate living and abundant riding. Typically, he set off from the little group of shielings across the pathless moorland to climb one of the Paps of Jura – an arduous task, for they rise steeply, and their massive screes present the walker with considerable difficulties. (Scree was a word which had not then entered the English language.) Pennant was in his late forties – not exactly a young man.

> Cross, on foot, a large plain of ground, seemingly improveable, but covered with a deep heath, and perfectly in a state of nature. See the arctic-gull, a bird unknown in South Britain, which breeds here on the ground: it was very tame, but, if disturbed,

flew about like a lapwing, but with a more flagging wing. After a walk of four miles, reach the Paps: left the lesser to the South East, preferring the ascent of the greatest, for there are three; Beinn-a-chaolois, or, the mountain of the sound; Beinn-sheunta, or the hallowed mountain; and Beinn-an-òir, or, the mountain of gold. We began to scale the last; a task of much labor and difficulty; being composed of vast stones, slightly covered with mosses near the base, but all above bare, and unconnected with each other. The whole seems a cairn, the work of the sons of Saturn. . .

Gain the top, and find our fatigues fully recompenced by the grandeur of the prospect from this sublime spot: Jura itself afforded a stupendous scene of rock, varied with little lakes innumerable. From the West side of the hill ran a narrow stripe of rock, terminating in the sea, called, the slide of the old hag. Such appearances are very common in this island and in Jura, and in several parts of North Britain, and in the north of Ireland, and all supposed to be of volcanic origin, being beds of lava. . .They frequently appear three or four feet above the surface of the ground, so that they are called on that account Whin-dikes, forming natural dikes, or boundaries. . .

To the South appeared Ilay, extended like a map beneath us; and beyond that, the North of Ireland; to the East, Gigha and Cara, Cantyre [Kintyre] and Arran, and the Firth of Clyde, bounded by Airshire; an amazing tract of mountains to the N.E. as far as Ben-lomond; Skarba finished the Northern View; and over the Western ocean were scattered Colonsay and Oransay, Mull, Iona, and its neighboring groupe of isles; and still further the long extents of Tirey and Col just apparent.

On the summit are several lofty cairns, not the work of devotion, but of idle herds, or curious travellers. Even this vast heap of stones was not uninhabited: a hind passed along the sides full speed, and a brace of Ptarmigans often favored us with their appearance, even near the summit.

The other paps are seen very distinctly: each inferior in height to this, but all of the same figure, perfectly mamillary. Mr Banks and his friends mounted that to the South and found the height to be two thousand three hundred and fifty nine feet: but Beinn-an-òir far over-topped it; seated on the pinnacle, the depth below was tremendous on every side.

The stones of this mountain are white (a few red) quartzy and composed of small grains; but some are brecciated, or filled with crystalline kernels, of an amethystine color.[34]

Pennant and his party then returned to the Sound of Islay, and crossed over to Port Askaig. He spent the next few days on Islay, staying with various gentlemen, from whom he received details of local history, and the flora and fauna, charms and cures, diversion and superstitions. By 6 July he was ready to rejoin his vessel.

Northward bound, the *Lady Frederick Campbell* sped with the tide up the narrow Sound of Islay, and from thence to the twin isles of Oronsay and Colonsay. The weather was exceedingly hot and calm, and after a tedious passage they anchored off Oronsay. Here Pennant explored the ruined monastry of St Oran, and wondered at the rich bird life — red-billed choughs, eider duck, and sheldrakes.

It was not until 8 July that Pennant rejoined ship to sail northwards again for Iona. Still the weather held. He enjoyed the stupendous views: the lofty mountains of Mull lay ahead, while to the south and southeast were Islay, Jura and Scarba, and the entrance to the 'gulph of Corryvrekan'. Beyond lay Lorn, and in the distance soared the high hill of Cruachan.

As they neared the Sound of Iona they began to hear the perpetual noise of breakers as the swell crashed on the Torran rocks — 'a tremendous chain of rocks'. Dusk was approaching. They spent the night hoved to, fearful of rocks.

The Paps of Jura. Thomas Pennant, who climbed the highest of the Paps, described them as 'the work of the sons of Saturn'. Aquatint by John Schekty.

About eight of the clock in the morning [of 9 July], very narrowly escape striking on the rock Bònirevor, apparent at this time by the breaking of a wave; our master was at some distance in his [rowing] boat, in search of sea fowl, but alarmed with the danger of his vessel, was hastening to its relief; but the tide conveyed us out of reach of the rock, and saved him the trouble of landing us; for the weather was so calm as to free us from any apprehensions about our lives. After tiding for three hours, anchor in the sound of Iona, in three fathoms water, on a white sandy bottom; but the safest anchorage is on the East side, between a little isle and that of Mull. [Pennant is referring to Bull Hole.] This sound is three miles long and one broad, shallow, and in some parts dry at the ebb of spring tides: it is bounded on the East by the island of Mull; on the West, by that of Iona, the most celebrated of the Hebrides.

Multitudes of gannets now fishing here: they precipitated themselves from a vast height, plunged on their prey at least two fathom deep, and took to the air again as soon as they emerged. Their sense of seeing must be exquisite; but they are often deceived, for Mr Thompson informed me, that he had frequently taken them by placing a herring on a hook, and sinking it a fathom deep, which the gannet plunges for and is taken.

The view of Iona is very picturesque: the East side, or that which bounds the sound, exhibited a beautiful variety; an extent of plain, a little elevated above the water, and almost covered with the ruins of the sacred buildings, and with the remains of the old town still inhabited. Beyond these the island rises into little rocky hills, with narrow verdant hollows between (for they merit not the name of vallies) and numerous enough for every recluse to take his solitary walk, undisturbed by society.[35]

Pennant then recounts in some detail the story of St Columba and the religious communities which had lived on the island. His journal then continues:

Took boat and landed on the spot called the Bay of Martyrs, the place where the bodies of those who were to be interred in this holy ground were received, during the period of superstition.

Walked about a quarter of a mile to the South, in order to fix on a convenient spot for pitching a rude tent, formed of oars and sails, as our day residence, during our stay on the island. . .

Having settled the business of our tent, return through the town, consisting at present of about fifty houses, mostly very mean, thatched with straw of bear [barley] pulled up by the roots, and bound tight on the roof with ropes made of heath. Some of the houses that lie a little beyond the rest seemed to have been better constructed than the others, and to have been the mansions of the inhabitants when the place was in a florishing state, but at present are in a very ruinous condition.

The [nunnery] church was fifty-eight feet by twenty: the roof of the east end is entire, is a pretty vault made of very thin stones, bound together by four ribs meeting in the centre. The floor is covered some feet thick with cow-dung; this place being at present the common shelter for the cattle; and the islanders are too lazy to remove this fine manure, the collection of a century, to enrich their grounds.

With much difficulty, by virtue of fair words, and a bribe, prevale on one of these listless fellows to remove a great quantity of this dung-hill; and by that means once more exposed to light the tomb of the last prioress. Her figure is cut on the face of the stone; an angle on each side supports her head; and above them is a little plate and a comb.[36]

Pennant describes in great detail all his discoveries, including the 'broad paved way', the 'large and elegant cross, called that of Maclean', the 'slight remains' that were all he could find of the tombs of the kings, and the tombs in the chapel of St Oran of both named warriors and priests, and 'numbers of other antient heroes, whose very names have perished, and they deprived of their expected glory: their lives were, like the path of an arrow, closed up and lost as soon as past; and probably in those times of barbarism, as fatal to their fellow creatures'. Finally, he comes to the ruined cathedral, which, with his customary exactitude, he measures and describes, though in a rather uninspired manner.

Pennant then proceeded to walk around the ruins of the monastery, the ruins of the abbot's gardens, the kiln (for drying grain) and mill, with the dried-out pool above it. The natives, he observed, 'neglect at present the convenience of the mill and use only the querns' (hand mills).

After carefully cataloguing the remains, Pennant, true to form, set out briskly to explore the isle:

Cross the island over a most fertile elevated tract to the S. West side, to visit the landing place of St Columba; a small bay, with a pebbly beach, mixed with a variety of pretty stones, such as violet-coloured Quartz, Nephritic stones, and fragments of porphyry, granite and Zoeblitz marble; a vast tract near this place

Iona Cathedral. Engraving after a sketch by Pennant's servant, Moses Griffith, from Pennant's *Voyage*.

was covered with heaps of stones, of unequal sizes: these, as is said, were the penances of monks who were to raise heaps, of dimensions equal to their crimes: and to judge by some, it is no breach of charity to think there were among them enormous sinners.

On one side is shewn an oblong heap of earth, the supposed size of the vessel that transported St Columba and his twelve disciples from Ireland to this island.

On my return saw, on the right hand, on a small hill, a small circle of stones, and a little cairn in the middle, evidently druidical, but called the hill of the angels, Cnoc nar-aimgeal; from a tradition that the holy man had there a conference with those celestial beings soon after his arrival.[37]

An interesting thing about this passage – as in so many other passages in the fascinating book – is the way Pennant writes down on paper, in many cases for the first time, oral traditions about places and people that had been handed down through many generations. Here, an illiterate people, living in abject poverty, with an apparently complete disregard for the historic ruins in which they squatted, nevertheless preserved in their oral traditions a rich and extensive heritage of folklore, historical materials and poetry of the highest order. (This last was not accessible to the English-speaking Pennant.)

Another fascinating thing is the extent to which later travellers and writers of guide books were to quarry materials from Pennant's *Voyage* – a book last printed in the year 1790, but repeated, sometimes word for word, in the pages of today's guides.

On 11 July Pennant once again set sail, northward bound. The *Lady Frederick Campbell*'s sails filled with a fresh southwesterly as they churned through a rising sea. The heavy swell breaking on rocky outliers prevented an approach to what looked like an interesting small island.

Thus did Pennant miss the biggest scoop of his tour – the fabulous cave of Fingal on Staffa. Only a month later, on 12 August 1772, in calm weather, an immensely rich young landowner, by the name of Joseph Banks, landed on Staffa and was not long in communicating his astonishing discovery to the world in the pages of the *Scots Magazine*. In the next chapter I quote from the journal of this lucky traveller – a journal that Pennant managed to incorporate in his own *Voyage*, for Banks was a friend and, like Pennant, a Fellow of the Royal Society.

It must have been galling for Pennant that he was so near to making a discovery of the first water – and yet so far. For unlike the rich and privileged Banks, Pennant was only able to finance modest expeditions, and depended on his popular travel writings to recoup his expenses. But for the freshening breeze, and the prudence of Mr Thompson, it might have been Pennant who had rowed over to Staffa and amazed the world with the romantic discovery.

The sky now grew black, there were 'gales of rain' and 'turbulent seas'. The mountains of Rhum disappeared in squally clouds, and it was a relief to find themselves, after such a rough passage, safe within Canna's delightful harbour, after rounding the dangerous reef that lies in wait for sailors coming in from the south.

At first sight, Pennant says, each shore

> appeared pleasing to humanity; verdant, and covered with hundreds of cattle: both sides gave a full idea of plenty, for the verdure was mixed with very little rock, and scarcely any heath: but a short conversation with the natives soon dispelled this agreeable error: they were at this time in such want, that numbers for a long time had neither bread nor meal for their poor babes: fish and milk was their whole subsistence at this time: the first was a precarious relief, for, besides the uncertainty of success, to add to their distress, their stock of fish-hooks was almost exhausted: and to[o] ours, that it was not in our power to supply them. The rubban [ribbons], and other trifles I had brought would have been insults to people in distress. I lamented that my money had been so uselessly laid out; for a few dozens of fish-hooks, or a few packs of meal, would have made them happy.[38]

Famine years in the islands were all too frequent. The abundant cattle were kept in order to pay the rapacious landlord. The owners of Canna were descendants of Clanranald (Alastair MacDonald's chief) who were being transformed by Eton into fit companions for the Prince Regent. The starving clansmen had no option but to fill the coffers of their greedy chiefs.

Commercial fishing was beyond the means of the impoverished islanders:

> Abundance of cod and ling might be taken; there being a fine sand-bank between this isle and the rock Heisker, and another between Skie and Barra; but the poverty of the inhabitants will not enable them to attempt a fishery. When at Campbeltown I enquired about the apparatus requisite, and found that a vessel of twenty tuns was necessary, which would cost two hundred pounds; that the crew should be composed of eight hands, whose monthly expences would be fourteen pounds; that six hundred fathom of long-line, five hundred hooks, and two Stuoy lines (each eighty fathoms long) which are placed at each end of the long-lines with buoys at top to mark the place when sunk, would all together cost five guineas; and the vessel must be provided with four sets; so that the whole charge of such an adventure is very considerable, and past the ability of these poor people.[39]

From the figures Pennant gives, it would appear that the money income of the poorest families on the isle was miserable: men servants could earn thirty shilling (£1.50) a year. Some money was raised by selling their cows (at about £1 a head) to drovers who visited the island. The money went almost entirely on rent of 'four and a half guineas each' (£4.72), in addition to forced labour of three days a quarter 'to the impoverishing and very starving of the wretched inhabitants'. Small wonder they could not even buy oatmeal or fish hooks.

Pennant's peregrinations far and wide – from Canna through the Kyles to Skye, and from thence ever northwards up the west coast of Scotland – gave him ample opportunity to observe the fisheries, and their enormous potential for exploitation. In one particularly striking passage he describes the annual migration of the herring – 'that great army that annually deserts the vast depths of the arctic circle, and comes, heaven-directed, to the seats of population, offered as a cheap food to millions'. The migration, Pennant records,

> is regular: their visits to the Western isles and coasts, certain: but their attachment to one particular loch, extremely precarious. All

have their turns; that which swarmed with fish one year, is totally deserted the following; yet the next loch to it is crowded with the shoals. These changes of place give often full employ to the busses [two or three-masted fishing boats], who are continually shifting their harbour in quest of news respecting these important wanderers.

They commonly appear here in July; the latter end of August they go into deep water, and continue there for some time, without any apparent cause: in November they return to the shallows, when a new fishery commences, which continues till January; at that time the herrings become full of roe, and are useless as articles of commerce. . .

The signs of the arrival of the herrings are flocks of gulls, who catch up the fish while they skim on the surface; and of gannets, who plunge and bring them up from considerable depths. Both these birds are closely attended to by the fishers.

Cod-fish, haddocks, and dog-fish follow the herrings in vast multitudes; these voracious fish keep on the outsides of the columns, and may be a concurrent reason of driving the shoals into bays and creeks. In summer they come into the bays generally with the warmest weather, and with easy gales. During winter the hard gales from the N. West are supposed to assist in forcing them into shelter . . .

In a fine day, when the fish appear near the surface, they exhibit an amazing brilliancy of colors; all the various coruscations that dart from the diamond, sapphire and emerald, enrich their tract: but during night, if they break, i.e. play on the surface, the sea appears on fire, luminous as the brightest phosphorus.

During a gale, that part of the ocean which is occupied by the great shoals, appear as if covered with the oil that is emitted from them.

They seem greatly affected by lightening: during that phenomenon they sink towards the bottom, and move regularly in parallel shoals one above the other.

The enemies that assail these fish in the Winter season are varied, not diminished: of the birds, the gannets disappear; the gulls still continue the persecutions; whales, pollacks (a small whale whose species I cannot determine) and porpesses are added to their number of foes: these follow in droves; the whales deliberately, opening their vast mouths, taking them by the hundreds. These monsters keep on the outside, for the body of the phalanx of herrings is so thick as to be impenetrable by these unwieldy animals.[40]

Pennant remarked that 'very few of the natives possess a boat and nets' and were prevented by their extreme poverty from taking advantage of these fertile fishing grounds, exept as hands and 'raw seamen'.

Pennant's *Voyage* is endlessly fascinating, for he visits so many seas, lochs, kyles and anchorages while his skilful pen sketches in vignette after vignette. He has a particularly good eye for scenery – unusual for the period when mountains were considered 'horrid' and the ideal was the bosky woods and lush meadows of an English country park – and for the changes and chances of voyaging under sail.

Pennant's *Voyage* ends with an account of a strange dream which, he claims, disturbed his rest on his last night in the Hebrides:

> A figure, dressed in the garb of an antient warrior, floated in the air before me: his target [targe, shield] and his claymore seemed no common size, and spoke the former strength of the hero. A graceful vigor was apparent in his countenance, notwithstanding time had robbed him of part of his locks, and given to the remainder a venerable hoariness. As soon as he had fixed my attention, he thus seemed to address himself to me:

Lochranza Bay, Arran. The ship is probably the *Lady Frederick Campbell*, used by Pennant, who witnessed hunts for basking sharks such as the one shown here. Engraving after Moses Griffith.

85

'A figure dressed in the garb of an antient warrior, floated before me . . .' Engraving from an 1806 edition of *The Poems of Ossian*.

'Stranger, Thy purpose is not unknown to me; I have attended thee (invisible) in all thy voyage; have sympathised with thee in the rising tear at the misery of my once-loved country; and sighs, such as a spirit can emit, have been faithful echoes of those of thy corporeal frame.

'Know, that in the days of my existence on earth, I possessed an ample portion of the tract thou seest to the North. I was the dread of neighbouring chieftains; the delight of my people; their protector, their father, their friend. No injury they ever received, passed unrevenged; for no one excelled me in conferring benefits on my clan, or in repaying insults on their enemies. A thousand of my kindred followed me in arms, wheresoever I commanded. I was (for nothing now can be concealed) fierce, arrogant, despotic, irritable; my passions were strong, my anger tremendous: yet I had the arts of conciliating the affections of my people, and was the darling of the numerous brave. They knew the love I bore them: they saw, on a thousand occasions, the strongest proofs of my affection. In the day of battle I have covered the weak with my shield; and laid at my feet their hostile antagonists.'[41]

Thus did the apparition recall the days when 'strong fidelity and warm friendship' reigned among them, and 'mutual hospitality' knit the clan. Then the apparition lamented the changes. Not the exchange of the targe and claymore for the 'arts of peace' which enabled his clansmen to learn 'to spread the net, to shoot the shuttle, or to cultivate the ground', but the dereliction of the chieftains:

The mighty Chieftains, the brave and disinterested heroes of old times, by a most violent and surprising transformation, at once sunk into rapacious landlords; determined to compensate the loss of power, with the increase of revenue; to exchange the warm affections of their people for sordid trash. Their visits, to those of their fore-fathers, are like the surveys of a cruel land-jobber, attended by a set of quick-sighted vultures, skilled in pointing out the most exquisite methods of oppression, or to instructing them in the art of exhausting their purses of sums to be wasted in distant lands. Like the task-masters of Egypt, they require them to make brick without straw. They leave them in their primaeval poverty, uninstructed in any art for their future support; deprived of the wonted resources of the hospitality of their Lord, or the plentiful boards of his numerous friends. They experience an instantaneous desertion: are flung at once into a new state of life, and demand the fostering hand as much as the most infant colony.[42]

86

Pennant, through the mouth of his dream figure, attacks the rapacious exploitation of the Highlands and Islands by anglicized lairds, who drained their estates dry in order to match the lifestyle of their models, the English aristocracy. The tragedy was that the wealth of the English landowner was sustained by advances in agriculture; in the Islands no such advances had been made. And when they came, they took the form of the clearances, with the burning of houses, and the introduction of sheep. Pennant did not foresee this. His pleas (through the dream figure) were different:

> Return to your country; inform them [your people] with your presence; restore to them the laudable part of the antient manners; eradicate the bad. Bring them instructors, and they would learn. Teach them the arts adapted to their climate; they would brave the fury of the seas in fishing. Send them materials for the coarser manufactures; they would with patience sit down to the loom; they would weave the sails to waft your navies to victory; and part of them rejoice to share the glory in the most distant combats. Select a portion of them for the toils of the ocean: make your levies, enroll them; discipline them under able veterans, and send annually to our ports the smaller vessels of your tremendous navy. Trust them with swords. . .

Alas, such pleas were to fall mainly on deaf ears. Even Pennant's more modest requests were sadly ignored:

> If you will totally neglect them; if you will not reside among them; if you will not, by your example, instruct them in the science of rural economy, nor cause them to be taught the useful arts. . .do not at least drive them to despair, by oppression: do not force them into a distant land, and necessitate them to seek tranquillity by a measure which was once deemed the punishment of the most atrocious criminals.[43]

Pennant's *Voyage* opened up the seas of the Hebrides, revealing an area of spectacular beauty, and a culture very different from the home counties, or even the little Welshman's Flintshire estate. But his grim forebodings were painfully fulfilled.

For the next fifty years Pennant's *Voyage* was read by every visitor to the Hebrides. It was brought out in three editions in his lifetime, as well as in a German translation. Its popularity was deserved: he was one of the most observant, entertaining and humane travel writers of his age.

6

THAT CATHEDRAL OF THE SEAS

Sir Joseph Banks, Fingal's Cave,
and MacPhearson's Ossian

THOMAS PENNANT was still in Scotland when, in the autumn of 1772, the *Scots Magazine* announced to a fascinated public the discovery of a huge cave of magnificent basalt columns. The discoverer was Mr (later Sir) Joseph Banks, who proclaimed the island of Staffa as

> one of the greatest natural curiosities in the world: it is surrounded by many pillars of different shapes, such as pentagons, octagons, etc. They are about 55 feet high, and nearly five feet in diameter, supporting a solid rock of a mile in length, and about 60 feet above the pillars. There is a cave in this island which the natives call the Cave of Fingal: its length is 371 feet, about 115 feet in height, and 51 feet wide; the whole sides are solid rock, and the bottom is covered with water 12 feet deep. The Giant's Causeway in Ireland, or Stonehenge in England, are but trifles when compared to this island, elegant drawings of which were taken on the spot.[44]

Fingal's Cave – 'that cathedral of the seas' – was destined to become the most famous and most romantic attraction of the Hebrides. It was to inspire Mendelssohn's famous Hebridean overture, and Turner's impressionistic seascape. The giants of the Romantic movement such as Wordsworth and Keats came to pay tribute (resulting in some rather poor verse), as have many thousands of more ordinary sightseers, lured by the magnetic name and glamorous reputation to chance the perilous seas and heavy swell that make landing at this remote island so difficult.

The original discoverers of Staffa are, of course, lost in the mists of antiquity. The Vikings gave the isle its name, 'Staffa Island', for its resembled the stout wooden staves used to build log cabins. To Banks, however, must go the honour of recognizing the extraordinary attraction of this 'wonderous isle'.

Joseph Banks was, at the time of his discovery, not yet thirty years old, and already a natural historian and explorer with an international repution. He was the only son of a wealthy Lincoln-shire landowner, who died while young Banks was still a gentleman commoner at Christ Church, Oxford. The young man, an Old Etonian with a reputation for being immoderately fond of sport and indifferent to the classical studies which were then the staple of a gentleman's education, refused to follow the normal lecture course. Instead he imported, at his own expense, a Cambridge lecturer on botany and astronomy.

Banks left Oxford without a degree, having come into a large fortune. At the age of 23 he was elected a Fellow of the Royal Society, in recognition of his outstanding interest in natural history. Three years later he obtained permission to accompany Cook on his first voyage of exploration (1768-71). At his own expense, Banks equipped a scientific team, consisting of himself, Dr Daniel Solander, two draughtsmen, and two attendants. Banks's journal of this three-year cicumnavigation of the globe in the *Endeavour* makes exciting reading. Banks's incessant curiousity was aroused by the numerous new species of plants and animals, including the kangaroo. A journey to collect specimens on the southernmost tip of South America almost ended in disaster, and but for Banks's energy his companions would have perished from exposure. At Tahiti, Banks was able to recover vital navigational instruments stolen by natives. In New Zealand six months were spent exploring the coast. Australia was next visited, and Banks christened Botany Bay, after the large number of new species discovered there. The *Endeavour* was wrecked on the Great Barrier Reef, and only saved by the expedients suggested by a young midshipman. The expedition was dogged with sickness, and at one time Banks and Solander were so desperately ill that they were put ashore at Batavia, and two female slaves were purchased to nurse them. They recovered, but three of Banks's party perished, one in Tahiti, and two in the passage to the Cape of Good Hope.

In spite of these disasters, Banks was eager to accompany Cook on his next trip, in 1772. He was disappointed in this plan, so instead visited Iceland in the summer of 1772, in the company of Dr Solander (himself an eminent scientist), and an Icelandic Bishop. Banks's party also included Zoffany the painter, three draughtsmen to make drawings of plants and animals, two secretaries, and nine other skilled assistants.

Sir Joseph Banks, the 'discoverer' of Fingal's Cave. Drawing by Thomas Lawrence.

89

The route to Iceland was the traditional one: via the Hebrides, the Faroes and thence westward along the Arctic Circle. So it was that in early August 1772 Banks found himself in the Sound of Mull. There he was hospitably entertained by MacLean of Drummen, where, according to Banks's journal, they met with 'an English gentlemen, Mr Leach, who no sooner saw us than he told us, that about nine leagues from us was an island where he believed no one in the highlands had ever been, on which were pillars like those of the Giant's-Causeway'.

The energetic Banks immediately 'resolved to proceed directly'. Clearly, the tiny island would offer no anchorage for the expedition's large vessel. Approach, he was advised, would only be possible in a small boat, probably the yawl shown in the illustration, which could be rowed by the crew.

Accordingly having put up two days provisions, and my little tent, we put off in the boat about one o'clock for our intended voyage, having ordered the ship to wait for us in Torbirmore [Tobermory], a very fine harbour on the Mull side.

At nine o'clock, after a tedious passage, having not a breath of wind, we arrived, under the direction of Mr. Mc. Leane's son, and Mr. Leach. It was too dark to see any thing, so we carried our tent and baggage near the only house upon the island, and began

The landing place at Staffa. This engraving, and that on the following page, were published in Pennant's *Voyage*, and were based on sketches made by John Cleveley Jnr, an artist employed by Sir Joseph Banks.

to cook our suppers, in order to be prepared for the earliest dawn, to enjoy that which from the conversation of the gentlemen we had now raised the highest expectations of.

The impatience which every body felt to see the wonders we had heard so largely described, prevented our morning's rest; everyone was up and in motion before the break of day, and with the first light arrived at the s.w. part of the island, the seat of the most remarkable pillars; where we no sooner arrived than we were struck with a scene of magnificence which exceeded our expectations, though formed, as we thought, upon the most sanguine of foundations: the whole of that end of the island supported by ranges of natural pillars, mostly above 50 feet high, standing in natural colonnades, according as the bays or points of land had formed themselves; upon a firm base of solid unformed rock, above these, the stratum which reaches to the soil or surface of the island, varied in thickness as the island itself formed into hills or vallies; each hill, which hung over the columns below, forming an ample pediment; some of these above 60 feet in thickness, from the base to the point, formed by the sloping of the hill on each side, almost into the shape of those used in architecture.

Compared to this what are the cathedrals or the palaces built by men! mere models or playthings, imitations as diminutive as his works will always be when compared with those of nature.

Fingal's Cave. Engraving after John Cleveley Jnr. The engraver found great difficulty in making sense of Cleveley's protrayal of the cave's columnar basalt walls and the contrasting roof of porous tufa, in which are embedded the stumps of columns.

91

James MacPhearson, author of *Fingal* and other poems supposedly translated from the Gaelic of Ossian. Engraving after Joshua Reynolds.

Where now is the boast of the architect! regularity, the only part in which he fancied himself to exceed his mistress, Nature, is here found in her possession, and here it has been for ages undescribed. . .

With our minds full of such reflections we proceed along the shore, treading upon another Giant's Causeway, every stone being regularly formed into a certain number of sides and angles, 'till in a short time we arrived at the mouth of a cave, the most magnificent, I suppose, that has ever been described by travellers.

The mind can hardly form an idea more magnificent than such a space, supported on each side by ranges of columns; and roofed by the bottoms of those, which have been broke off in order to form it; between the angles of which a yellow stalagmitic matter has exuded, which serves to define the angles precisely; and at the same time vary the color with a great deal of elegance, and to render it still more agreeable, the whole is lighted from without, so that the farthest extremity is very plainly seen from without, the air within being agitated by the flux and reflux of tides, is perfectly dry and wholesome, free entirely from the damp vapours with which natural caverns in general abound. . .

We asked the name of it [the cave]. Said our guide, the cave of Fhinn; what is Fhinn? said we. Fhinn Mac Coul, whom the translator of Ossian's works has called Fingal. How fortunate that in this cave we should meet with the rememberance of that chief, whose existence, as well as that of the whole Epic poem is almost doubted in England.[45]

What is Finn? – what an extraordinary question to ask in 1772! For Fingal was a cause célèbre throughout the literary world, a talking point among the drawing rooms of London and Edinburgh, a literary scandal which rocked the western world and in some sense was to launch the Romantic movement. Everyone who was anyone in 1772 knew of Fingal. And the romantic linking of the name of Fingal with this magnificent cave was to fuel the controversy about the epic poem entitled *Fingal*.

Ten years before Banks 'discovered' Staffa and Fingal's cave a 26-year-old Scot, James MacPhearson, published a volume he entitled *Fingal, an Ancient Epic Poem. . .composed by Ossian*. No doubt the young Joseph Banks, then an undergraduate at Oxford, read this fantasy which was soon topping the bestsellers. MacPhearson claimed his epic was a literal translation of Ossian's poems. Ossian was reputed to be the son of Finn, an historic figure who

92

died in a battle in Ireland in 283 AD. If MacPhearson had indeed discovered and translated this epic of Homeric proportions, it was the oldest British literary survivor from the Dark Ages. It was contemporary with the last period of the Roman Empire. Was it possible that this poem could have survived for fifteen centuries? The poem set literary Europe agog. MacPhearson was lionized. But, said his critics, could he be believed?

MacPhearson was an unsuccessful, hard-up young would-be poet. Born on the edge of the Highlands, he had a sprinkling of Gaelic – enough for him to understand some of the tales which were the mainstay of the ceilidh, the fireside story-tellings that whiled away the long dark winter nights. 'Have you any new tales of Finn and his warriors, the Feinne?' was the question put to every Gaelic-speaking stranger, for all were avid for tales of this legendary hero. Bards and story tellers recounted the feats of Finn and his band. The poems and legends were of heroism, courtships, voyaging, of battle and the hunt; of cruel enemies, of witchcraft, of wild boars; of passion and rivalry, of love and nobility. Truth triumphed over falsehood, loyalty was stronger than death, good vanquished evil.

The blind Ossian singing, accompanying himself on the harp. Alexander Runciman's sketch for his magnificent ceiling at Penicuik House, Midlothian (1772). The house was destroyed by fire.

93

'Fingal, tall in his ship, stretched his bright lance before him. Terrible was the gleam of the steel: it was like the green meteor of death, setting in the heath of Malmor . . .' The engravings on these two pages are from an 1806 edition of *The Poems of Ossian*.

The fight of Fingal and Swaran: 'Terrible is the battle of the kings; dreadful the look of their eyes . . .'

Many of these tales were ascribed to Ossian, Finn's son. Ossian, it was fabled, had been seduced by a fairy princess and persuaded to spend three marvellous days with her in Tir nan Og – the land of the ever young, which lies beneath the western waves. Three days they had seemed. But when he returned to earth he found three centuries had passed, and none now knew of Fingal and his exploits. So the ancient white-bearded bard swept the strings of his *clarsach* – his harp – with his knarled fingers and sang of the heroes of his youth and unforgettable tales passed on down the generations.

Thus it was that this material was available to young MacPhearson. He presented some half-remembered tales as a 'translation'.

Encouraged by his success he set out in 1760 to search the Highlands and Islands for

> what remains of the works of the old bards, especially those of Ossian, the son of Fingal, who was the best, as well as the most ancient, of those who are celebrated in tradition for their poetic compositions.[46]

MacPhearson was, as he says, 'not unsuccessful':

> Several gentlemen in the Highlands and isles generously gave me all the assistance in their power; and it was by their means I was enabled to compleat the epic poem.

'There Comala sits forlorn! . . . She turns her blue eyes toward the fields of promise. Where art thou, O Fingal?'

Almost certainly, MacPhearson had obtained some ancient Gaelic manuscripts, including the famous *Book of the Dean of Lismore*, which he later deposited with his bookseller. His Gaelic was halting. The Dean's book was almost indecipherable, alas. But he heard – or claimed to hear – echoes of an epic fit to rival the *Odyssey*, authentic despite the hazards of centuries of oral transmission. From this rich seam he quarried.

MacPhearson's 'translation', *Fingal, an Ancient Epic Poem*, was a runaway bestseller. It was soon translated into Italian, German, French, Spanish, Danish, Russian, Swedish, Dutch, Czech, Hungarian, and Polish. It enjoyed immense popularity. For it met a deeply felt need. The eighteenth century – the Age of Reason – was more than half over. A new feeling was astir. What we now call the Romantic movement was just below the horizon. The conventions of classicism were beginning to be challenged by a new, freer attitude to poetry. The artificiality of urban civilization was to give way to a new sensitivity to the wonders of nature, especially of mountain, cliff, wild seas and grandiose scenery.

Fingal symbolized the ancient, the primitive, the grand and romantic, the wild and remote. No wonder that Banks found it fitting that this magnificent cave should be named after this heroic chieftain. For in legend the great Finn and his band the Feinn used caves for their hide-outs. Indeed, folk say that he sleeps yet in some dark cave, with his men and his noble hunting dogs. About his neck is slung his mighty hunting horn. Three blasts would wake the sleeping warriors, but it is death to him who sounds that blast.

Sir Joseph Banks – he was created a baronet in 1781 – may have later regretted the credibility he lent to young MacPheason by naming the cave after Fingal. For James MacPhearson was un-

Felix Mendelssohn, whose visit to Staffa in 1829 inspired his overture *The Hebrides*, popularly known as *Fingal's Cave*.

masked as an egoistic, unscrupulous mountebank who fabricated more and more fantastic evidence as the years passed to shore up his shaky claim to have translated an ancient masterpiece. And Sir Joseph Banks, his voyaging days over, increasingly became a member of the establishment. He was a distinguished, and highly autocratic, president of the Royal Society for over forty years, was invested with the Order of the Bath, and sworn of the Privy Council in 1797.

And yet. . .surely Banks's instinct was right. He may even have misheard the name of the cave. But what does it matter? By some subtle chemistry the romantic legend and the marvellous cave created an elixir that transformed literary history, and our attitude to wild and romantic places. Fingal's Cave became a place of pilgrimage for the Romantics: for Wordsworth, Keats and Sir Walter Scott amongst poets; young Mendelssohn among musicians; Turner and William Daniell among painters. Queen Victoria ventured here in 1847.

Perhaps the finest evocation of the cave is in Mendelssohn's overture, *The Hebrides*, popularly known as *Fingal's Cave*. Those great surges of wave-like music haunt us still, recreating for us 'that vast cathedral of the sea, with its dark lapping waters within, and the brightness of the gleaming waters without' (to quote Mendessohn's own description).

And MacPhearson's Ossian? Who reads his epic now? No one. You may chance upon a copy in the dusty stacks of an old-fashioned library: leather bound, elegant, a first edition – once cherished, then cast aside as an embarrassing scandal. Turn the pages, so long unread, of a book that had once made literary history. Does this prose poem deserve a better fate? The clash of arms still rings in your ears as you read the last page. The heroic Gaels have triumphed in battle over the Viking invaders from faraway Lochlann. Now their thoughts turn to peace. Fingal, King of Morven (which lies to the east of Mull's Sound), addresses his friend and ally, the legendary Cuchullin of Skye:

> Spread now thy white sails for the isle of mist, and see thy lover, Bragela, leaning on her rock. Her tender eye is in tears, and the winds lift her long hair from her heaving breast. She listens to the winds of night to hear the voice of thy rowers; to hear the song of the sea and the sound of thy distant harp. . .
>
> Spread the sail, said the king of Morven, and catch the winds

that pour from Lena. – We rose on the wave with songs, and rushed, with joy, through the foam of the ocean.[48]

Thus ends MacPhearson's masterpiece. In his life acclaimed, it was reviled in his dying days. 'Poetry', he wrote, 'like virtue, receives its reward after death.' After his death, as the full extent of his disastrous forgery was revealed, both his poem and his reputation were destroyed.

Yet we owe him a debt. The violent controversy over 'Ossian' resulted in a desperate search for manuscripts and oral literature. Undoubtedly many priceless manuscripts were preserved just as the culture of the Highlands and Islands was coming under increasing threat from those who followed in Banks's wake. Moreover, as Sir Walter Scott observed in his review of the 1805 *Report on Ossian*, which, after half a century, at last gave a definitive evaluation of MacPhearson:

> While we are compelled to renounce the pleasing idea 'that Fingal lived, and that Ossian sung', our national vanity may be equally flattered by the fact that a remote and almost barbarous corner of Scotland produced, in the 18th century, a bard, capable not only of making an enthusiastic impression on every mind susceptible of poetic beauty, but of giving a new tone to poetry throughout all Europe.[49]

But for MacPhearson's *Fingal*, as we shall see in the following chapter, our next pair of travellers, Dr Samuel Johnson and his faithful Boswell, would probably never have undertaken their tour of the Hebrides. Johnson carefully ascribed his interest to his perusal of Martin Martin's *Description of the Western Isles*, given to him by his bookseller father half a century earlier. But there can be little doubt that the announcement in 1772 of Banks's discovery of Fingal's Cave also played a significant part in Johnson's decision the following year to set off on his Hebridean jaunt.

7

A-ROVING IN THE HEBRIDES

Samuel Johnson and James Boswell

Johnson. 'I am not disputing that you may have poetry of great merit; but that McPherson's is not a translation from ancient poetry. You do not believe it. I say before you, you do not believe it, though you are very willing that the world should believe it.'—Mr. McQueen made no answer to this—Dr. Johnson proceeded, 'I look upon McPherson's *Fingal* to be as gross an imposition as ever the world was troubled with. Had it been really an ancient work, a true specimen how men thought at that time, it would have been a curiosity of the first rate. As a modern production, it is nothing.'[50]

DR JOHNSON and his faithful biographer Boswell were in the Hebrides. It was the year 1773 – just twelve months since the historic voyages of Thomas Pennant and Joseph Banks. And here was the confirmed Londoner seated in a small rowing boat crossing from Skye to Raasay, and arguing, against the sound of the waves, with the Reverend Mr McQueen on the authenticity of MacPhearson's Ossianic tales of Fingal.

Here, from the pen of Boswell, are portraits of the passengers. First, Dr Johnson:

His person was large, robust, I may say approaching to the gigantick, and grown unwieldy from corpulency. His countenance was naturally of the cast of an ancient statute, but somewhat disfigured by the scars of the *evil*, which, it was formerly imagined, the *royal touch** could cure. He was now in his sixty-fourth year, and was becoming a little dull of hearing. His sight had always been somewhat weak; yet, so much does mind

---

* The 'king's evil' – scrofula – was a form of tuberculosis which affected the lymphatic glands; Johnson was 'touched' by Queen Anne as a small child, but without receiving a cure.

govern, and even supply the deficiency of organs, that his perceptions were uncommonly quick. His head, and sometimes also his body, shook with a kind of motion like the effect of a palsy: he appeared to be frequently disturbed by cramps, or convulsive contractions, of a nature of that distemper called *St Vitus's* dance. He wore a full suit of plain brown clothes, with twisted-hair-buttons of the same colour, a large bushy greyish wig, a plain shirt, black worsted stockings, and silver buckles. Upon this tour, when journeying, he wore boots, and a very wide brown cloth great coat, with pockets which might have held the two volumes of his folio dictionary; and he carried in his hand a large English oak stick.

'If', Boswell continues, somewhat apologetically,

he was particularly prejudiced against the Scots, it was because they were more in his way; because he thought their success in England rather exceeded the due proportion of their real merit. . .He was indeed, if I may be allowed the phrase, at bottom much of a *John Bull*; much of a blunt *true-born English-man*. There was a stratum of common clay under the rock of marble. He was voraciously fond of good eating.[51]

Johnson's description of Boswell is briefer: in him he found

a companion, whose acuteness would help my inquiry, and whose gaiety of conversation and civility of manners are suffi-cient to counteract the inconveniences of travel.[52]

Accompanying Johnson and Boswell were two Skye gentlemen, Donald McQueen and Malcolm Macleod, whom Boswell describes in his Journal thus:

Mr. Donald McQueen [is] a decent minister, an elderly man with his own black hair, courteous, and rather slow of speech, but candid, sensible and well informed, nay learned. Along with him came, as our pilot, a gentleman whom I had a great desire to see, Mr. Malcolm Macleod, one of the Rasay [Raasay] family, cele-brated in the year 1745-6. He was now sixty-two years of age, hale, and well proportioned,—with a manly countenance, tanned by the weather, yet having a ruddiness in his cheeks, over a great part of which his rough beard extended.—His eye was quick and lively, yet his look was not fierce, but he appeared at once firm and good-humoured. He wore a pair of brogues,—Tartan hose which came up only near to his knees, and left them bare,—a purple camblet [a mixture of wool and silk] kilt,—a black waistcoat,—a short green cloth coat bound with gold cord,—a yellowish bushy wig,—a large blue bonnet with a gold thread button. I never saw a figure that gave a more perfect representation of a Highland gentleman. . .

Boswell continues:

We got into Rasay's *carriage*, which was a good strong open boat made in Norway. The wind had now risen pretty high, and was against us; but we had four stout rowers, particularly a Macleod, a robust, black-haired fellow, half-naked, and bare-headed, something between a wild Indian and an English tar. Dr. Johnson sat high on the stern, like a magnificent Triton. Malcolm sung an Erse song, the chorus of which was '*Hatyin foam foam eri*' with words of his own. The tune resembled '*Owr the muir amang the heather*'. The boatmen and Mr. McQueen chorused, and all went well. At length Malcolm himself took an oar, and rowed vigorously. We sailed along the coast of Scalpa [Scalpay], a rugged island, about four miles in length. Dr. Johnson proposed that he and I should buy it, and found a good school, and an episcopal church, (Malcolm said, he would come to it,) and have a printing-press, where he would print all the Erse that could be found.

The cathedral at Iona (above). 'That man is little to be envied, whose patriotism would not gain force upon the plain of *Marathon*, or whose piety would not grow warmer among the ruins of *Iona!*' Aquatint by William Daniell.

Here I was strongly struck with our long-projected scheme of visiting the Hebrides being realised. I called to him, 'We are contending with seas;' which I think were the words of one of his letters. 'Not much,' said he; and though the wind made the sea lash considerably upon us, he was not discomposed. After we were out of the shelter of Scalpa, and in the sound between it and Rasay, which extended about a league, the wind made the sea very rough. I did not like it.—*Johnson*. 'This now is the Atlantick. If I should tell at a tea-table in London, that I have crossed the Atlantick in an open boat, how they'd shudder, and what a fool they'd think me to expose myself to such danger?'. . .

Ardnamurchan 'the height of the great seas' (below). Storms off this coast nearly put paid to the literary careers of Johnson, Boswell and James Hogg. Aquatint by William Daniell.

The approach to Rasay [Boswell continues in his *Journal*] was very pleasing. We saw before us a beautiful bay, well defended by a rocky coast; a good family mansion; a fine verdure about it;. . .and beyond it hills and mountains in gradation of wilderness. Our boatmen sung with great spirit. Dr. Johnson observed, that naval musick was very ancient. As we came near the shore, the singing of our rowers was succeeded by that of reapers, who were busy at work, and who seemed to shout as much as sing, while they worked with bounding activity.[53]

Dr Johnson gives, in his *Journey to the Western Islands*, his own description of this scene:

Two poignant evocations of the desolation of forced exile: *The Last of the Clan* (above) by Thomas Faed, and *Lochaber No More* (right), an engraving after J. Watson Nichol. 'No man willingly left his native country', a Highlander told Dr Johnson, and Boswell remarked on the 'melancholy sight' of the emigrant ships. Despite the indignation of travellers such as Johnson and Boswell at the 'rage for emigration', the clearances were to continue for another hundred years, inflicting untold miseries on the people of the Highlands and Islands.

102

The corn of this island [Raasay] is but little. I saw the harvest of a small field. The women reaped the corn, and the men bound up the sheaves. The strokes of the sickle were timed by the modulation of the harvest song, in which all their voices were united. They accompany in the Highlands every action, which can be done in equal time, with an appropriate strain, which has, they say, not much meaning; but its effects are regularity and cheerfulness. The ancient proceleusmatick [consisting of a metrical foot of four short syllables] song, by which the rowers of gallies were animated, may be supposed to have been of this kind. There is now an *oar-song* used by the *Hebrideans*.[54]

(How typical is Dr Johnson's ponderous classical reference!)

Awaiting the sage of London and his faithful Scots biographer was a large party. Boswell lists them: Raasay himself (chiefs were always given the title of their lands), and a dozen gentlemen:

We were welcomed upon the green, and conducted into the house, where we were introduced to Lady Rasay, who was surrounded by a numerous family, consisting of three sons and ten daughters. The laird of Rasay is a sensible, polite, and most hospitable gentleman. I was told that his island of Rasay, and that of Rona, (from which the eldest son of the family has his title,) and a considerable extent of land which he has in Sky, do not altogether yield him a very large revenue; and yet he lives in great splendour; and is so far from distressing his people, that, in the present rage for emigration, not a man has left his estate.

It was past six o'clock when we arrived. Some excellent brandy was served round immediately, according to the custom of the Highlands, where a dram is generally taken every day. They call it a *scalch*. On the side-board was placed for us, who had come off the sea, a substantial dinner, and a variety of wines. Then we have coffee and tea. I observed in the room several elegantly-bound books, and other marks of improved life. Soon afterwards a fiddler appeared, and a little ball began. Rasay himself danced with as much spirit as any man, and Malcolm bounded like a roe. Sandie Macleod, who has at times an excessive flow of spirits, and had it now, was, in his days of absconding, known by the name of *McCruslick*, which it seems was the designation of a kind of wild man in the Highlands, something between Proteus and Don Quixote; and so he was called here. He made much jovial noise. Dr. Johnson was so delighted with this scene, that he said, 'I know not how we shall get away.' It entertained me to observe him sitting by, while we danced, sometimes in deep

103

The route of Johnson and Boswell, 1773.

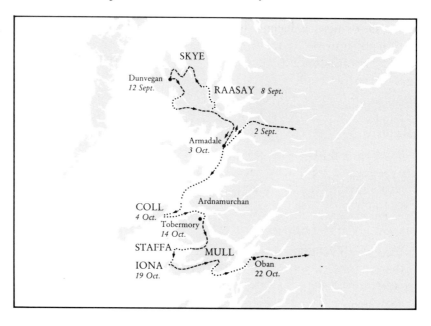

On foot/ horseback ----------

Voyages ....

meditation,—sometimes smiling complacently,—sometimes looking upon Hooke's Roman History,—sometimes talking a little, amidst the noise of the ball, to Mr. Donald McQueen, who anxiously gathered knowledge from him. He was pleased with McQueen, and said to me, 'This is a critical man, sir. There must be great vigour of mind to make him cultivate learning so much in the isle of Sky, where he might do without it. It is wonderful how many new publications he has. There must be a snatch of every opportunity.'. . . Soon after we came in, a black cock and grey hen, which had been shot, were shewn, with their feathers on them, to Dr. Johnson, who had never seen that species of bird before. We had company of thirty at supper; and all was good humour and gaiety, without intemperance.[55]

So ended a memorable day — the first truly Hebridean day of Johnson's visit. (Johnson had earlier stayed with Sir Alexander MacDonald of Sleat and completely failed to 'rouse the English-bred Chieftain. . .to feudal and patriarchal feelings'.) Here was the combination of the wild and uncouth, of gentility and manners, of romance and heroism with the lingering memory of the '45. It had been a most exciting day.

But what, it may be asked, were Dr Johnson and his faithful Boswell doing in the Hebrides? The eccentric philosopher, sage and conversationalist, a legend in his own time, was not the most obvious of tourists. Corpulent, short-sighted and somewhat deaf, at 64 he was scarcely a fit man able to withstand the rigours of a rainy autumn so far from the tea tables and coffee houses of literary London. Johnson's subject was the human race, and in the Hebrides he hoped to find a society essentially feudal, 'ignorantly proud and habitually violent' (to quote Johnson):

> We came thither [to the Hebrides] too late to see what we expected, a people of peculiar appearance, and a system of antiquated life. The clans retain little now of their original character, their ferocity of temper is softened, their military ardour is extinguished, their dignity of independence is depress-ed, their contempt of government subdued, and the reverence for their chiefs abated. Of what they had before the late conquest [i.e. the Hanoverian suppression after the '45] of their country, there remain only their language and their poverty. Their language is attacked on every side. . .[56]

Yet Johnson acknowledged, as late as 1783, that he had acquired 'more ideas' by the trip 'than anything I remember: I saw quite a different system of life'.

Secondly, the claims of MacPhearson's Ossianic epic, *Fingal*, had whetted his appetite. Johnson was unwavering in his contempt for MacPhearson's preposterous claims. In this he was right. Besides, *Fingal* fitted ill with his classicism and the culture of eighteenth-century London, and Johnson sensed that it threatened civilized values. He expected a journey to the Hebrides to disprove Mac-Phearson's claims, and came away well satisfied that Gaelic, or, as it was then known, Erse

> . . .never was a written language; that there is not in the world an Earse manuscript a hundred years old; and that the sounds of the Highlanders were never expressed by letters. . .*Earse* merely floated in the breath of the people, and could therefore receive little improvement. . .
>
> The state of the Bards was yet more hopeless. He that cannot read, may now converse with those that can; but the Bard was a barbarian among barbarians. . .
>
> . . .the poems of Ossian. . .never existed in any other form than that which we have seen. . .

The Scots have something to plead for their easy reception of an improbable fiction: they are seduced by their fondness for their supposed ancestors. A Scotchman must be a very sturdy moralist, who does not love *Scotland* better than truth.[57]

Not that Johnson was a lover of Scotland. Boswell had to humour his 'outrageous contempt of Scotland'. He had long doubted whether it would be possible to prevail on Dr Johnson 'to relinquish, for some time, the felicity of a London life'. Moreover, a journey to the Hebrides was a somewhat daunting proposition for both Johnson the Londoner and Boswell the Lowlander. Even, says Dr Johnson

> to the southern inhabitants of Scotland, the state of the mountains and the islands is equally unknown with that of *Borneo* or *Sumatra*: Of both they have only heard a little, and guess the rest. They are strangers to the language and the manners, to the advantages and wants of the people, whose life they would model, and whose evils they would remedy.[58]

There would be, at the very least, Boswell reckoned, 'some inconveniences and hardships, and perhaps a little danger; but these we were persuaded were magnified in the imagination of every body'. For had not the rebellious clansmen been pacified and disarmed, the gentry anglicized, the mountains mapped, the seas charted, roads built, customs and excise laws enforced – in short, had not the Highlands and Islands begun to benefit, with the rest of Scotland, from the happy results of the Act of Union of 1707? Whereas once their tables (to quote Johnson) 'were as coarse as the feasts of Eskimeaux, and their houses as filthy as the cottages of Hottentots', the Union (so he said) 'made them acquainted with English manners', and, he added, 'they must for ever be content to owe to the English that elegance and culture'. So while many looked on the 'curious expedition' as difficult and dangerous, they were not proposing to travel quite beyond the bounds of the civilized world.

They were a curiously assorted pair of travelling companions. Dr Johnson's character, as Boswell says, was well known to all his readers in its 'religious, moral, political, and literary' gravity:

> a sincere and zealous christian, of high-church of England and monarchical principle. . .; correct, nay stern in his taste; hard to please, and easily offended; impetuous and irritable in his temper, but of a most humane and benevolent heart; having a mind stored

with a vast and various collection of learning and knowledge, which he communicated with peculiar perspicuity and force, in rich and choice expression. . .He was conscious of his superiority. He loved praise when it was brought to him; but was too proud to seek it. He was somewhat susceptible of flattery. . .yet, though grave and awful in his deportment, when he thought it necessary or proper,—he frequently indulged himself in pleasantry and sportive sallies. . .He had a loud voice, and a slow deliberative utterance, which no doubt gave some additional weight to the sterling metal of his conversation.

To Boswell, Dr Johnson was

that Wonderful Man, whom I venerated and loved while in this world, and after whom [Boswell wrote in 1785] I gaze with humble hope, now it has pleased Almighty God to call him to a better world.[59]

No doubt Boswell's almost obsessive admiration commended him to Johnson, who may have yearned for the son he never had, and found in the young Scotsman a filial piety which enabled the older man to gloss over the younger's youthful peccadillos – a weakness for wine, women and song, extravagant spending, and an enthusiasm for Scotland. Boswell was a delightful companion, and well connected (he was an up-and-coming young lawyer, and heir to Lord Auchinleck).

But let us return to the travels of Johnson and Boswell. From Raasay they travelled to Dunvegan in Skye, meeting on their way with none other than Flora MacDonald. Dr Johnson, at heart a Jacobite sympathizer (though he accepted a pension from King George III), describes Flora, now married to MacDonald of Kingsburgh, as 'a woman of middle stature, soft features, gentle manners, and elegant presence'. Hers, he says, is

a name that will be mentioned in history, and if courage and fidelity be virtues, mentioned with honour.[60]

At Dunvegan, and at Talisker, the two travellers were entertained in great style. Johnson was particularly impressed by Dunvegan's medieval fortress, and the ancient traditions. The urbane Londoner, so much a man of his times, was nonetheless struck by the outlandish and fascinating Celtic atmosphere:

The fictions of the *Gothick* romances were not so remote from credibility as they are now thought. In the full prevalence of the

107

Johnson and Boswell visit Flora MacDonald. Hers was a name, according to Johnson, 'that will be mentioned in history, and if courage and fidelity be virtues, mentioned with honour'. Painting attributed to Allan Ramsay.

feudal institutions, when violence desolated the world, and every baron lived in a fortress, forests and castles were regularly succeeded by each other, and the adventurer might very suddenly pass from the gloom of woods, or the ruggedness of moors, to seats of plenty, gaiety, and magnificence. Whatever is imagined in the wildest tales, if giants, dragons, and enchantments be excepted, would be felt by him, who, wandering in the mountains without a guide, or upon the sea without a pilot, should be carried amidst his terror and uncertainty, to the hospitality and elegance of Raasay or Dunvegan.[61]

It was, in particular, the social delights of the company found in these great houses that entranced Johnson and his youthful companion. Dr Johnson sharpened his wits on the gentlemen he met (and the faithful Boswell noted the exchanges in his diary, and

108

allowed his venerable friend to make any necessary corrections). And Johnson too enjoyed mild flirtations with the ladies:

> He [writes Boswell] was quite social and at ease amongst them; and, though he drank no fermented liquor, toasted Highland beauties with great readiness. His conviviality engaged them so much, that they seemed eager to shew their attention to him, and vied with each other in crying out, with a strong Celtick pronunciation, 'Toctor Shonson, Toctor Shonson, your health!'
>
> This evening one of our married ladies, a lively pretty little woman, good-humouredly sat down upon Dr. Johnson's knee, and, being encouraged by some of the company, put her hands round his neck, and kissed him.—'Do it again, (said he,) and let us see who will tire first.'—He kept her on his knee some time, while he and she drank tea. He was now like a *buck* indeed. All the company were much entertained to find him so easy and pleasant. To me it was highly comick, to see the grave philosopher. . .toying with a Highland beauty.[62]

Boswell's sins were more reprehensible. One evening he caroused with several of the younger gentlemen into the small hours. One bowl of punch followed another until five had been drunk. Boswell was not in bed until five in the morning. The next day, Sunday 26 September, he expected retribution:

> I awaked at noon, with a severe head-ache. I was much vexed that I should have been guilty of such a riot, and afraid of a reproof from Dr. Johnson. I thought it very inconsistent with that conduct which I ought to maintain. . .About one he came into my room, and accosted me, 'What, drunk yet?'—His tone of voice was not that of severe upbraiding; so I was relieved a little.—'Sir, said I, they kept me up.'—He answered, 'No, you kept them up, you drunken dog:'—This he said with good-humoured English pleasantry. Soon afterwards, Corrichatachin, Col [Coll], and other friends assembled round my bed. Corri had a brandy-bottle and glass with him, and insisted I should take a dram.—'Ay, said Dr. Johnson, fill him drunk again. Do it in the morning, that we may laugh at him all day. It is a poor thing for a fellow to get drunk at night, and sculk to bed, and let his friends have no sport.'[63]

The repentant Boswell rose, and donned his clothes. Anxious to make amends, he found a prayer book, and read the epistle for the day. 'And be not drunk with wine, wherein is excess,' he read. 'Some,' he comments, 'would take this as a divine interposition'.

'I awaked at noon, with a severe headache.' The hungover and repentant Boswell confronts an indulgent Dr Johnson. From *The Picturesque Beauties of Boswell* by Thomas Rowlandson (1786).

By now, as will have been noticed, they were almost at the end of September. It was the season of equinoctial storms, and they were still on Skye. Johnson had been anxious to include in his itinerary a visit to Iona, and so the plan was to sail from Sleat, the southern wing of Skye, to Mull, and from thence make the journey across that island on horseback. Fortunately, among those now entertaining Johnson, was 'young Col' – Maclean of Coll. He had taken a great liking to the grand old man, and to Boswell (who joined him in his cups on more than one occasion). Coll was determined to escort the travellers, and, as will be seen, it was as well that he did so.

They were, at last, able to take advantage of a break in the weather on Sunday, 3 October. Johnson notes briefly,

Having waited some days at *Armidel* [Armadale in Skye], we were flattered at last with a wind that promised to convey us to Mull. We went on board a boat that was taking in kelp, and left the Isle of *Sky* behind us. We were doomed to experience, like others, the danger of trusting to the wind, which blew against us, in a short time, with such violence, that we, being no seasoned sailors, were willing to call it a tempest. I was sea-sick and lay down. Mr *Boswell* kept the deck. The master knew not well whither to go; and our difficulties might perhaps have filled a very pathetick page, had not Mr. *Maclean* of *Col*, who, with every other qualification which the insular life required, is a very active and skilful mariner, piloted us safe into his own harbour.[64]

Boswell performing a Highland dance on the top of Dun Caan, Raasay. Engraving by Rowlandson.

Such is Dr Johnson's account. Fortunately, 'Bozzy' was less incapacitated with sea sickness, and gives a far livelier account of a harrowing experience, in which the whole party nearly lost their lives (a loss which would have deprived us of Johnson's own *Journey to the Hebrides*, Boswell's far more entertaining *Journal of a Tour to the Hebrides*, and one of the greatest literary biographies in English, Boswell's *Life* of Dr Johnson). For the voyage was nearly a disaster. The month was October. Daylight hours were short, the winds high, and the seas heavy. In particular, the seas around Ardnamurchan Point have an evil reputation. The irregular, shallowing seabed causes prodigious seas as the swell and breakers roll in and dash themselves against the massive dark cliffs. This 'height of the great seas' – which is what Ardnamurchan means — is a menacing coastline, bleak and harbourless.

But let Boswell tell his tale:

When we got in full view of Ardnamurchan, the wind changed, and was directly against our getting into the sound. We were then obliged to tack, and get forward in that tedious manner. As we advanced, the storm grew greater, and the sea very rough. Col then began to talk of making for Egg [Eigg], or Canna, or his own island. Our skipper said, he would get us into the Sound. Having struggled for this a good while in vain, he said, he would push forward till we were near the land of Mull, where we might cast anchor, and lie till morning; for although, before this, there had

111

been a good moon, and I had pretty distinctly seen not only the land of Mull, but up the Sound, and the country of Morven as at one end of it, the night was now grown very dark. Our crew consisted of one McDonald, our skipper, and two sailors, one of whom had but one eye; Mr. Simpson himself, Col, and Hugh McDonald his servant, all helped. Simpson said, he would willingly go for Col, if young Col or his servant would undertake to pilot us to a harbour; but, as the island is low land, it was dangerous to run upon it in the dark. Col and his servant appeared a little dubious. The scheme of running for Canna seemed then to be embraced; but Canna was ten leagues [about thirty sea miles] off, all out of our way; and they were afraid to attempt the harbour of Egg. All these plans were successively in agitation. The old skipper still tried to make for the land of Mull; but then it was considered that there was no place there against the storm. Much time was lost in striving against the storm.

At last it became so rough, and threatened to be so much worse, that Col and his servant took more courage, and said they would undertake to hit one of the harbours in Col.—'Then let us run for it in God's name,' said the skipper; and instantly we turned towards it. The little wherry which had fallen behind us, had hard work. The master begged that, if we made for Col, we should put out a light to him. Accordingly one of the sailors waved a glowing peat for some time. The various difficulties that were started, gave me a good deal of apprehension, from which I was relieved, when I found we were to run for harbour before the wind. But my relief was but of short duration; for I soon heard that our sails were very bad, and were in danger of being torn in pieces, in which case we should be driven upon the rocky shore of Col. It was very dark, and there was a heavy and incessant rain. The sparks of the burning peat flew so much about, that I dreaded the vessel might take fire. Then, as Col was a sportsman, and had powder on board, I figured that we might be blown up. Simpson and he appeared a little frightened, which made me more so; and the perpetual talking, or rather shouting, which was carried out in Erse, alarmed me still more. A man is always suspicious of what is saying in an unknown tongue; and, if fear be his passion at the time, he grows more afraid. Our vessel often lay so much on one side, that I trembled lest she should be overset; and indeed they told me afterwards, that they had run her sometimes to within an inch of the water, so anxious were they to make what haste they could before the night should be worse.

112

As the small vessel drew away from Mull's wild but sheltering cliffs, it was more and more exposed to the wind and boisterous seas. I estimate that they would have had to sail about eleven sea miles from the Sound of Mull to Loch Eatharna (Arinagour) on Coll: plenty of time for poor Boswell to reflect on his predicament:

I now saw what I never saw before, a prodigious sea, with immense billows coming upon the vessel, so that it seemed hardly possible to escape. There was something grandly horrible in the sight. I am glad I have seen it once. Amidst all these terrifying circumstances, I endeavoured to compose my mind. It was not easy to do it; for all the stories that I had heard of the dangerous sailing among the Hebrides, which is proverbial, came full upon my recollection. When I thought of those who were dearest to me [Boswell had a young wife and infant children], and would suffer severely, should I be lost, I upbraided myself, as not having sufficient cause for putting myself in such danger. Piety afforded me comfort. . .

. . .but we will pass over Boswell's pious reflections.

Fortunately, Maclean of Coll was able to offer poor Boswell a practical diversion. Since shortly before midnight they had been running before the storm, with the terrifying fear of being pooped (overwhelmed by a following sea). Boswell was anxious to be of assistance to the harrassed crew:

As I saw them all busy doing something, I asked Col, with much earnestness, what I could do. He, with happy readiness, put into my hand a rope, which was fixed to the top of one of the masts, and told me to hold it till he bade me pull. If I had considered the matter, I might have seen that this could not be of the least service; but his object was to keep me out of the way of those who were busy working the vessel, and at the same time to divert my fear, by employing me, and making me think that I was of use. Thus did I stand firm to my post, while the wind and rain beat upon me, always expecting a call to pull my rope.

The man with one eye steered; old McDonald, and Col and his servant lay upon the fore-castle, looking sharp out for the harbour. It was necessary to carry much *cloth*, as they termed it, that is to say, much sail, in order to keep the vessel off the shore of Col. This made violent plunging in a rough sea. At last they spied the harbour of Lochiern [Loch Eatharna], and Col cried, 'Thank God, we are safe!' We ran up till we were opposite it, and soon afterwards we got into it, and cast anchor.

113

'Thus did I stand firm to my post, while the wind and rain beat upon me, always expecting a call to pull my rope.' Engraving by Rowlandson.

It sounds so easy. A glance at a plan of Loch Eatharna, however, shows how the way in is between skerries and isolated rocks, none of them then buoyed, over which tremendous seas must have been breaking. It is an anchorage that is tricky in daylight with light winds; in darkness and lashed by southeasterlies, only a superb and experienced seaman like young Coll would dare it.

Meanwhile, Boswell recounts:

> Dr. Johnson had all this time been quiet and unconcerned. He had lain down on one of the beds, and having got free from sickness, was satisfied. The truth is, he knew nothing of the danger we were in: but fearless and unconcerned, might have said, in the words which he has chosen for the motto to his *Rambler*,
>
> *Quo me cunque rapit tempestas, deferor hospes**
>
> Once, during the doubtful consultations, he asked whither we were going; and upon being told that it was not certain whether to Mull or Col, he cried, 'Col for my money!'—I now went down, with Col and Mr. Simpson, to visit him. He was lying in philosophick tranquillity, with a greyhound of Col's at his back, keeping him warm.[65]

The real hero of his voyage was young Maclean of Coll. But for his courage and seamanship, neither Johnson nor Boswell would have survived to write their recollections. Maclean of Coll was a fine

---

* For as the tempest drives, I shape my way. [Boswell's note]

example of a new generation of chiefs. His father had moved to Aberdeen to further the education of his large family, leaving his son and heir to care for his estates. The young man is described as a great sportsman, extremely lively and vivacious, and most popular with his tenants on Coll. He had travelled widely, and had spent a long period learning farming in Hertfordshire and Hampshire, where he learnt every operation by doing it with his own hands.

An island like Coll in the eighteenth century was an almost entirely self-sufficient community, deeply conservative, but with a very fragile economy. Johnson describes the island of Coll as 'one continued rock, of a surface much diversified with protuberances, and covered with a thin layer of soil'. While the clan could withstand the almost annual famine that came with the spring, when last year's supplies were exhausted, the social fabric and the economy were to prove unable to bear rents imposed to sustain a higher standard of life for landowners and their factors.

Young Coll's intention was to 'improve. . .without hurting the people or loosing their ancient Highland fashions'. He introduced newfangled ideas – a road for wheeled carriages, grass to stabilize sand dunes. But Johnson found many old customs practiced – the fosterage of children (young Coll had been fostered by Macsweyn of Grishipoll on Coll); festivities at New Year, involving a man dressed in a cow's hide; folk tales of heroes; and above all the status of the chieftain's heir and representative, young Coll himself:

> Wherever we roved, we were pleased to see the reverence with which his subjects regarded him. He did not endeavour to dazzle them by any magnificence of dress: his only distinction was a feather in his bonnet; but as soon as he appeared, they forsook their work and clustered about him: he took them by the hand, and they seemed mutually delighted. He has the proper disposition of a Chieftain, and seems desirous to continue the customs of his house. The bagpiper played regularly, when dinner was served.[66]

The combination of the traditional virtues of a well-loved chief, with the new skills of an agricultural improver, made him an ideal landlord. The island, said Johnson, was 'without any of the distresses, which Mr *Pennant*, in a fit of simple credulity, seems to think almost worthy of an elegy by Ossian'. Small wonder the 'evil of emigration' was unknown on Coll.

Above all, Johnson and Boswell were delighted with the young

Laird. 'Col,' said Dr Johnson, 'does every thing for us: we will erect a statue to Col.' Later, writes Boswell,

> Young Col told us he could run down a grey-hound; 'for, (said he) the dog runs himself out of breath, by going too quick, and then I get up with him'. I accounted for his advantage over the dog, by remarking that Col had the faculty of reason, and knew how to moderate his pace, which the dog had not the sense to do. Dr. Johnson said, 'He is a noble animal. He is as complete an islander as the mind can figure. He is a farmer, a sailor, a hunter, a fisher: he will run you down a dog: if any man has a *tail*, it is Col. He is hospitable; and he has an intrepidity of talk, whether he understands the subject or not. I regret that he is not more intellectual.'[67]

The tragedy was that young Col was drowned a year later, on his way to visit his betrothed, the daughter of Sir Allan Maclean of Inchkenneth. Many of his fine ideas, and warm concern for his clan, died with him. Within a few generations the exasperated owners of Coll found their island perpetually overpopulated, impoverished, and unrewarding. How could they sustain a standard of living suitable for a gentleman on the miserable rents, always in arrears, of their tenantry?

But to return to 1773.

From Coll, Johnson and Boswell sailed, still under the protection of the young Laird, to Tobermory, on Mull. From thence they rode on horseback across Mull's bleak hills (it was mid-October) to Inchkenneth, where their host was Sir Allan Maclean, Coll's father-in-law to be. Here once more were the paradoxes of the Hebrides:

> Romance [observes Johnson] does not often exhibit a scene that strikes the imagination more than this little desert in these depths of Western obscurity, occupied not by a gross herdsman, or amphibious fisherman, but by a gentleman and two ladies, of high birth, polished manners, and elegant conversation, who, in a habitation raised not very far above the ground, but furnished with unexpected neatness and convenience, practiced all the kindness of hospitality, and refinements of courtesy.[68]

In the evening one of the ladies played her harpsichord, and there was Scottish dancing. But when they went to bed, though the beds were 'elegant', Johnson found on undressing that his feet were 'in the mire: that is, the clay-floor of the room, on which he stood before he went to bed, was wet, in consequence of the windows being broken, which let in the rain'. The fact was that the Macleans, once among the greatest chiefs, were now impoverished, their lands having been forfeit following the '45. Yet the extraordinary hold of the clan chief on his clan is illustrated in this little scene on Iona, which Maclean had sold to the Duke of Argyll, and had not visited for fourteen years. A local lad had failed to send his chief some rum. Angrily, Sir Allan reproved him.

> 'Refused to send rum to me, you rascal! Don't you know that if I order you to go and cut a man's throat, you are to do it?'—'Yes, an't please your honour! and my own too, and hang myself too.'[69]

And, added Boswell, these professions were no mere pretence. They were the truth.

Iona, or Icolmkill, to give it the more correct name, was the high point of their journey. From Inchkenneth the party had sailed (on Johnson's estimation) about forty miles, following the indented coastline of Mull the day long. 'If this is not *roving among the Hebrides*, nothing is,' remarked Johnson. But let us follow this final stage in Dr Johnson's own narrative:

> The evening was now approaching, and we were yet at a considerable distance from the end of our expedition. . .The day soon failed us, and the moon presented a very solemn and pleasing scene. The sky was clear, so that the eye commanded a wide circle: the sea was neither still nor turbulent: the wind neither silent nor loud. We were never far from one coast or another, on which, if the weather had become violent, we could have found shelter, and therefore contemplated at ease the region through which we glided in the tranquility of the night, and saw now a rock and now an island grow gradually conspicuous and gradually obscure. . .
>
> We were very near an Island, called *Nun's Island*, perhaps from an ancient convent. Here is said to have been dug the stone that was used in the buildings of *Icolmkill*. Whether it is now inhabited we could not stay to inquire.
>
> At last we came to *Icolmkill*, but found no convenience for landing. Our boat could not be forced very near dry ground, and our Highlanders carried us over the water.[70]

Boswell tells us that he and the Doctor embraced cordially once ashore. The islanders ran to greet the party from the hovels built in and around the ruinous cathedral and monastery. After their long sail, the travellers were weary:

> We were accommodated [Boswell writes] this night in a large barn, the island affording us no lodging we should have liked so well. Some good hay was strewn at one end of it, to form a bed for us, upon which we lay with our clothes on; and we were furnished with blankets from the village. Each of us had a portmanteau for a pillow. When I awaked in the morning, I could not help smiling at the idea of the chief of the McLeans, the great English Moralist, and myself, lying thus extended in such a situation.[71]

There was only time to spend the morning exploring the historic ruins. It was Wednesday, 20 October, and Dr Johnson was eager to return to civilization. Ahead lay a few more days of hard travel, by sea, and on horseback across the highest part of Mull to Loch Buie. From thence they would sail in a small open boat across the Firth of Lorn – a considerable distance – to the tiny village of Oban. Within a fortnight Boswell – ah, happy man! – would be able to entertain the eminent sage in his elegant home, where Johnson met Boswell's father, Lord Auchinleck.

But let us take our leave of the travellers on Iona, with the memorable and solemn rhetoric of Dr Johnson's celebration of the isle still ringing in our ears:

> We were now treading that illustrious Island, which was once the luminary of the *Caledonian* regions, whence savage clans and roving barbarians derived the benefits of knowledge, and the blessings of religion. To abstract the mind from all local emotion would be impossible, if it were endeavoured, and would be foolish, if it were possible. Whatever withdraws us from the power of our senses; whatever makes the past, the distant, or the future predominate over the present, advances us in the dignity of thinking beings. Far from me and from my friends, be such frigid philosophy as may conduct us indifferent and unmoved over any ground which has been dignified by wisdom, bravery, or virtue. That man is little to be envied, whose patriotism would not gain force upon the plain of *Marathon*, or whose piety would not grow warmer among the ruins of *Iona!*[72]

8

THE SAILING OF THE
WHITE-SAILED SHIPS

The Voyage of the Hector

'**N**O MAN,' an indignant Highlander told Dr Johnson, 'No
man willingly left his native country.' Yet (he continued)
with his rent having risen from five to twenty pounds in
the course of 25 years (when prices were stable), he was being forced
to consider emigration. Twenty pounds was more than double the
annual income of a farm labourer.

Every traveller to the Hebrides for the next century, and more,
was to remark on the emigrant ships.

> In the morning I walked out [writes Boswell], and saw a ship, the
> *Margaret* of the Clyde, pass by with a number of emigrants on
> board. It was a melancholy sight.[73]

Brief though their visit was, the pair saw several such ships,
including the *Nestor* at Portree.

Dr Johnson, like many observers, viewed the 'rage for emigration' with alarm.

> The topic of emigration being again introduced [writes Boswell],
> Dr. Johnson said, that 'a rapacious Chief would make a wilder-
> ness of his estate'. Mr Donald McQueen told us, that the
> oppression . . .was owing to landlords listening to bad advice in
> the letting of their lands; that interested and designing people
> flattered them with golden dreams of much higher rents than
> could reasonably be paid; and that some of the gentlemen *tacks-
> men*, or upper tenants, were themselves in part the occasion of the
> mischief, by over-rating the farms of others. That many of the
> *tacksmen*, rather than comply with exorbitant demands, had
> gone off to America, and impoverished the country, by draining
> it of its wealth.[74]

Among those families with whom Dr Johnson and Boswell

Armadale Castle
in Skye, seat of
Sir Alexander
Macdonald of
Sleat, whose
indifference to his
clansmen infuri-
ated Dr Johnson.
Aquatint by John
Schekty.

stayed was that of Sir Alexander MacDonald of Sleat, on the island of Skye. Most of Dr Johnson's comments on Sir Alexander were unprintable. He and Boswell were 'full of the old Highland spirit, and were dissatisfied at hearing of racked rents and emigration; and finding a chief not surrounded by his clan'. Johnson was infuriated by the Chief's superficial charm, his anglicized manners, and his supercilious indifference to his clansmen.

The fact was that Sir Alexander represented a new breed of chieftains. Like his two brothers, he had been educated at Eton. In 1764, when he had attained the age of about eighteen, he had been offered a most attractive opportunity: the chance to travel extensively on the Continent with two other young men roughly the same age as himself – Henry Scott, the third Duke of Buccleuch, and Hew Campbell Scott, younger brother to the Duke. The young men were in the charge of a tutor, engaged by Charles Townshend, Buccleuch's stepfather – the arrogant, brilliant and disastrous Chancellor of the Exchequer whose taxes precipitated the revolt of the American colonists. The tutor was a Glasgow professor, a scholarly and immensely hard-working don. A 50-year-old batchelor, he had been living quitely with his mother, whom he adored. His name was Adam Smith. He had been glad enough to exchange his professor's chair for several years' travel, particularly in France (then renowned for its philosophers and intellectuals), with all expenses paid, and a salary of £300 a year for life (compared with roughly £200 a year which he had earned as a professor).

The significance of young Alexander MacDonald's grand tour of Europe under the tutelage of Adam Smith is this. Scotland, and in particular, the Highlands and Islands, were in an age of transition. Many of the problems were common to all European nations at the time (and are currently being experienced by the Third World in our own day). They included land hunger and overpopulation; landlordism, peasant recalcitrance and famine; the effects of modernizing forces pitted against traditional cultural values; the clash of a pastoral, summer-nomadic cattle-keeping economy with arable farming and intensive sheep rearing. These problems were made the more acute by the breakdown of traditional clan patterns. But the problems were not unique to the Highlands and Islands. They were felt all over Europe. And different countries sought a variety of solutions: for example, in Denmark, peasant farmers were forced into small producer cooperatives.

Adam Smith, sometime tutor to Sir Alexander Macdonald. In the hands of landlords in the Highlands and Islands, Smith's economic theories led to the ruthless eviction of thousands of tenants. Portrait by an unknown artist.

What made the solution imposed in the Highlands and Islands unique was the naked and ruthless self-interest of the landlords, resulting, in due course, in the systematic clearance of land through the eviction of the clansmen. Smith taught, in the *Wealth of Nations* (1776), that self-interest is the prime motive in economic affairs, but that an 'invisible hand' ensures that, mysteriously, the actions of self-interested men produce the greater good for the community. He must often have discussed this with his charges in the two and a half years they travelled together, for he was writing the *Wealth of Nations* during this period.

It was a brutal and callous age. Evictions were commonplace throughout Britain. But what was beginning to occur, in the remote northerly fringe of the British Isles, was something more akin to the systematic extermination of a racial minority by landlords now divorced from their people. The clan system, being in a state of collapse, offered few safeguards.

The government had followed the devastation of the glens by fire and the sword in the immediate post-Culloden period with a series of Acts of Parliament designed to destroy those features of Highland life which had made the uprisings of 1715 and 1745 possible. Those chiefs who supported the Jacobite cause were exiled. Their estates were forfeit to the Crown, and administered by agents of the government. (Much of the revenue went into commendable enterprises, including the building of canals, such as the Crinan and Caledonian Canals, and of harbours like that at Tobermory.) Chiefs were no longer hereditary justices. The Highlanders were disarmed, and made to swear a terrible oath against the wearing of their Highland dress:

> I, A.B., do swear as I shall answer God at the great day of judgement, I have not, nor shall have in my possession any gun, sword, pistol or arm whatever, and never use tartan, plaid, or any part of the Highland garb; and if I do so, may I be cursed, may I never see my wife and children, father, mother or relations, and lie without Christian burial in a strange land, far from the graves of my forefathers and my kindred; may all this come across me if I break my oath.[75]

With what unerring and terrible insight into the Gael's character was this dire oath framed.

Perhaps even more effective – from the government's viewpoint – was the requirement, as much by social pressures as anything else, on the chiefs to educate their sons and heirs at the English public schools. Within one or two generations the chiefs had been transformed into playboys and racketeering landlords. The expenses of London living, with the gambling debts and free-spending mistresses, the town houses and liveried servants, the string of race horses and the jewellery required to grace the hands and throats of wives and daughters, were more than the barren acres of moor and glen could supply. From their huge Scottish estates the descendants of the Lords of the Isles could wring but a paltry sum. Agricultural innovations which had enriched the English land-owning classes yielded lower returns under the dour skies of Scotland. The money exacted flowed south to London, further depleting the coffers of the Highlanders. The ancient feudalism of the clans disappeared, making way for a new, harsher economic feudalism of absentee lairds. It was to lead to an uncontrolled exploitation of resources, both of land and of human life. While the price of Highland cattle held up, the land was just able to sustain the luxurious new generation of chieftains. But a price drop in the late 1760s threatened their expensive pastimes. The bad harvests of 1768, 1769, 1772 and 1773 brought famine to the isles. Starving groups of islanders roamed the beaches, subsisting on raw shellfish and seaweed.

Thousands probably died. For many the alternative to death was emigration – sometimes voluntary, often compulsory, occasionally brutally enforced.

'There is a serious charge,' remarked one of the Royal Commis-

Lord Macdonald's evictions at Boreraig, Skye. From Donald Ross's *Real Scottish Grievances* (1854).

sioners in 1883, at a hearing when the clearances in South Uist were under investigation,

a serious charge in the paper [submitted as evidence to the Commission] which requires a little explanation. It is said in reference to the emigration of the people that they were 'compelled to emigrate to America; some of them had been tied before our eyes; others hid themselves in caves and crevices for fear of being caught by authorized officers'. Did you see any of these operations?'

Interpreter: 'Yes; he [the witness] heard of them, and saw them. He saw a policeman chasing a lad named Donald Smith. . .in order to send him aboard the emigrant ship lying at Lochboisdale; and he saw a man who lay down on his face and knees on a little island to hide himself from the policeman, who had dogs searching for him in order to get him aboard the emigrant ship. The man's name was Lauchlan Macdonald. The dogs did not find this unfortunate youth, but he was discovered all the same in a trench, and was taken off.'

Question: 'Do you really say that those people were caught and sent to America, just like an animal going to market?'

Answer: 'Just the same way. Angus Johnston. . .had a dead child in the house, and his wife gave birth to three children, all of whom died. Notwithstanding this, he was seized, and tied on the pier at Lochboisdale, and kicked on board. The priest interfered, and said, "What are you doing to this man? let him alone; it is against the law."

'There were many hardships and cruelties endured in consequence of these evictions. . .'

123

He remembered seeing people forced into the emigrant ships at Lochboisdale by policemen and others. He saw a man named William Macpherson forced by four men to the waterside and put into the ship. Everyone of the family was sent away, including the blind father. . .There were many such cases. . .Seventeen hundred persons were, he believed, sent off, all belonging to the Gordon estate.[76]

The estates of Colonel Gordon covered Barra and the isles to the south, and South Uist. The date of this incident was about 1850 – but the events were not untypical.

Force was not always necessary, however. Many were lured by specious promises. Some were reasonably prosperous – tacksmen, tenants with some small savings. But many were landless, hungry, despairing. They had had their roofs burned down, their homes made uninhabitable, their rights to arable land and grazing destroyed. They faced starvation. They had no option but to emigrate.

What this meant is best understood by following just one such group of emigrants. In the year 1773, an emigrant ship, the *Hector*, left Loch Broom, with about two hundred souls on board. The *Statistical Account of Scotland*, a 21-volume survey of the length and breadth of Scotland based on information supplied by parish ministers in the years 1791-98, provides evidence that no less than twenty thousand Highlanders and Islanders emigrated in the twelve years 1763-75. So those who sailed on the *Hector* are an insignificant number. But it so happens that a very complete record of the voyage was assembled from oral traditions, gathered from the descendants of the *Hector's* human cargo almost a century later by Alexander MacKenzie, the editor of the *Celtic Magazine*. And this provides us with the earliest picture of life aboard the 'white-sailed ships' that carried away tens of thousands of evicted clansmen over the century that followed.

'We shall,' writes Alexander MacKenzie in 1883,

> We shall here give a few instances of the unspeakable suffering of those pioneers who left so early as 1773, in the ship *Hector*, for Pictou, Nova Scotia, gathered from trustworthy sources during the author's late visit to that country.
>
> The *Hector* was owned by two men, Pagan and Witherspoon, who brought three shares of land in Pictou, and they engaged a Mr. John Ross as their agent, to accompany the vessel to Scotland, to bring out as many colonists as they could induce, by

misrepresentation and falsehoods, to leave their homes. They offered a free passage, a farm, and a year's free provisions to their dupes.

On his arrival in Scotland, Ross drew a glowing picture of the land and other manifold advantages of the country to which he was enticing the people. The Highlanders knew nothing of the difficulties awaiting them in a land covered with dense unbroken forest; and, tempted by the prospect of owning splendid farms of their own, they were imposed upon by his promise, and many of them agreed to accompany him across the Atlantic and embraced his proposals.[77]

The specious promise of a free passage, free provisions and a free farm easily duped the unsophisticated Highlanders; in fact, they were destined to be little better than slaves on the agent's land, selling him their produce, buying from the company store. They were exchanging economic dependence on a heartless chief for economic dependence on a ruthless company. (Records at the Home Office show that there were even slave ships plying the Minches at this very date: kidnapping of young men and boys from the beaches was by no means uncommon.)

The *Hector's* first Scottish port of call was Greenock, where she picked up three families and five single men. MacKenzie continues:

> She then sailed to Lochbroom, in Ross-shire, where she received 33 families and 25 single men, the whole of her passengers numbering about 200 souls. This band, in the beginning of July, 1773, bade a final farewell to their native land, not a soul on board having ever crossed the Atlantic except a single sailor and John Ross, the agent. As they were leaving, a piper came on board who had not paid his passage; the captain ordered him ashore, but the strains of the national instrument affected those on board so much that they pleaded to have him accompany them, and offered to share their own rations with him in exchange for his music during the passage. Their request was granted, and his performances aided in no small degree to cheer the noble band of pioneers in their long voyage of eleven weeks, in a miserable hulk, across the Atlantic.[78]

The *Hector* – if other emigrant ships are anything to go by – would have been perhaps ninety foot long. She was almost certainly a cargo vessel, used in the lumber trade from the St Lawrence River. Homeward bound for Britain, her holds would be filled with timber. Outward bound, they were crowded with emigrants, sleeping

The pier at Tanera, Loch Broom, from where the *Hector* departed in 1773 with two hundred emigrants aboard. Aquatint by William Daniell.

on rough tiers of berths hastily run up. Men, women and children would be housed together in the holds, with minimal cooking facilities, and the most primitive sanitation – the lee rail for the fit, slop buckets for the sick.

Despite the appalling conditions, which were worse than those on many slave ships in terms of space, the emigrants were at least a close-knit community, with resources developed by their hardy life in the Hebrides:

> The pilgrim band kept up their spirits as best they could by song, pipe-music, dancing, wrestling, and other amusements, through the long and painful voyage. The ship was so rotten that the passengers could pick the wood out of her sides with their fingers. They met with a severe gale off the Newfoundland coast, and were driven back so far that it took them about fourteen days to get back to the point at which the storm met them. The accommodation was wretched, small-pox and dysentery broke out among the passengers. Eighteen of the children died, and were committed to the deep amidst such anguish and heart-rending agony as only a Highlander can understand. Their stock of provisions became almost exhausted, the water became scarce and bad; the remanent of provisions left consisted mainly of salt

126

meat, which, from the scarcity of water, added greatly to their sufferings. The oatcake carried by them became mouldy, so that much of it had been thrown away before they dreamt of having such a long passage; but, fortunately for them, one of the passengers, Hugh MacLeod, more prudent than the others, gathered up the despised scraps into a bag, and during the last few days of the voyage his fellows were glad to join him in devouring this refuse to keep soul and bodies together.[79]

At last the *Hector* entered the great estuary of the mighty St Lawrence. Their destination was Pictou, on the northern shores of Nova Scotia, opposite Prince Edward's Island. It was late September when, after nearly three months at sea, the *Hector* dropped anchor in the harbour opposite Pictou – then a small clearing on the edge of the forest. The descendants of the emigrants told Mackenzie that they arrived full of hope – hope soon to be cruelly dashed:

Though the Highland dress was then proscribed at home, this emigrant band carried theirs along with them, and, in celebration of their arrival, many of the younger men donned their national dress – to which a few of them were able to add the *Sgian Dubh* and the claymore (the two handed Highland sword) – while the piper blew up his pipes with might and main, its thrilling tones, for the first time, startling the denizens of the endless forest, and its echoes resounding through the wild solitude. Scottish immigrants are admitted upon all hands to have given its backbone of moral and religious strength to the Province, and to those brought over from the Highlands in this vessel is due the honour of being in the forefront – the pioneers and vanguard.

How different was the reality to the expectations of these poor creatures, led by the plausibility of the emigration agent, to expect free estates on their arrival. The whole scene, as far as the eye could see, was a dense forest. They crowded on the deck to take stock of their future home, and their hearts sank within them. They were landed without the provisions promised, without shelter of any kind, and were able by the aid of those few before them, to erect camps of the rudest and most primitive description, to shelter their wives and children from the elements. Their feelings of disappointment were most bitter, when they compared the actual facts with the free farms and the comfort promised them by the lying emigration agent. Many of them sat down in the forest and wept bitterly; hardly any provisions were possessed by the few who were before them, and what there was among them was soon devoured; making all – old and new comers – almost destitute. It was now too late to raise any crops that year. To make matters worse they were sent some three miles into the forest, so that they could not even take advantage with the same ease of any fish that might be caught in the harbour. The whole thing appeared an utter mockery. To unskilled men the work of clearing seemed hopeless; they were naturally afraid of the Red Indians and of the wild beasts of the forest; without roads or paths, they were frightened to move for fear of getting lost in the unbroken forest. Can we wonder that, in such circumstances, they refused to settle on the company's lands? though, in consequence, when provisions arrived, the agents refused to give them any. Ross and the company quarrelled, and he ultimately left the newcomers to their fate. The few of them who had a little money bought what provisions they could from the agents, while others, less fortunate, exchanged their clothes for food; but the greater number had neither money nor clothes to spend or exchange, and they were soon left quite destitute.[80]

So passed the first cruel winter, in severity far worse than any ever experienced in Scotland or the Isles. Many left. Others, fathers, mothers and children, bound themselves as indentured farm labourers into virtual slavery in other settlements, in return for food. The nearest town, Truro, was many days' walk away, through trackless forests. Those who went thither to buy potatoes or flour had to drag the heavy sacks back through the snow to their shacks, where their ill-clad, famished families huddled. 'The remembrance of these terrible days,' remarks Mackenzie, 'sank deep into the minds of that generation.' When he visited the families still living in Pictou, a century later, he was to hear the tales of the 'cruel hardships' still recounted, in all their graphic details, by the grandchildren of the settlers.

Although Mackenzie found the descendants of the survivors 'prosperous and happy', he remarks bitterly,

> But who can think of these early hardships and cruel existences without condemning – even hating – the memories of the harsh and heartless Highland and Scottish lairds, who made existence at home even almost as miserable for those noble fellows, and who drove them in thousands out of their native land, not caring one iota whether they sank in the Atlantic, or were starved to death on a strange and uncongenial soil? Retributive justice demands that posterity should execrate the memories of the authors of such misery and horrid cruelty.[81]

The grim story of the clearances and emigrations was to continue for the whole of the period covered by this book and well beyond.

> From the lone shieling of the misty island
>   Mountains divide us, and the waste of seas –
> Yet still the blood is strong, the heart is Highland,
>   And we in dreams behold the Hebrides.[82]

Thus, according to an early nineteenth-century traveller in Canada (possibly John Galt), thus sang the exiled oarsmen, still yearning for their native isles.

Were the clearances, the emigrations, the only solution to the overpopulation and impoverishment of the isles?

Highlanders being forced into exile. From *Livingstone's Caledonian Critic*, 1852.

THE SILVER DARLINGS

John Knox of the British Fisheries Society

HERRING, the 'silver darlings' in their teeming shoals, seemed to offer to the Hebrides an escape from abject poverty and the twin evils of emigration and overpopulation. In 1786 the newly founded British Society for Extending the Fisheries dispatched a certain John Knox (no relation to the Calvinist reformer) northwards to explore the potential of these rich fisheries. Their object was humanitarian and commercial: a combination of philanthropy and entrepreneurial stimulation of local industry not dissimilar to the operations of Oxfam in the Third World today.

John Knox congratulated the noblemen and gentlemen who had founded this well-intentioned agency (he was himself one of the moving spirits) on the launch of the Society, 'an event,' he wrote in his dedicatory epistle to his *Tour of the Highlands of Scotland and the Hebride Isles*,

> an event which, while it reflects immortal honour on your humanity and patriotic spirit, will contribute, in a most eminent degree, to the security and prosperity of these kingdoms.[83]

The British Fisheries Society would, Knox assured his distinguished backers, inaugurate a new age in the Highlands and Islands, bringing to an end the misery he so graphically describes in his book:

> A very considerable part of this island was lying almost in a state of nature; the riches of its shores, tho' more important to great national purposes than the mines of Mexico and Peru, were scarcely sought after. A great body of people, having no means of employment, were rendered torpid by idleness; they were frequently exposed to famine; and many of them forced, through necessity, to abandon their barren, but beloved wilds.
>
> To you, my Lords and Gentlemen, Britain owes the great national acquisition that is before us. To you, the naked, the hungry, and the helpless; the desponding parent, the husband,

and the widow, will look up in transports of gratitude. When necessity and despair had thinned many districts, and threatened more, you voluntarily stept forth, with the benevolent resolution to procure that relief which the circumstances of the country and the people required. The Public have caught the generous flame, and, from present appearances, there is every reason to believe, that the year MDCCLXXXVI [1786] will form an æra in the British annals.[84]

Knox's tour of the Hebrides was not merely a pleasure cruise. He had been commissioned by the British Fisheries Society to make a survey of and write a report on the prospects for fisheries on the west coast of Scotland. The Society was prepared to invest some £7,000 – a very considerable sum in those days – in benevolent undertakings which would improve the fisheries and the condition of the people.

Knox is an interesting example of an eighteenth-century benefactor. A Scot by birth, he had made a fortune in the bookselling trade, and his shop in the Strand, in central London, had allowed him to mix with the rich, learned and noble. He retired from the trade in 1764, when only 44 years of age, and devoted the rest of his long life and his hard-earned fortune to good works. Between 1764 and 1775 he made no less than sixteen tours through Scotland, in connection with projects aimed at economic development.

His proposals were far-sighted. He championed the building of three canals, all of which were constructed within the next thirty years: the Forth-Clyde Canal, across the Lowland waist of Scotland connecting the ancient capital of Edinburgh to the burgeoning industrial city of Glasgow; the Crinan Canal, from the Clyde to the Sound of Jura, which began the opening of the west coast; and the Caledonian Canal, through the Great Glen from Fort William to Inverness, which offered a route from east to west bypassing the perilous seas of the Pentland Firth. He also interested the British Fisheries Society in the construction of small fishing villages, with their own pier, inn, school house and church. Best known of these is the delightful village of Tobermory on Mull.

Thus it was that the stout-hearted old gentleman (he was 66 years old) found himself in the summer of 1786 in the Hebrides. His self-appointed mission was to explore the potential of the seas of the Hebrides; to get to know the skippers of the vessels that plied on those seas, the state of the fishing fleets, the anchorages and

John Knox's voyage round the Hebrides, 1786.

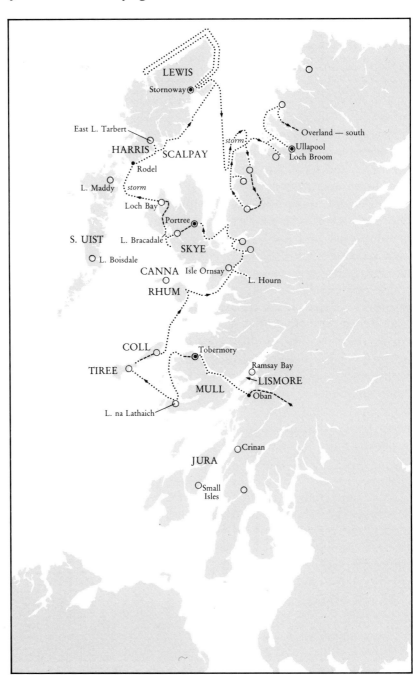

Voyages ············

Overland - - - - - - - -

Proposed fishing
stations ○

harbours, and the island landlords, on whose interest and commitment the success of the enterprise would depend.

One such was Captain Alexander Macleod, of Rodel, on the Isle of Harris in the Outer Hebrides. Knox had, rather typically, voyaged to this destination more by chance than by good judgement. He had reached Skye by a roundabout route – such are the vagaries of sailing in small boats (as Knox was wont to do) – which sailed hither and thither, according to the whims of the skipper or the passenger if the weather was fine, but at the mercy of wind and tide when, as so often occurs in the Hebrides, the weather deteriorates. Now he determined to cross the Minches to the Long Island (the Outer Hebrides) – a voyage roughly equivalent to sailing across the English Channel, although the Minches are more prone to gales. The ferry, a packet boat which sailed fortnightly with the mail, had already sailed, so he was glad to accept a passage in a small open boat, manned by a Macleod with a crew of three. It was to be an eventful voyage.

The morning fixed for Knox's departure dawned 'wet, thick and boisterous'. The wind was a southwesterly, so they would have to beat all the way to Benbecula (Knox's supposed destination). Deceived by the shelter afforded by Loch Bay (in the northwest corner of Skye), Knox insisted they set sail. Soon they found themselves

> very unequally matched against the great swell of the open Atlantic. The storm increased, and the violence of the rain occasioned a general thickness in the atmosphere, which soon deprived us of any guide from the land, by which to steer our course.—There was fortunately a compass on board, and Mr Macleod, who seemed to be master of his business, managed the helm, and gave directions to his men, without ceasing.
>
> A mason, who had, for reasons which I did not enquire into, come into the boat, laid himself down upon his back, under the half deck, and continued in that position with his hands lifted up, and seemingly in fervent prayer, through the whole voyage.
>
> I had taken my station near Macleod, at the stern, where I was not wholly idle. His attention was much engaged, in observing the sails, and giving directions to the men, who were fully employed, between the rigging and the pump, which they took by turns. My department was to observe the approach of every successive wave, and to give timely notice, that we might rise and fall with it, the only means of preserving us from being buried

133

under a watery mountain. Yet neither Macleod's skill, nor my vigilance, could prevent us from getting a brush now and then, *en passant*, which made Macleod stagger, set the compass a-swimming, and knocked myself down more than once.[85]

As the men became more and more exhausted, it became clear that they would never make Benbecula against a head wind. They changed course for Loch Maddy, in North Uist, but still were prevented by huge seas whipped up by adverse winds. At last there was nothing for it but to run before the wind northwards, to Loch Rodel in Harris where Macleod's master, Captain Macleod, resided.

The name Rodel (or 'Rowdil' as Knox spells it) put new heart into his crew, and they gained the point before sunset. It had been an epic voyage, and Captain Macleod of Harris, who, Knox tells us, had often passed the Cape of Good Hope, declared he would rather go there again 'than come across from Skye, in such a day, with an open boat'.

Captain Alexander Macleod was the former captain of the East Indiaman *Mansfield*, and had indeed rounded the Cape of Good Hope many a time. He had amassed a considerable fortune in the orient, and in 1780, when about 70 years of age and considering retirement, he purchased Harris from his kinsman for £15,000 – a huge sum in those days. Knox was extremely impressed with the energetic improvements to Rodel's tiny hidden anchorage, Poll an Tighmhail. (The name means Pool of the House of Mail – the Armoury – and goes back to medieval times. This anchorage, which is virtually unchanged since Macleod's improvements, is very popular with the more adventurous yachtsmen, and well known to tourists who visit St Clement's church, Rodel, with its famous tomb of Alasdair Crotach.)

> About four years ago [wrote Knox] captain Macleod came to settle in Harris, and fixed upon Rowdil Bay as the best adapted to his views; that place being situated on the south-east side of the island, and contiguous to the Sound of Harris. Within the bay of Rowdil, on the north side, there is an opening, through a channel of only 30 yards wide, to one of the best sheltered little bays in the Highlands; from which, on the opposite side, there is an opening of the same dimensions to the sea. This has water for any vessel to enter or depart at any time of the tide. [Knox is wrong here: the sea channel is only passable with difficulty, due to the rocks

The Shiant Islands, where the bodies of Annie Campbell and her lover were washed up by the tides (see page 169). Aquatint by William Daniell.

Two carefully authenticated costumes designed by John Francis Campbell of Islay for the Queen's Ball in 1845. That on the left was for Campbell himself, who in time was to become the leading authority on the folklore of the Highlands and Islands.

135

Daniell's view of Loch Coruisk, Skye (above), contrasts with Turner's more turbulent vision (below). 'It is as exquisite a savage scene', wrote Sir Walter Scott, 'as Loch Katrine is a scene of romantic beauty.'

136

which clog it, at high tide.] Captain Macleod has deepened the south passage to fifteen feet at common spring tides. The circumference of this little harbour or bason is nearly an English mile; and here ships lie always afloat, and as safe as in Greenland Dock. Here the captain has made an excellent graving bank, and formed two keys [quays], one at the edge of the bason, where ships may load or discharge afloat, at all times of the tide; the other on the graving bank.

He has also built a store-house for salt, casks, meal, &c. and a manufacturing house for spinning woollen and linen thread, and twine for herring nets, which he makes for his own use. He has procured some East Coast fishers, with Orkney yawls, to teach the inhabitants; and has built a boat-house, sixty feet long by twenty wide, capable of containing nine boats. . .

He has raised, or rather repaired, a very handsome church, out of the ruins of an old monastry, called St. Clements. He has also built a school house and public house; and he is now carrying on good cart roads from the keys to the village, and from thence though the country, to facilitate the communications with the west side of the island. He has done something in the planting way, and he finds that the hazel and sycamore thrive best.

He brought with him the model of a press, corn, and fulling mill, to work under the same roof; the two latter to go by one water wheel. He also brought the iron work for these machines.

He fitted out a fine cutter, sounded the coast, and found a bank half way between Harris and Sky, where many boats have caught cod and ling. In August, 1785, he made a trial of the banks of St. Kilda, which lies fifty-four miles west from the nearest land of the Long Island.[86]

Knox continues at length about the many projects of this imaginative and energetic man, who was making extensive trials of various banks and promoted the fisheries with an enthusiasm that matched Knox's own.

After a week staying with Captain Macleod, Knox was anxious to be on his way to Stornoway. Captain Macleod, who 'was not behind the gentlemen of the Highlands in civilities', offered to accompany Knox:

His vessels being at the fisheries, one at St. Kilda, and the other at Loch Broom, we embarked in the largest boat that remained in the harbour, and were accompanied by a pinnace, well manned, one of whom was equally qualified for managing the sails or the bagpipe, which he carried with him.

Rodel, Harris,
where the
landlord, Captain
Alexander Mac-
leod, made many
improvements
much approved of
by Knox. His
quays and boat-
houses, shown in
this aquatint by
William Daniell,
survive little
changed.

In our way thither we entered every bay or loch, and found them so safe and commodious for shipping of all sizes, and of such easy access, that the old navigator every now and then exclaimed, 'What a treasure this would be on the coast of Coromandel!' At other times he lamented the want of such harbours on the coast of England. But none of them are comparable, either in magnitude or safety, to East Loch Tarbert, which. . .I expressed a desire to explore minutely, and Captain Macleod readily acquiesced.

For this purpose we landed on the island of Scalpay, or as it is sometimes called, Elen Glass [Eilean Glas], and staid the night with Mr. Campbell, a tacksman under captain Macleod. As this island lies immediately in the course of ships that pass through the outer channel to and from the Baltic, and being near several clusters of rocks, it was judged a proper station for a lighthouse; and in 1786, a bill passed for that purpose.[87]

The lighthouse at Eilean Glas, Scalpay, was almost the first to be built on the whole west coast of Scotland. Begun by Mr Campbell without an official go-ahead in 1787, it was completed by Thomas Smith, founder of the famous Stevenson dynasty of lighthouse builders, in 1789, the first of a string of 'northern lights'.

While at Loch Tarbert, Knox and Captain Macleod attended the

wedding of a young couple. After the ceremony there was the dancing typical of a Highland wedding:

> The whole company [Knox recounts] were decent and orderly. Old and young danced, and among the rest, captain Macleod, who, notwithstanding his years, stepped up to the bride with a gallant air, took her by the hand, and acquitted himself nobly upon the floor; but he put the poor woman and some others to the blush soon after. I had asked him in a whisper, how he like the bride; he answered in a voice rather loud, that, 'she was too old; and that he liked her maid much better'. The bride seemed to be about thirty-six, and his own age seventy. His father married at seventy-five, had ten children, who are mostly married, and he died above ninety, when his youngest child was little more than an infant.[88]

Knox now continued northwards in the company of the excellent Captain Macleod. Whether the latter married or not is unknown. But he was an old-fashioned paternalistic laird:

> In every loch, bay or creek, he stations men and boats, proportioned to the extent of each water, who are to fish through the whole year when the weather permits. He allows them cottages and potato-ground rent free; he furnishes them with necessaries

The lighthouse at Eilean Glas, Scalpay. Completed in 1789, it was one of the first such lights on the west coast of Scotland. Aquatint by William Daniell.

at prime cost [i.e. wholesale prices], including freight; and he takes their fish in payment, at the market price.

This conduct will in time line the coast with a numerous race of expert fishermen, comfortable in their circumstances, whose wants will take off the produce of the neighbouring farms, and gradually raise the value of lands.

It ought to be a model for some proprietors in the Highlands, who, blinded by the representations of factors, and misled by their influence, have never permitted their tenantry to raise their heads, and are continually crushing them, by new impositions upon their industry and upon every appearance of improvement; by which they are stripped of the fruits of their labour, to which the improver, and not the master, has in common justice the best right. The consequence of this squeezing system has invariably proved a fictitious, instead of a real rent-roll well paid; and thus each party impoverishes the other.[89]

How much happier would have been the history of the Highlands and Islands had proprietors followed the example of the good Captain Macleod, rather than the advice of rapacious factors, or the policies of self-interest advocated by Adam Smith in his recently published *Wealth of Nations*.

The voyagers were now nearing their destination:

Towards evening [writes Knox] we discovered land on the north side of the bay of Stornoway. This is an almost detached wing, called the Point of Aird, that lies off the main island, to which it is only joined at high water by a peninsula of a few hundred feet in width. It is six miles in length by two in breadth, and forms a striking contrast to the shores upon the east side of the Long Island.

Knox was delighted with the potential of the town:

First, the shipping, of which there were thirteen at anchor, one of them 600 tons burthen. Secondly, the town of Stornoway, which being rebuilt with houses of stone, lime, and slate, makes a handsome appearance. One wing or street is built on a narrow peninsula that stretches out a considerable way into the bay, and adds greatly to the beauty of the landscape. Lastly, Seaforth Lodge, which is built on a lawn that rises gradually from the head of the bay, and being perfectly white, has a good effect.

However, he was disappointed to discover

that noble port [is] without a key [quay]; and it appeared still more strange, when we were informed that £12-1500 [£1,200-£1,500] had been granted several years ago, by the trustees at Edinburgh for building a sufficient key, and for raising cottages for fishermen along the shores of the island.

Something had indeed been erected here in the name of a key, and even that is so much out of repair, that the vessels load and unload upon the beach, or in the bay, by means of boats.[90]

Captain Macleod decided that they should stay at the inn, 'being unwilling, he said, to dress and go among company'. But they were prevented by the Earl of Seaforth, who 'carried [them] irresistibly to the lodge'. The next morning Knox was delighted to awake to a fine morning and delightful views from his chamber window:

The small craft were afloat at the head of the bay, with their sails up to dry after some rains; behind, was the point stretching across the bay, and covered to the very extremity with neat, white-washed houses. Beyond these, in the outer bay, were the shipping with their sails up; while some were going out, and others coming in. Upon the north side of the bay were sloping fields of ripe corn; on the south, were lofty hills; and, to crown this matchless scenery, the far distant mountains of Ross-shire conveyed the idea of a country that had been convulsed into a chaos.

When the church and spire shall be built, with a small spire also upon the town-house, and other ornaments which Seaforth's fertile imagination may easily conceive, this place will merit the pencil of the first landscape painter in the kingdom.[91]

Seaforth proposed an expedition to Loch Roag. Like Macleod, Seaforth was an experienced seaman. He had served when young in the Royal Navy; but his career seems to have been cut short by deafness:

While he was ill with a fever [Knox explains], an engagement happened between the fleet on which he was on board and that of the French, when the noise of the cannon totally deprived him of his hearing, under which calamity he still remains. The usual way of conversing with him is by writing, or by the fingers, at which his family and intimate acquaintance are very expert, and he is equally quick in anticipating their meaning.

Knox was quick to agree to the expedition, and 'a boat was manned and stored with provisions, wine, spirits, and malt liquor'. The weather continued fine, and the party set out in holiday spirits:

In coasting along we kept in many parts within a few yards of the

The Earl of
Seaforth, who
treated Knox to a
splendid picnic on
Lewis. Portrait by
John Sobieski
Stuart, after an
unknown artist.

rocks, where a large fish called lyth are generally caught with the hook. They are esteemed by the natives to be more delicate than cod, ling, or whiting, and they generally weigh seven or eight pound. We caught two of them to furnish an additional dish at dinner, for which our stomachs pointed very strongly.

For this purpose it was unanimously agreed that we should encamp upon one of the little islands, where, having arrived at a snug little creek, we left a man in charge of the boat, and scrambled up the lofty shore.

Here all hands were employed in landing the cargo, and carrying it to the place of encampment. Some brought up fire arms; others carried the provisions and liquors; and the rear followed with kitchen utensils. The island was covered with heath, and a fire was instantly kindled under a little rock, where the fish was to be cooked. Every man now took his station. Seaforth cut up one of the lyth, which he gutted, washed, and put into the kettle.

The department chosen by captain Mackenzie was to attend to the kettle and supply the fire with heath, which, being dry, made a fine blaze, and facilitated the business on hand.

We laid in a small salmon, just caught, of which captain Macleod took charge. Having performed the previous opera-

142

tions, he cut it in slices of about half a pound each, which he wrapped in paper, and cooked with great attention, and with great satisfaction to those who ate of it.

My office consisted in pulling heath for the supply of our kitchen, which consumed no small quantity, and the boatmen had various works on their hands.

When dinner was nearly ready to be served, Seaforth spread a large table cloth upon the ground; opened his hampers and kanting [canteen]; laid the knives, forks, and plates; took out his stores of cold tongue, tame and wild fowl, roast beef, bread, cheese, butter, pepper, salt, vinegar, pickles, &c. also wine, spirits, ale, and porter.[92]

Fishing boats in the Bay of Barrisdale, Loch Hourne. Aquatint by William Daniell.

Much as Knox enjoyed hobnobbing with the aristocracy, he was also unusually sensitive to the needs of ordinary people at a time when the sufferings of the poor were accepted with a complacency which we reserve for people in Third World countries. In his journal we frequently find references to the six or seven-man crews of native Hebrideans in their Highland boats returning from their fisheries.

The wind being contrary [he writes of one such fleet] these poor people were forced to labour at the oars from ten to twenty, or

143

twenty-five miles, before they could reach their respective huts. They take the oars alternately, and refresh themselves now and then with water, though generally in a full sweat. They sing in chorus, observing a kind of time, with the movement of the oars. Though they kept close upon the shore, and at a considerable distance from our vessel, we heard the sound from almost every boat. Those who have the bagpipe, use that instrument, which has a pleasing effect upon the water, and makes these poor people forget their toils.

They were returning to their families, with their little captures of herrings, or with what they were able to buy, and with a very disproportionate quality of salt, which, in the fishing season, is generally above their abilities to purchase, and sometimes it cannot be procured at any price. For these herrings, the value of which might not, upon an average, exceed fifty shillings per boat, six or seven men must have been from home a week or ten days, in moderate weather, and double that time had the weather been stormy, with contrary winds. If successful, they do not repine at the loss of so much time, the fatigue which they have gone through, or the dangers which they have been exposed, in navigating the main ocean with boats, not much longer than a London sculler, and many of them, called Norway skiffs, about that size. But when, after all these delays, toils, and hazards, they return without herrings, which is often the case, the disappointment to their half-starved families is easier to be conceived than expressed, and they soon have the same work to perform again, as soon as herrings are heard of, within the distance of fifty miles. Even then, disappointment sometimes follows; the report may have been false, or the herrings may have disappeared before the people, struggling with the contending elements, could have reached the fishery. If, at the same time, these people should be thus compelled to wander from place to place, upon the turbulent ocean, through positive necessity, arising from the immediate wants of subsistence, or from the urgent calls of those by whom they have been supplied upon credit, with meal and necessaries, they must, when the fishery fails, dispose of their property, and shift every one for himself; some in the Lowlands, and others to incessant labour, in the wilds of America.[93]

On his return from his long and perilous tour – on at least three occasions Knox came within a hair's-breadth of shipwreck in conditions that would have spelt almost certain death – Knox published his *Tour through the Highlands of Scotland and the*

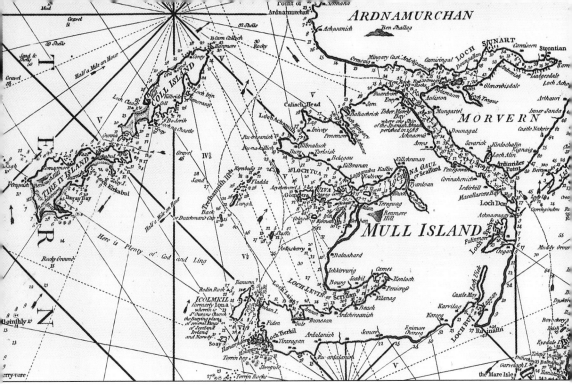

Hebride Isles in 1786, which was in fact the text of his survey of the west coast on behalf of the British Fisheries Society. The Society successfully brought pressure to bear on the British government, and 1787 saw a change in policy: bounties were from thenceforth paid not only to the larger vessels, which came mainly from the Clyde and the east coast, but also to small local vessels. A considerable amount of money (for those days) was spent from government funds (the revenue from the estates forfeited after the 1745 rebellion) in building both canals and providing piers and harbour facilities. Thomas Telford, the famous civil engineer, made his first *Survey and Report on the Coast of Scotland* in 1794, and this was followed in 1801 and 1803 by his first and second *Highland Surveys and Reports*. Many of the small stone piers in hebridean anchorages are the direct result of Telford's work, and most were designed and erected under his personal supervision. The value of these modest piers can be best understood in the light of Knox's experience. Here he is, attempting to get on board a small vessel, on a blustery October morning:

> Our only difficulty in this voyage [across Loch Inver] happened at the first setting out. The wind blew fresh from the sea, which sent in a high swell that rolled furiously along the beach, and dissolved in a cloud of white foam.

A detail from Joseph Huddart's chart of the west coast of Scotland, prepared for the British Fisheries Society and published in 1791.

145

Having dragged the boat to a proper station on the shore, it was resolved that Mr. Mackenzie, the boatman, and myself, should go on board before she was launched; that the people on shore, of whom there were a croud of men, women, and children, should be prepared to push the boat out, between the wave that had just passed, and that which was following, before it had time to break.—In effecting this, some of the people were almost up to their shoulders in water and foam, while those in the boat were straining every nerve to keep her out, by means of oars and poles. The tongues, the noise, and the bustle upon this occasion resembled, we may suppose, the confusion at Babylon; and this work, when the wind blows from certain points, is to be repeated upon the launch of every fishing boat; merely from the want of a small pier, a conveniency almost unknown in the Highlands, and which proves a great impediment to fisheries.[94]

The most permanent memorial to Knox and the British Fisheries Society are the villages or 'fishing stations' which the Society was instrumental in founding. Foremost among these are Oban (then an almost uninhabited bay); Tobermory, surely one of the prettiest villages on the west coast, with its pier built by Telford; and Ullapool in Loch Broom, once the Mecca of herring fleets. Crinan, destined to be the entrance to the canal, and Jura's justly popular Harbour of the Small Isles, were also among his nominees, along with two score other candidates. Not all were in fact adopted by the Society, for, alas, the great herring shoals, for reasons we do not understand, moved further out to sea.

Knox died, at the age of 70, three years after the publication of his *Tour*. At the time of his death the old philanthropist was still actively canvassing support for his schemes and full of new projects.

For the people of the Hebrides, despite the efforts of Knox and the British Fisheries Society, a century of unspeakable oppression lay ahead. As the old lairds died out, their sons and grandsons, land-rich and purse-poor, educated in English schools and aping London society, turned their glens over to sheep and abandoned their clansmen to the mercy of the seashore and a starvation diet of shellfish and seaweed.

The Wandering Shepherd

James Hogg

The jaws of sheep have made the land rich,
but we were told by the prophecy
that sheep would scatter the warriors
and turn their homes into a wilderness.
The land of our loves lies under bracken and heather,
every plain and every field is untilled,
and soon there will be none in Mull of the Trees
but Lowlanders and their white sheep.[95]

IN THE GREY DAWN of 22 May 1804, a shepherd from Ettrick Forrest, the rich Border uplands where the green hills were covered with great flocks of sheep, set out for the Hebrides in search of a sheepwalk. James Hogg, the 'Ettrick Shepherd', was 32. His travelling companion, William Laidlaw, was a boyhood friend, the son of Mr Laidlaw of Yarrow who had employed young Hogg for ten years as a shepherd. Both men had the tanned, weatherbeaten features and sturdy build of farm labourers, and the steady gait of men who are used to walking great distances. They travelled on foot, staff in hand, their tartan cloaks or plaids flying open when the sun shone, or close wrapped when it rained. They took it in turns to carry the small portmanteau which contained all they would require for a four-week trip to the Hebrides: 'a clean shirt, and a change of stockings, a pocket travelling map, and a few neck-cloths.'

It was not Hogg's first visit to the Highlands. As a younger man in 1793 he had accompanied a drover northwards with a flock of sheep. The beauty of the scenery had made a deep impression. For the past two years he had made an annual journey north in search of pastures new. For in 1803 his parents' tenancy in the family's farm had come to an end. Hogg was seeking 'a cheap and quiet retreat in the bosom of some sequestered glen where, unawed by the proud, or unenvied by any, I would nourish and increase my fleecy store and awaken, with pipe and violin, echoes which had slept for a

147

The route of James Hogg, 1804.

On foot ----------

Outward
bound   ....

Homeward
bound   .—.—.—.-

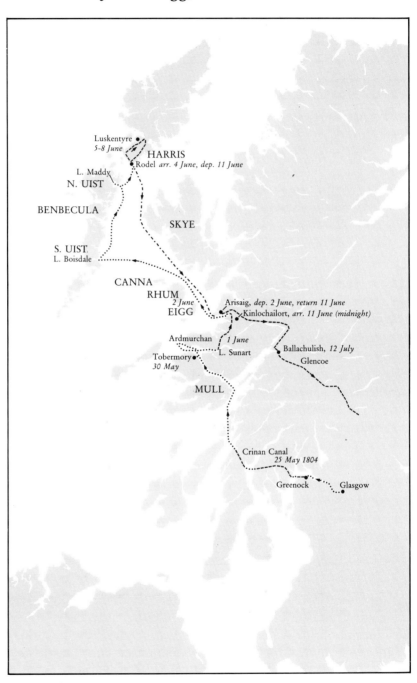

Luskentyre •
5-8 June

HARRIS
• Rodel *arr. 4 June, dep. 11 June*

L. Maddy
N. UIST

BENBECULA

SKYE

S. UIST
L. Boisdale

CANNA
RHUM
2 June
EIGG

Arisaig, *dep. 2 June, return 11 June*
• Kinlochailort, *arr. 11 June (midnight)*

Ardmurchan
1 June
L. Sunart

Tobermory•
30 May

Ballachulish, *12 July*
Glencoe

MULL

Crinan Canal
25 May 1804

Greenock • • Glasgow

thousand years, unless aroused to a transient hum by the voice of the hunter, or the savage howl of the wild beast of the desert'.[96]

The bens and glens of the Highlands and Islands were being thrown open to the shepherds from the south, with their prize flocks of Cheviots. But the land that they were seeking to occupy, at the behest and to the great profit of the clan chieftains now turned lairds, belonged to the clansmen by tradition. They were being cleared in the most brutal way, with thatches burned over the heads of the sick, the elderly, and little children. The people had been driven to the seashores, to make way for the 'four-footed clansmen' – the sheep – and their Sassenach shepherds.

Yet we cannot entirely blame Hogg and his companion. He too had been dispossessed in the name of 'improvement'.

James Hogg has left us a journal of this trip to the Islands, so we are able to follow him. He was not, after all, a completely ordinary shepherd. True, he had had virtually no schooling, and from the age of 7 had spent most of his childhood in the hills herding his father's flocks. Obviously a highly intelligent man, he had taught himself to read and write, but much of his education had come from the traditional folksongs and the rich vein of the old Border ballads. So when Scotland lost her national poet with the early death of Robert Burns, the ploughman from Ayrshire, Hogg felt the mantle fall on him. He began by contributing ballads to the collection begun by Walter Scott. He seems to have passed off as traditional a good many of his own compositions, which Scott uncritically accepted and printed in his *Minstrelsy of the Scottish Borders*. Hogg by 1804 had accumulated £200 – a considerable sum for a simple shepherd – through this and other literary ventures. It was this capital which he proposed to invest in a sheep farm in Harris which belonged to a neighbouring farmer. How he fared will unfold with his account of his travels, which takes the literary form of a series of letters to Walter Scott, which the far more famous poet was able to place for Hogg in the pages of the *Scots Magazine*.

So James Hogg and Will Laidlaw stepped out that May morning in high hopes. A third member of the party, Mr John G., joined the walkers in Glasgow. They had great hopes of a 'pleasing and delightful excursion':

What romantic bays, and inchanted islands, have we in fancy already visited! what verdant pastures, vernal woods, and sweet blooming blushing maids! What pretty compliments have we

James Hogg, the 'Ettrick Shepherd'. Portrait by William Bewick, 1824.

149

already etched out as best suiting the illustrious highland chieftains at whose boards we should be quaffing the delicious nectar![97]

With these expectations the young men set off. They had a rough passage down the Clyde, and a tough walk from Dunoon across the Cowal peninsula. From thence, by ferry (on which they flirted with some buxom country lassies) and on foot they travelled through the rain. Their luck turned when they were able to join, in the Crinan Canal, the *Johnson* of Greenock, 'bound for the Isle of Skye with a valuable cargo of luxuries'. With her, they sailed northwards from Crinan.

Hogg's letters to his friend and patron, Mr (later Sir) Walter Scott, have a freshness and panache of their own. 'Dear Sir,' he writes to Scott, on 30 May 1804, from Tobermory,

Dear Sir,—We set sail on the morning of Tuesday with a fine southern breeze, which carried us out of Loch Crinan. About a mile off the point of Craignish we witnessed a very singular phenomenon. A phenomenon, James! little things are such to you when on a journey: pray what was it? Your honour will not guess; not if you should do nothing else but try for a year. It was, however, what I never before saw or heard of;—being a boat well manned, fishing up cows in the open sea. Aye look back at the word again; it is just *Cows*. But I am to this day unable to account for it in the least, or how such a valuable fishery came to be there; but it was literally as follows:

On reaching the sound of Jura, we steered to the northward: where the wind beginning to sink, and the tide meeting us like a mighty river, we advanced very slow. To the westward about half a mile, we saw a large wherry crouding sail to the South, and then, a good way ahead of here, a black thing came on with the tide, which we soon discovered, with the help of the spyglass, to be an excellent black highland cow. We approached quite near them, and saw them overtake her, when they immediately dropped their sail and threw coils of rope around her, endeavouring with all their might to haul her into the boat: this however they were unable to effect, for she splashed like a whale; and the boat was like to turn its keel uppermost; but they lashed her to the stern.

Just about this time, when the noise of Gaelic in the boat began to abate, in a moment a dun cow emerged from below the waves about forty yards to the N.W. of us. She was grown very weak, was swimming with her side uppermost, and blowing like a porpoise; but the tide bare her rapidly away from us, and very near straight for them. I cannot describe to you the noise and hurry which ensued in the boat on the appearance of this second prize: some hauled up the sails, others hung strenuously by that which they had got, being unwilling to lose a certainty for a chance. They at last with some difficulty succeeded in securing that also, when they made slowly toward the land.[98]

Hogg and his companions were 'lost in conjecture from whence these cows could have come'. Probably they were cattle on their way to market. The economy of the islands depended much on the black Highland cattle, raised in the Isles, which were often swum across from island to island till they reached the mainland. From thence they were herded by drovers across the Highlands to fairs such as that at Falkirk. The unfortunate beasts Hogg saw had, no doubt, been swept down by the tide – 'the furious tide' which now seemed to threaten the *Johnson*:

We were now in no very agreeable situation, being surrounded to the southward by numbers of rocky islets, without any means in our power of eschewing them, and were greatly alarmed to see ourselves borne full upon a large one in the mouth of Loch Crinan! The sailors plied the oars to force the vessel from its longtitude, but their efforts for a long time proved abortive. I, for my own part, had no apprehension of being wrecked on that rock, and strove with all my rhetorick, to persuade them that it was impossible the tide could run us ashore on the island, unless it had a passage under it. . .A small breeze now coming from the s.w. we stood into the bay of Craignish, and the breeze afterwards increasing, we again beat up, doubled the point of Craignish a second time, and the tide turning in our favours, went on swimmingly.[99]

So they sailed northwards on the great tidal race, out past Pladda (also spelt Fladda), and into the Firth of Lorn. That night, fearing the tide-rip off Lady Rock at the entrance to the Sound of Mull, they anchored off Loch Don, and so it was not until ten o'clock on the following day that they dropped anchor in the bay of Tobermory, where the master of the *Johnson*, Mr McAlister, had business to transact. Hogg went ashore despite the 'violent rain'. The weather seemed unpromising for a departure, but Hogg and his friends were eager to make progress:

Mr. McAlister having settled his business at Tobermory, we left

151

Two shepherds on a journey. Illustration from a 1788 edition of Allan Ramsay's *The Gentle Shepherd*. Hogg modelled himself to some extent on Ramsay's popular hero.

at about 3 o'clock p.m. contrary to the ardent remonstrances of an old sailor named Hugh; and I still believe that our importunity to get forward influenced the master too much to set out. The wind was now shifted to the West, the day cleared up, and every five minutes the sky wore a more gloomy aspect; the consequence was, that before we passed the bloody bay, where one of the large vessels of the Spanish Armada was ruined, every countenance was stamped with marks of apprehension; but as it still continued tolerable we held on.

When we reached the point of Ardnamurchan, we were obliged to tack twice in order to weather it, and had already got to the windward of it, when the sea growing prodigiously heavy, and the wind continuing to increase, the sailors were affrighted, and though ten or twelve miles advanced, turned and run again for Tobermory. It was not long until we found ourselves off the mouth of the harbour, but the wind, which was now increased to a gale, blowing straight out of it, and the passage betwixt the island and the rocky point being so narrow that it was dangerous to tack, the getting in became a serious concern: the *Johnson* though a strong English-built sloop, is certainly the most unwieldy vessel of her size that ever was made. They now made a strong effort to weather the straits, putting her about almost

152

every three minutes; all hands assisted in hauling in the sheets; and after a struggle of nearly two hours, they succeeded in working her through the narrows, and expected at the next stretch to gain the harbour. There being ten in all on board, and the deck rather throng, I stepped below to prevent confusion and write this letter; but my two companions assisted with all their might, not without imminent danger to their persons, for the boom overthrew Mr. John every time it was dragged in, and very nearly threw him overboard, he not having experience how to manage himself. I was at length alarmed by an unusual noise and bustle above, but still kept tenaciously by my birth [berth] in the cabin, until I heard Mr. McAlister cry out in great agitation, O! Lord! she will go in a thousand pieces!—O! my God! my God! cried the man at the helm. What's the matter now, thought I; and setting my head out of the compeignan [companion] door, saw every man riveted to the spot awaiting his fate in silent horror. In truth, my dear Sir, you need not envy the present feelings of

Your most obedient servant, James Hogg[100]

Walter Scott would have had to wait for several days to learn from his correspondent of his fate. The next letter, dated Friday 1 June, begins:

Dear Sir,—I took leave of you in my last at a very alarming crisis, when we were all expecting in a few moments to be plunged in the deep, and in all probability into eternity.

Providentially, the vessel 'whirled clear of the rocks', and they stood out to sea:

It was now wearing late, and I shall never forget the stormy appearance of that awful night: the sun, when about to sink into the waves beyond the isles of Barra, frowned upon us through a veil of pale vapour, and seemed to swell to three times his ordinary size. The atmosphere was all in a ferment, having a thin white scum settled steadfastly on its surface, over the face of which, at short intervals, small clouds flew with amazing velocity.

In desperation, they turned and ran before the gale down Loch Sunart:

a most dangerous place, being. . .interspersed with rocks, islands, and narrow rugged points.[101]

The tempest, vividly described, increased in violence, until the ship

153

was driven into a rocky creek. To avoid shipwreck the crew cast out anchors to hold the vessel off the jagged rocks on either side. The fury of the storm abated, and Hogg regaled the crew with whisky as they celebrated their deliverance.

In the early dawn he surveyed the view:

> This Loch-Sunnart, and its environs, is a very wild scene, and though not destitute of beauty, it is rather of the savage kind, being a group of precipitate rocks, green hollows, and wild woods; with the sea winding amongst them in every direction; and the background shaded by the range of black-topped mountains, embosomed in which the mean hamlets lie hid from all the rest of the world.[102]

The three young men – unwisely, as events were to prove – left the storm-bound *Johnson* in Loch Sunart, and decided to make their way on foot across the Ardnamurchan peninsula:

> We mounted the braes of Ardnamurchan at the farm house of Borrowdale, by a small foot track that soon vanished. Here there are many green patches amongst the woods and alongst the shore, but higher on the hills, the soil is wholly moss, with heather and ling.
>
> In ascending this hill, we were riveted to a certain spot a good while, listening to the most mellifluous music, which came floating on the breeze from a neighbouring wood, sometimes in a cadence so soft and low as scarcely to be heard, and at other times in full concert, so loud that all the hills rang. This proceeded from a great number of people, of both sexes, who were cutting and peeling wood at that place; and being assembled at their breakfast, had joined in singing a Gaelic song, in the chorus of which they all joined: and though their notes were wild, and, as we thought, irregular, yet by reason of the distance, and the fine echo of the woods and rocks, the effect was excellent.[103]

They passed through 'a stock of good short sheep belonging to a Captain Cameron', but the young shepherd was too bedraggled by the incessant rain, and muddied by scrambling up and down inaccessible 'precipices and ravines' to call on that gentleman. Hogg had written a book on the management of flocks, and considered himself to be something of an expert, so he frequently comments on the flocks that were, as the clearances progressed, being introduced to the Highland and Island braes and glens:

> In all these districts the sheep stocks are well attended to, and the

154

breeds were, on many farms, above mediocrity; they are all of the blackfaced breeds, and some of the smaller farmer's stocks retain too striking marks of their consanguinity to the old degenerate highland breed. Smearing with tar and grease* is becoming more general, but even those which we saw unsmeared were not much ragged in their fleeces: the frost there is never very intense, when the salt impregnated vapours are unfavourable to the breeding of vermin upon them. . .[104]

It was not on the mainland of Scotland, however, that James Hogg planned to set up as a sheep master, but on distant Harris, across the stormy Minches. So the friends took ship from Arisaig. Their vessel, the *Hawk*, was a fine sailer, but of very shallow draught, and so rolled 'most violently' on the swell. Soon the party were suffering from nausea, an early symptom of which is often 'the most voracious appetite for food'. In particular, Mr John grew quite desperate, and pleaded in his broad Scots with the three Gaelic-speaking seamen:

'Sirs, have you ainy bridd?' said Mr. J. 'Hu, she, she,' said Angus. 'I wish you would gie me a small piese,' returned he. Angus either did not understand, or took no notice of him, for the request was never granted.—The worm continued to gnaw. 'There will be nothing for it,' said I, 'but to eat oakum [old rope] and drink bilge water;' 'Faith,' said Mr. W., 'we'll lick meal and eat cheese.' 'L—d preserve us,' said Mr. J. Angus now struck up a good fire, and put on a pot full of ugly ill-washed potatoes, with six salt herrings. I have seen the day when Mr. W. would have thought them next to poison; but now he started a doubt that they were not meant for us, as they did not really belong to us; this was a piece of heavy news, and I strove to corroborate it by unanswerable evidence. 'I believe it is the case,' said Mr. J., 'but 'tis no matter, we must just mutiny, and take them by force, for I can put off no longer:' 'D—n them,' said W., 'if they don't give us their potatoes, we'll give them none of our gin.' We were, however, invited to partake of this delicious fare, 'and snapt them up, baith stoop an' roop [i.e. completely, entirely]'; we began at the tails of the herrings, and ate them off at the nose, leaving nothing but the two eyes.

We continued to move slowly on, and got some very striking

---

* Grease and tar had long been used in England. Shakespeare speaks of shepherds' hands being 'greasy' and 'tarred over with the surgery of our sheep' (*As You Like It*, III. ii). The practice had little to commend it.

views of Egg [Eigg], which hath a very romantic appearance from some points, especially from the N.W.; on the other hand, the stupendous mountains of Coulan [Cuillin] in the forest of Sky, with some of the bold promontories of that island, formed a scene of the wildest grandure. As we approached the coast of Rum, we saw four or five whales playing in the mouth of the bay, one of which was amongst the largest of them that frequent those seas. In the evening we were quite becalmed a little off the north-east coast of Rum, when we retired all three to our hammocks, and slept soundly until about two in the morning; when I got up, being somewhat disgusted at having arrested an overgrown louse which was traversing one side of my beard: it was then beginning to blow fresh out of the s.w. and a dark fog hid everything from our eyes.[105]

The weather now deteriorated. There were gale-force winds. The sea grew rough and 'the ship rolled amain'. Hogg's unlucky companions grew increasingly sick:

Mr. W. on awakening and perceiving our condition. . .spoke none; his colour was as pale as if the cold hand of death had been upon him; and his mouth has assumed an exact resemblance in shape to a long bow, the nether lip being the string. . .

The motion of the vessel had also by this time thrown Mr. J. into a morbid lethargy; he still kept this hammock, and puked at times so violently, that I though his chest should have rent.[106]

Meanwhile, up on deck, Hogg was expostulating with the seamen. Not that he understood the finer points of seamanship, but it was clear enough that they were miles off course. Instead of making Harris, they were not far from Loch Boisdale, having been 'considerably mistaken in their bearings':

We now run before the wind with great velocity, keeping in a straight line with the headlands of South Uist, Benbecula, and North Uist, for upwards of fifty miles. The whole of these coasts presented nothing to our eyes but naked desolation: the sea seems to have washed away everything but the solid rocks, and to have forced itself into the country in innumerable creeks, in spite of every other impediment. The predominant colour on the face of the Uists is that of the grey rock, and where soil of any kind prevails, it is only a turf of moss. On the western shore, indeed, there are a few bays, round which there is a mixture of sand, where crops are raised equal to any in these barren regions. The coasts are bold and rocky, but low in comparison with those of

Sky. We looked into Loch Eynard [Eynort], when we were first certified where we were; and I could scarcely prevent the sailors from running into it for shelter, as I never could apprehend any danger while we were on a weather shore, and plenty of sea-room. About mid-day we opened Loch-Madi [Maddy] in North Uist, when no arguments could move them to proceed further; so they run the vessel up into it, and anchored beside other two large ones that had taken shelter there. It is not easy to conceive a more dreary and dismal-looking scene, than the environs of this harbour exhibit; the whole country is covered with moss, or grey stones, without the smallest green spot; the sea runs into the country nearly the whole breadth of the island, and spreads itself into a thousand branches, stretching in every direction, which renders travelling completely impracticable; and indeed there is not the smallest semblance of a road. We were, however, agreeably surprised at finding a good slated inn, of two stories, where we took up our residence during the remainder of the day, and the following night.

I continue, Sir, as usual

Your affectionate, Etterick Shepherd[107]

A Highland drover's departure for the south, by Edwin Landseer.

157

In his next letter, dated Wednesday 13 June, Hogg's narrative moves forward apace:

Dear Sir,—After having detained you so long reading a voyage, which, though rendered somewhat interesting by the many cross dispensations attending it, is, nevertheless, trifling, and fraught with very little information, I shall hasten to a conclusion, or at least to places which I have not heretofore visited.

You would lose all patience, were I to detail the whole of our adventures in Uist, which are nevertheless well worthy of a place; and if you had not found fault with me in this respect, you should have heard such a story! What should I have heard, James? You should have heard what a curious waiter we had;—how he clasped his hands above his head whenever he could not comprehend our meaning;—how much we were at a loss for want of Gaelic;—how we hunted the rabbits;—tired of waiting at Kersaig, and set out to traverse the country on foot to its northern extremity, and there procure a passage for Harries [Harris]. You should have heard our unparalleled embarrassments and difficulties, and how we fell out with the natives and were obliged to return;—how we arrived again at the place where we set out in the morning, both completely drenched and fatigued;—how the house, and every part about it, was crowded with some hundreds of Lord Macdonald's people, who were assembled to pay their rents;—what an interesting group they were, and how surprised my two friends were at seeing such numbers in a place they had judged a savage desert, and unfit for the nourishment of intellectual life. You should likewise have heard how our crew fell asleep on board, and could not be awakened;—of Donald's despair: and many other interesting particulars, of which you must now live and die in ignorance.

We at length left Loch-Madi with a fair wind, and, in two hours, found ourselves in the great bason [basin] at Rowdil in Harries, which is one of the greatest curiousities in these countries. There are three narrow entrances into it, but the middle one is impassable, and very dangerous to strangers, as it is the only one which is seen; and had not the inhabitants of Rowdil observed us in a critical minute, *we* had infallibly been dashed to pieces, as we were entering it in full sail: but they, joining in a general shout, tossed their bonnets up into the air, and thus opened our eyes to our imminent danger; nor was it with small difficulty that we then got the vessel put safely about, on the very brink of the sunk rocks. A pilot soon after arriving, we got safely in by the south entrance, and lodged that night at the inn in the village of Rowdil, where we got plenty of everything, and were well refreshed. Here we all manifested considerable satisfaction at having gained in safety the place to which we were bound, after having struggled so long with conflicting elements.[108]

James Hogg does not disclose, in these letters as he edited them for publication, exactly what transpired on the isle of Harris. It will be remembered that Hogg and his companions had set out to explore the feasibility of leasing a farm on Harris, stocking it with Cheviot sheep, and setting up as master of the flock. But it would seem that James Hogg was disappointed. The title to the land was uncertain, and after three days in Luskentyre, on the Atlantic seaboard of Harris, the trio returned deeply disheartened. It must have been a shattering blow, for the chartering of the *Hawk*, and other expenses incurred on the journey, had squandered the hard-earned £200 which Hogg had saved up to invest in his venture:

> Thus terminated the *unfortunate journey*. . .Nor will you refuse your assent to the propriety of the denomination, when you consider that it was not productive of one good effect: that we never, in our way out, walked an hour without being drenched to the skin, and mudded to the knees: that we never went to sea, though but for a few miles, without encountering storms, accidents, and dangers: nor even, after leaving Gourock, proceeded one day by the route we intended, but either lost our way by land, or were thwarted by the winds and the sea.[109]

Hogg failed in his project to obtain a sheepwalk. Other men were more fortunate. And the implications for the native Hebrideans were ominous. The factors ruthlessly cleared their masters' estates of all that cumbered the land, to make way for the flocks and their shepherds. Here is a description of one such eviction – one of the thousands of clearances that were occurring all over the Highlands and Islands in the latter half of the eighteenth and throughout the nineteenth century. The witness is Sir Alexander Giekie, who in his autobiography recalled this scene:

> One of the most vivid recollections which I retain of Kilbride [in Skye] is that of the evictions and clearance of the crofts of Suishnish. The corner of Strath between the two sea inlets of Loch Slapin and Loch Eishort had been for ages occupied by a community that cultivated ground where their huts formed a kind of scattered village. The land belonged to the wide domain of

159

Lord Macdonald, whose affairs [due to extravagant expenditure] were in such a state that he had to place himself in the hands of trustees. These men had little knowledge of the estate, and though they doubtless administered it to the best of their ability, their main object was to make as much money as possible out of rents. . .The interests of the crofters formed a very secondary consideration. With these aims, the trustees determined to clear out the whole population of Suishnish and convert the ground into one large sheep farm, to be placed in the hands of a responsible grazier, if possible, from the south country.

I had heard rumours of these intentions, but did not realise that they were in the process of being carried into effect, until one afternoon as I was returning from my ramble, a strange wailing sound reached my ears at intervals on the breeze from the west. On gaining the top of one of the hills on the south side of the valley, I could see a long and motley procession winding along the road that led north from Suishnish. It halted at the point of the road opposite Kilbride, and there the lamentation became long and loud. As I drew nearer, I could see that the minister with his wife and daughters had come out to meet the people and bid them all farewell. It was a miscellaneous gathering of at least three generations of crofters. There were old men and women, too feeble to walk, who were placed in carts; the younger members of the community on foot were carrying their bundles of clothes and household effects, while the children, with looks of alarm, walked alongside. There was a pause in the notes of woe as the last words were exhanged with the family of Kilbride. Everyone was in tears; each wished to clasp the hands that had so often befriended them, and it seemed that they could not tear themselves away. When they set forth once more, a cry of grief went up to heaven, the long plaintive wail, like a funeral coronach [lament], was resumed, and after the last of the emigrants had disappeared behind the hill, the sound seemed to re-echo through the whole valley of Strath in one prolonged note of desolation. The people were on their way to be shipped to Canada. I have often wandered since then over the solitary ground of Suishnish. Not a soul is to be seen there now, but the greener patches of field and the crumbling walls mark where an active and happy community once lived.[110]

11

THE SOLITARY REAPER

William Wordsworth and the Songs of the Isles

Behold her, single in the field,
Yon solitary Highland Lass!
Reaping and singing by herself;
Stop here, or gently pass!
Alone she cuts, and binds the grain,
And sings a melancholy strain;
O listen! for the Vale profound
Is overflowing with the sound.

No Nightingale did ever chant
More welcome notes to weary bands
Of travellers in some shady haunt,
Among Arabian sands:
A voice so thrilling ne'er was heard
In spring-time from the Cuckoo-bird,
Breaking the silence of the seas
Among the farthest Hebrides.

Will no one tell me what she sings?—
Perhaps the plaintive numbers flow
For old, unhappy, far-off things,
And battles long ago:
Or is it some more humble lay,
Familiar matter of to-day?
Some natural sorrow, loss or pain,
That has been, and may be again?

Whate'er the theme, the Maiden sang
As if her song could have no ending;
I saw her singing at her work,
And o'er the sickle bending;—
I listened, motionless and still;
And, as I mounted up the hill,
The music in my heart I bore,
Long after it was heard no more.[111]

THERE CAN BE few more poignant and evocative images than this, William Wordsworth's solitary reaper.

Who was she? We will never know. Wordsworth saw her, heard her sweet singing, while on a walking tour in Scotland in 1803. Together with his beloved sister Dorothy, and fellow poet Samuel Taylor Coleridge, the 30-year-old Lakeland poet had come to visit Walter Scott, already famed for his *Minstrelsy of the Scottish Border*. It was at Scott's suggestion that the party then went north and west, to the Trossachs, Loch Lomond, and the west coast of Scotland. It was to be the first of a number of visits, and, in poetic terms, the most productive for Wordsworth.

The solitary reaper may well have been an Island girl. Many travellers have described how, every summer, bands of women and girls set out from the Islands for the Lowlands of Scotland:

> In the low countries the harvest is over before that in the Highlands begins, which enables the Highland men and women to profit by two harvests. A traveller in June will continually meet groups of Highlanders trudging south; the women with . . . their sickle on their arm . . .; thus they march on, for perhaps a hundred miles to the earliest harvest districts, and work their way back to the north and west by degrees, as the climate retards the ripening season, and arrive at their homes in good time for gathering in their own crops.[112]

The pay, according to contemporary sources, was about fourpence a day.

In the Highlands and Islands, music was the accompaniment for every task. Here is how one old woman -- a contemporary of Wordsworth's reaper – many years later recalled the songs of her girlhood. She is speaking to Alexander Carmichael (1832-1912), himself Island-born and a Gaelic speaker, of the times before the clearances, or the 'putting out' of the people.

> In my own time, and before we were 'put out' of Ben More, there was much of old lore and old customs and old ways of thought among the old people—prayers and charms, songs and hymns, tales and music and dancing from Monday to Sunday. Whatever the people might be doing, or whatever engaged in, there would be a tune of music in their mouth. When they would arise in the morning . . . there could always be heard a man here and a woman there, a lad yonder and a maiden at hand, with the cheerful strain of music in the mouth of each; whether they would

162

be shaking corn in the kiln or feeding cattle in the byre, fetching in a stoup of water or bringing home a creel of peat, from each one's mouth came his own croon. . . . O Mary Mother, sweet indeed it was to hear them early on a spring morning, speeding their labour—the thrush here in the thicket, the mavis yonder on the rock, the lark aloft in the sky, the radiant golden yellow sun illuminating the high slopes of the mountains and bathing the surface of the waves, the seagull seeking the seed, and the porpoises raising the spray and blowing yonder in the sea of Canna. . .[113]

William Wordsworth. Portrait by R. Hancock, 1798.

What more natural for the girl reaping alone than to sing, to sing one of the lovely island melodies, in time with the slow sweep of her sickle.

'Will no one tell me what she sings?' pleaded the English poet. But the Highland lass sang on, in Gaelic, and listening to that haunting strain, with the minor keys of the ancient modes, the poet could only surmise:

> Perhaps the plaintive numbers flow
> From old, unhappy, far-off things
> And battles long ago:
> Or is it some more humble lay,
> Familiar matter of to-day?
> Some natural sorrow, loss, or pain,
> That has been, and may be again?

Many years later, when Carmichael was himself nearly 70, and Wordsworth's reaper, and many of Carmichael's informants, slept beneath the turf of island graveyards, the first volumes of the *Carmina Gadelica* began to appear: a collection of Gaelic hymns, incantations and songs, collected by Carmichael from the bearers of the great Gaelic tradition. It was to be followed by other notable collections from which I will also quote – in translation, with the inevitable losses.

Here, then, are just a few of the songs that may have been on the lips of Wordsworth's reaper, as that 'thrilling voice' poured out. For songs were shared and preserved with the care that non-literate societies give to their most precious inheritance, their oral culture. And yet each performance was also, in a sense, a unique personal event: motifs and imagery could be re-used to create a new song when some great event – like a bereavement – called forth a response. So the songs preserved by Carmichael, and other folklorists, are representative rather than definitive.

163

First then, here is a fragment from a very old lullaby, composed (it is said) by the foster mother of Donald Gorm, the Chieftain of Sleat who was alive in the early seventeenth century. (Fostering was a common practice, especially in noble families.) Each line has midway a break in the rhythm, as the cradle rocks to and fro:

Donald Gorm's Lullaby – Tàladh Dhomhnaill Ghuirm

. . .Naile naile | naile to travel
early tomorrow. | Then asked the woman
of the other woman, | 'What ship is yon
west of the coast | in the sea of Canna?'
Starvation take ye! | Why should I hide it?
What ship, but Donald's | the ship of my baby,
the ship of my king, | the ship of the Islands.
Heavy I think it, | the lading that's in her;
a rudder of gold | three masts of willow,
a well of wine | down at her quarter,
a well of pure water | up at her shoulder. . .

Might of the brightness | might of the sunbeam
be between Donald Gorm | and his raiment,
might of the cornshoot | in the Maytime,
might of the billows | heavy, heroic,
might of the salmon | headlong, leaping,
might of Cuchulann | in full war-gear,
might of the seven bands | the host of the Fiann,
might of sweet Oisein, | of valorous Oscar,
might of the storm | and the tearing tempest,
might of the thunder | and the hideous lightening,
might of the great sea-monster | blowing
might of the elements | and the hosts of heaven
be between Donald Gorm | and his raiment;
each one of those | and the might of God's son.[114]

In contrast with the magic of this lullaby is a very tender but practical song, composed by a mother as she sailed across one wild day from sea-girt Haskeir to North Uist. The Haskeir group, low-lying islets, lie to the west of the Uists, on the exposed Atlantic side of the Outer Hebrides. Once inhabited by twenty or so families, the islets have now been abandoned. The six-mile crossing, through the heavy swell, breaking surf and dangerous currents, across the kyles to the sea-swept beaches of North Uist is a dangerous one even in calm weather. The singer is Rachel, daughter of Alexander – a tall woman, and of great strength. The song dates from the 1750s. It was collected by Rachel's descendant, seven generations later.

Chorus: O hi u i ho u bho
        Let's raise a tune and sing a boat song;
        trim the lines of the boat
        That's coming today from Heisgeir;
        O hi u i ho u bho.

No thin spurts from fountains cold
The mother's milk that fed my laddies;
No handling a crooked load
Their legacy when sailing. [Chorus]

The first in line is Donald Don,   [Donn =
My first-born and darling laddie;   brown-haired]
My love with his curly head,
Who's worthy of a maiden. [Chorus]

To the windward is Angus Roo-a,   [Roo-a = Ruadh
With hair that's curled in many ringlets; = red-head]
Happy is he on the salt sea,
And worthy of a maiden. [Chorus]

Around her bow the snore of waves
Is keeping time with sailing ditties,
Sung so high by Alasdair Ban,   [Ban = fair haired]
Who's worthy of a maiden. [Chorus]

It's young John who's near the mast,
To reach dry land is what he hopes for;
Spume of spindrift on his hair,
And worthy of a maiden. [Chorus]

On my knee is Allan Peck,   [Beag (pronounced
He chatters of the ocean's fury;   Peck) = little]
His eye lively, kind and warm,
He's worthy of a maiden. [Chorus]

So, little laddies, sing your song;
Though many waves will strike her planking;
The next tack we take with her,
Puts Currachag to our windward. [Chorus]

Currachag, Angus Macdonald (the descendant of little Allan) reminds us, is 'a sunken rock out from the Balranald shore. It would be a dangerous spot on a stormy trip from Heisgeir.'

Women reaping in Skye. Illustration from C.F. Gordon Cumming's *In the Hebrides* (1883).

Carmichael commented on the extraordinary courage and hardiness of these men and women:

> These people of warmest emotion are of the coolest composure in danger. The writer observed this many times during his long residence in those stormy Isles of the Atlantic. Many times among those wild seas, among the bristling rocks, roaring reefs and mountainous waves, when death appeared inevitable, the people remained cool and calm, neither cry nor clamour from man or woman, but only a murmured prayer for the soul and a tear for those behind.[116]

Many of the songs that women sang when reaping, or in the communal labour of shrinking cloth (waulking), were centred on the fears and hopes of the watchers on shore. Here is the song of a girl for whom the outcome was joyous.

> I was sad and so lonely, waiting here on the hill,
> Far, so far from my dear ones, while storm stayed in this place,
> Till I saw the fine birlinn with her sails fully set
> Coming round Ardmore Point, the hero's son at the helm . . .
>
> Son of heroes is steering, coming towards the Head,*
> Home through the narrows now swelling, seas that rise to the deck;
> And your hand is so skilful, it's lost none of its strength,
> Though rough seas that are blue-black spread in floods o'er the ship . . .

---

*Dunvegan Head, on Skye.

166

Unafraid of the ocean, your appearance so calm,
Though the seas are white-crested, and the angry waves roar;
Though the reef is a danger in the squalls and the gales,
Still your courage keeps steady and you weather the storm . . .[117]

The 'hero's son' of this song was Archibald MacLean, Laird of
Haskeir in the mid-eighteenth century. He was noted as a fine
sailor, and the master of a fast sailing vessel. He was also the 'darling
of maidens', and left at least one broken heart when he was forced to
emigrate to Canada:

> And your boat is now drawn up,
> On the sandy white machair.
>
> And I'm feeling so saddened,
> In the bent grass and sand drift.[118]

Here is a far older celebration of the prowess of the young heroes
of Clan MacNeil, who sailed out in their galley from Kismul Castle.
The hauntingly beautiful tune of this fine song is justly famous.

> *Chorus (repeated after every line):*
> Fair all al o, ro ho bhi o,
> Hoireann is o, ho ro bhi o ho
> Hi ri ho ro ho bha, o haodh.

> One day on the Misty Mountain,
> Rounding up the sheep to get them. . .
> 'Twas I myself beheld the vision,
> Seeing thy galley going past me,
> Setting her head to the wide ocean
> From McNeil of Barra's country,
> Out of Ciosamul's joyful castle
> Where we used to be a-feasting,
> Drinking wine from dawn till nightfall,
> Shouts of men their ale a-drinking,
> With women wearing brown silk dresses;
> 'Tis I indeed who am afflicted
> If Clan Neil's boat has passed me . . .[119]

The second part of this song is about when the singer was 'a girl
'neath the sheen of her tresses', and her lover who hunted antlered
deer in the rush-covered valley. Many are the songs of frank and
tender love. One such is this lament of a Barra girl for her lost lover,
John Campbell, once a hardy member of the crew of Clan Neil's

galley. The song goes through the stages of the girl's passion for her beloved: her joy in their love; her pride in her lover's seamanship; her grief that he is dead and coffined; her agony of jealousy lest another should claim him as lover; and then the girl recapitulates her love. After every half line there is a short refain of musical syllables, when the other women would join in the chorus.

Walk my beloved, [*refrain*] hu ill o ro | white-armed
   youth, [*refrain*] ho i ibh o,
Remember me | to the Isle of Harris,
To John Campbell | my brown haired-lover,
And say to him | that I am healthy,
That I have put | the winter past me.
Often I lay | beneath your covering,
If I did so | 'twas not at home,
In a secret valley, | in a dell of birch-trees,
It was the birds | who were our watchmen
With clear fresh water | cold and healthy
Like proud wine | being poured in glasses.
We mouth to mouth | I'd not be lying,
Your sweet lips | my breath drinking,
With me beneath | your plaid of tartan,
Beneath the gunwale | of your galley,
Within earshot | of deer a-calling.

Wet is the night | tonight, and chilly,
Clan Neil have taken | to the ocean,
If I am right, | I can see then,
With their galleys | bare and speedy,
With their banners | blue and green,
With their pulleys | round and hard,
My love himself | is on the weather side,
His grip's on the helm | when it's hardest;
'Twas no left-hander | who'd take it from you,
Nor a right-hander | man who's shivering.
I'll tell the truth | it is no comfort,
You are the man | I most am liking,
Who trod on grass | or on cornfield,
Who on his right | or left side lay,
Or who put his foot | in shoe or stocking.

'Tis I indeed | who am not healthy
From the Shrove Tuesday | beginning of spring time,
My brown-haired youth | is against the wall,

The back of your head | on a plank of oak,
With only a slender | shroud of linen.
Doctor's not needed | in your homestead,
Though he's not | a shroud is needed,
Also many | many white candles.
'Tis I indeed | who am shattered,
Tormented I | and torn to pieces,
Going tomorrow | with you from the village,
If I am, 'tis | not to your wedding,
But to bury you | in earth covered.
Despite who lives | and who survives not,
I spent last night | at your wake vigil,
I'll spend the night | tonight there also,
There will be no smooring | of white candles
Till earth is put | on the eyes of my lover,
Earth on the eyes | of my first secret sweetheart.

Betrothal tonight | in the upper village,
If I can | I'll take advantage,
Amorous eyes | in the heads of maidens;
If I heard | your name linked with another
I'd tear my hair | out by the roots,
My flesh would turn | into green vapour.
You are my honey | my own honey,
My sugar and | my violin music,
My harp music | high and low,
My marigolds | in the corn fields.[120]

Whatever personal tragedy lay behind this lament, it was kept alive by the women who made it their own. So too it was with one of the most famed of laments, the song of Annie Campbell of Scalpay for her betrothed, Ailein Duinn (brown-haired Allan). The tale is that Allan Morrison, son of Roderick Morrison of Stornoway, was a sea captain who plied his trade between Stornoway and the Isle of Man. In the spring of 1786 he set sail for the little island of Scalpay, off Harris, where he was to go through the ceremony of a marriage contract with Annie Campbell, daughter of Campbell the tacksman of Scalpay. Not far short of their destination, Captain Morrison and his crew were overtaken by a violent storm, and the ship foundered with all hands. Broken-hearted, Annie wasted away with grief, and died within a few months. Her body was taken to Rodel, on Harris, for burial in the ancient church, but on the voyage the boat was almost overwhelmed by a furious storm. To lighten the ship the

A cottar's wife, nursing her hungry child as she sings. Engraving after John Frederick Miller, from Pennant's *Voyage*.

coffin had to be cast overboard. Not long after, Captain Morrison's body was found on a beach on the lonely Shiant islands (the enchanted isles, to translate the Gaelic). A few days later the girl's corpse was also washed up on the same beach, swept thither by the strong tidal currents.

Here is a version of this song which was still widespread in the present century. The chorus or refrain is repeated every other line.

Chorus: Brown-haired Allan, o hi, I would go with thee;
Ho ri ri u ho, e o hug hoireann o,
Brown-haired Allan, o hit, I would go with thee.

I am tormented
I have no thought of merriment tonight
But only for the sound of the elements
And the strength of the gales
Which would drive the men
From the harbour.
And brown-haired Allan, my darling sweetheart,
I heard you had gone across the sea
On a slender black boat of oak,
And that you had gone ashore in the Isle of Man.
That is not the harbour I would have choosen
But Caolas Stiadair in Harris
Or Loch Miabhaig amongst the hills.
My prayer to God in heaven,
Let me not be put in the earth or in a shroud,
In a hole in the earth or a secret place,
But in the spot where you have gone, Allan!

Brown-haired Allan, my heart's darling,
I was young when I fell in love with you.
Tonight my tale is wretched.
It is not the death of cattle in the bog
But of the wetness of your shirt
And of you being torn by whales. . .
I heard you had been drowned,
Alas, O God, that I was not beside you
On whatever skerry or rock you were cast,
On whatever wrack the high-tide had left you.
I would drink a drink, in spite of everyone,
Of your heart's blood, after you had been drowned.[121]

This lament has many very ancient motifs, which often appear in laments for the drowned. In another version, the bereaved bride sings:

If sand is your pillow,
If seaweed is your bed,
If the fish are your white candles,
If the seals are your deathbed watchers,
I pray God in Heaven, let me be
In the spot where you have gone, Allan![122]

Death in the Isles was never far away. Famine stalked the land, year after year, for by late spring the previous year's harvest was all but used up – only the seed corn and seed potatoes remained. Many infants and children perished of starvation in bad years. The winter months, with their long nights and wild gales, were the months when the great herring shoals visited the isles. Brave men put out to sea in their frail boats to try to win food for their wives and children. But some boats never returned.

Many of the songs of labour were, inevitably, laments. I will end with translations of two magnificent elegies. The first is the highly personal lament of Rachel MacDonald, widowed in the middle of the eighteenth century, when her husband's fishing vessel, the *Canarag* (The Young Dolphin) failed to return to the island of Haskeir after a fishing expedition to the Rockall banks.

Lament for the Canarag

But where are the men who sailed so gaily on *Canarag*?
That cleared from Port Roy on Tuesday evening,
With James and Norman and Charles and Alasdair,

Seamen that were as strong as any in Scotland
At trimming the sails when the weather was stormiest;
Great-hearted heroes they were when action was needed,
When waves wildly breaking would crash over *Canarag* . . .

I stood as I promised on Lyndal and prayed for you
When you sailed on west to the setting of the sun;
Brave men were aboard of her to handle her properly,
And Alasdair was steering her close to the wind;
Devout was my prayer to Christ that you would return
From the storm of the ocean and the roar of the blast,
From Rockall fishing banks filled with harvest from the sea,
We'd see you in Cnoic here with heroes' reward.

Your conduct, my James, was discerning, distinguished,
Intense was your loving and kind was your wish;
The shade of your memory keeps you alive for me,
Death can never freeze up the warmth of your kiss;
Our love was still fragrant and secret our rendezvous,
'Twas sweet of you to whisper loving words in my ear . . .

Your love of the sea was what lulled you to sleep in it,
With love of the sea in your blood and your breast;
The rest you wished for rather than sleep in the grave-yard,
The clean, the clear, the restless and musical sea;
A poor and sad mourner I – and hard it is to confess –
No surety or care for them, no handful of earth;
No kind fold around them when the tempest o'erwhelmed them,
And death rode his Black Steed through the fiery atmosphere;
O God, since you willed it, it's vain to complain of it,
Though sad for those they left so weak and so young;
Our love shall not grow cold but live and be ever new,
While ocean's ceaseless movement rocks them in their sleep.[123]

It is difficult to match this moving lament – the work, it needs to be remembered, of a great poet, though she could neither read nor write. In another poem, Rachel speaks of her love of the sea, the life-giver and life-taker:

O, beautiful ocean and eternal,
I've given you so much love. . .
I have bent my knee to you,
Worshipping you with devotion. . .
Till I am laid in the turf
I shall bear good-will toward you,
Though you have left me bruised

And taken from me my honey-comb. . .
It is my desire truthfully
That it shall be told
Through the elements of eternity
That I did not withhold my love from you.[124]

While laments like that of Rachel, daughter of Neil of Haskeir, were handed down within families, some of the greatest folk poetry of the Hebrides comes down to us over the generations with no known author, and no date. Such is 'Seathan', the 'queen of the waulking songs'. A moving and expressive lament, it belongs to a legendary past. Seathan the wanderer, 'own son to my king of Tyrconnel', is a figure from medieval or earlier times. The Gaelic is that of the sixteenth century, but the shape and metric pattern may well be much earlier. As water rounds and polishes pebbles on the beach, so successive generations of singers may have polished the phrases of this powerful poem. For, like all the other songs in this chapter, this poem, composed by a woman, was passed from generation to generation of women, floating (to quote from Dr Johnson) on the breath of the people.

Here then is the version collected and translated by Alexander Carmichael. Wordsworth's solitary reaper would certainly have known 'Seathan' – time was when no Highland or Island waulking was complete without it – although she may not have have known all the lines of the soloist, but only have joined in the refrain. 'Where did you hear this song?' Carmichael asked Janet MacLeod of Eigg, one of the tradition-bearers. And she replied, in Gaelic,

I have heard it from many a person, and many a time have I sung it myself lustily at the waulking frame. My father's people, the tribe descended from the Counsellor, were famous for old songs and things of that kind,—was it not about them it was said that they never forgot any poetry or lore, but were constantly adding to the cairn? And when my father came to Trotternish, whether or not he brought any property with him from MacLeod's Country, he at least brought with him enough poetry and lore to fill the world.

That legacy was not worth much! [exclaimed Carmichael]

Was it not? I would not say so! Everything that endures is good. 'Shared gold goes not far, but shared song lasts a long time.' A gold coin does not go far in company, but a good song will suffice for a whole world of people. But what I was going to say was that 'Seathan Son of the King of Ireland' was the choice of waulking songs. The women to-day have only fragments of it;

when I first remember, 'Seathan' by itself would be sufficient to complete the waulking, however tough the cloth. I myself remember but little of it to-day, compared with what I knew when no waulking was complete without me. . .[125]

Fragmentary or not, 'Seathan' has a highly distinctive emotional drive. The telling imagery, the rich use of motifs, the pulse of the intricate metric pattern, with the rhyming paragraphs of varying length, the controlled passion – all suggest a single author, a woman poet of exceptional power and imagination.

Seathan Son of the King of Ireland

Woe to him who heard of it and did not tell it,
  Hu ru na hur i bhi o
woe to him who heard of it and did not tell it,
  Na bhi hao bho hao bhi o an
that my darling was in Minginish;
if thou wert, my love, thou hadst returned long since:
I would send a great ship to seek him there,
with a famed crew, fresh and bright and expert,
young men and lads would be there
he would visit here when he returned,
I would spend a festal day dallying with him,
I would sit on a knoll and engage in sweet converse,
I would curl thy hair as I did oft-times,
I would lie in thy arms and keep the dew from thee,
I would wash a fine-spun shirt full white for thee,
so long as any water remained in the pool,
and I would dry it on a moorland branch.

But Seathan to-night is a corse,
a sad tale to the men of Scotland,
a grievous tale to his followers,
a joyous tale to his pursuers,
to the son of the Hag of the Three Thorns.

Dear Seathan of the tranquil eyes,
oft didst thou redden the hillocks:
it was not with the blood of cattle or horses,
or the blood of the swift deer,
or the blood of the roe in a nook of the corn-field,
but the blood of thine enemy bent on strangling thee.

When I thought thou wast giving chase,
thou wast dead in the conflict,

borne on the shoulders of the young men,
and on the point of being buried . . .

My love thy right hand, though now cold,
oft did I have it, seldom was it away from me,
oft did I have a present from it,
and never with aught that was mean,
it was not with stick or cudgel,
it was not with abuse or quarrelling,
but with green satin and fine silk,
with the noblest of gifts.

O brown-haired Seathan, calf of my love,
I would go far away with thee, my love,
I would go with thee through the branchy wood
where the birds are wont to warble,
I would cross the Irish Sea with thee
where the swelling ocean surges,
I would cross the Sea of Greece with thee,
the haunt of swarthy corsairs.

Women waulking (shrinking and fulling cloth) and using the quern (handmill) near Talisker in Skye. Engraving after Moses Griffith. Waulking was more often done by hand, rather than by foot as shown here, and was accompanied by a particular type of song.

I and Seathan traversing mountains,
I was weak, but Seathan was strong,
I could endure but little clothing,
a russet coat to the middle of my thigh,
a kerchief of fine pure-white linen,
as I fared with my darling Seathan.

O Seathan, Seathan, bereft of life,
own son to my king from Tyrconnel,
oft have I lain beneath thy cloak;
if I did, it was not in a homestead,
but in a green hollow in a tree-sheltered field,
under the slope of the rugged blue peaks,
the wind from the mountains sweeping over us,
the wind from the glens with a sough taking
its fill of the first burgeoning of spring.

Many a glen and ben we traversed,
I was in Islay and in Uist with thee,
I was in Sleat of the yellow-haired women with thee,
I was in Iona of the nuns with thee,
I was in the land of birds and eggs with thee,
I was in Ireland, I was in Latium with thee,
I traversed Brittany and Burgundy,
I traversed the Continent and the Mearns with thee,
I traversed the Boyne, I traversed Munster with thee,
I heard Mass in Cill Chumha with thee,
I heard the music of the fairy-mansions with thee,
I drank a draught from the well of wandering with thee,
I was the day before yesterday and last year with thee,
I was from cape to cape with thee,
I was in Kildonan of the pines with thee.
I was three years on the hills with thee.

I kept watch for a day in the treetops with thee,
I kept watch for two days in the sea wrack with thee,
I kept watch for a night on a sea rock with thee,
I kept watch, my love, and I did not regret it,
wrapped in a corner of thy tartan plaid,
the spindrift ever breaking over us,
water that is very pure, cool and wholesome.

My love is Seathan of the tranquil eyes,
I would lie with thee on any uneasy bed,
a bed of heather with my side on stones;

dearer Seathan in a coil of heather rope
than a king's son on a bed of linen;
dearer Seathan behind a dyke
than a king's son in silks on deal flooring,
though he should have a restful bed
which had been well-planed by wrights,
and protected by power of druids;
dearer Seathan in the birch wood
than to be in Magh Meall with Airril,
though he had satin and silk under his feet,
and pillows lustrous with red gold.

If Seathan were seen as he arose
in shade of hill on a May morning,
a short kilt to the middle of his thigh,
a narrow black belt about his tunic,
his foster-mother's love, his wife's darling,
the sight seven times dearest to his own mother,
a secret lover he is to me.

O brown-haired Seathan thou gentle hero,
small is the place in which I would put thee,
I would put thee on the very top of my head,
I would put thee between my breasts,
between Bride and her soft kerchief,
between a young maiden and her snood,
between a fair virgin and her silken mantle,
between myself and my shirt of linen.

But Seathan is in the lonely chamber,
without drinking of cups or goblets,
without drinking of wine from splendid silver tankards,
without drinking of ale with his cronies and gentlemen,
without drinking to music, without kiss from seductive
    woman,
without music of harp, without listening to melody,
but strait bands on his shoulders,
and looped bands on the bier poles.

I am a sister of Aodh and yellow-haired Brian,
I am a kinswoman of Fionn son of Cumhall,
I am the wife of brown-haired Seathan, the wanderer,
but alas! for those who said I was a joyous wife,
I am a poor, sad, mournful, sorrowful wife,
full of anguish and grief and woe.

Spinning wool in
Skye, c. 1900.

My father put me in a distressing place
on that night he made a wedding-feast for me,
alas, O King! that it were not my lyke-wake,
that the linen shroud had not been cut for me,
that the pine planks had not been polished for me,
that the loops had not been tied on me,
that I had not been hidden in the mould,
for fear I should be alive on earth.
There is many a table where I shall be slighted,
where my teeth shall no more chew bread,
where my spoon shall no more draw,
where my knife shall no more cut,
where my fancy shall no more linger.

If Seathan could be but redeemed
the ransom could be got like rushes,
silver could be got like ashes,
gold could be got on the fringe of meadows,
wine could be got like spring water,
beer could be got like a cool verdant stream;
there would not be a goat in rock or stony upland,
there would not be a young she-goat in meadow,

there would not be a sheep on rocky shelf or mountain
    top,
there would not be cattle on plain or in fold,
there would not be pig or cow in pastures;
the salmon would come from the sea,
the trout would come from the river-banks,
the geldings would come from the rushes;
there would not be a black or white-shouldered cow
high or low in the fold,
at the edge of township or in stall,
that I would not send, my love, to redeem thee,
even to my green plaid,
though that should take the one cow from me,
and it was not the one black cow of my fold,
but herds of white-shouldered cattle,
of white-headed, white-backed, red-eared cattle.

But Seathan is to-night in the upper town,
neither gold nor tears will win him,
neither drink nor music will tempt him,
neither slaughter nor violence will bring him from his
    doom,
neither tumult nor force will wake him from his slumber;
and my heart is broken and distraught,
my tears flow like a well,
uneasily I sleep on a pillow,
for thou has no one who pities thee
save me, running to and fro.

O Seathan dear! O Seathan dear!
I would not give thee to law or king,
I would not give thee to the gentle Mary,
I would not give thee to the Holy Rood,
I would not give thee to Jesus Christ,
I would not, for fear I would not get thee myself.

O Seathan, my brightness of the sun!
alas! despite me death has seized thee,
and that has left me sad and tearful,
lamenting bitterly that thou art gone;
and if all the clerics say is true,
that there is a Hell and a Heaven,
my share of Heaven—it is my welcome to death—
for a night with my darling,
with my spouse, brown-haired Seathan.[126]

12

THE BEAUTIES OF SCOTLAND

Mrs Sarah Murray

'THE PICTURE of the outset':
A very good house facing the Sound of Mull; near it a ruin of what was once a castle, by which runs a river romantically enough. Mrs. Murray appears, accompanied by gentlemen and ladies, dressed in a red leather cap trimmed with brown fur, and the habit of Tartan such as is worn by the 42nd regiment of Highlanders. She mounts a white horse, with a Fingalian stick in her hand, cut out of the woods of Morven. Her horse led by an honest Highlander. Then comes a sheltie with creels [paniers] on his back, containing the baggage, on which sat a Highland lad.

Thus moved Mrs. Murray's first cavalry expedition in the island of Mull, and laughable enough it was.[127]

The year is 1800. A new century has dawned. Conditions have so far improved in the Hebrides that it is possible for a female tourist to travel far and wide.

Mrs Sarah Murray, at the time of her travels, was a sprightly widow nearing 60. She was cheerful, somewhat eccentric, and perhaps a trifle plump (the stone staircase in Dunstaffnage Castle, she complained, was 'so narrow and winding' that she could only just squeeze herself up the stairs).

The lady was already a well-known authoress, for she had published *A Companion to the Beauties of Scotland* in the year 1799. Mrs Murray was a romantic in search of the picturesque; cascades were her passion, but mountains, lakes, woodland, rocks and trees also excited her enthusiasm for natural beauty. She wrote, she claimed, neither for fame nor for bread, but in the hope of being 'really useful to travellers'. For, though she was tireless in her search for 'those objects worthy of notice', she nevertheless had an immensely practical streak. Other travellers loftily moved from place to place with little attention to the means of locomotion and the expense. Not Mrs Murray. She devoted at least a third of her first volume to good advice to the traveller: how to turn your carriage into a sort of caravan; whether to take bedding and towels; how far it was from inn to inn, and what the accommodation was like ('a shocking inn'; 'inn rather bad, but beds tolerably clean'), and whether the inn keeper was welcoming, the food good, and the beds free of 'the hopping gentry'. She gives advice on where to hire horses, or engage ferries, and what to pay. This more practical section precedes her descriptions of her own travels, the scenery she saw, and the people she met.

The success of her first volume encouraged her to attempt a second, on the Hebrides.

She proposed to travel far and wide on horseback and by open boat. The ferries of those days were tiny rowing vessels. There were no carriage roads on the Inner Hebrides (nor, for that matter, the Outer). There were almost no tracks across the islands, except a few rough stony paths which hurt the tender unshod feet of the Highland ponies. Most burns and rivers had to be forded. It could sometimes rain all day. She proposed to cross wild stretches of mountainous country in which there was no human habitation. She was prepared to travel, quite alone, unattended by a maid or manservant, entrusting herself to the local people, whose language she could not speak (the Murrays were a Perthshire family).

The result of her travels in the Hebrides was a second volume to add to her *Beauties of Scotland* – a guidebook and travelogue to the Hebrides, to which she made a series of voyages between 1800 and 1803.

Here then are some vignettes from her travels.

First, let us return to her progress on horseback, which, at that time, was the commonest mode of travel across the roadless isles. Here she is crossing Mull. As she approached Loch na Keal, her guide warned her that they were approaching a particularly difficult part. Naturally, as a lady, she was riding side-saddle: 'I came,' she writes,

> to what my guide had told me would be a very bad step; but I might remain, he said, on my saddle for he would answer for my safety. The step rises on a pointed rock hanging over the lake, and the shelf on which the horses tread is thickly strewed with huge stones standing and lying in every direction. These stones have fallen, and are every day falling, from a perpendicular huge mass rising to a vast height on one side of the shelf. The horse in going up and down this rocky broken shelf went cautiously, and

The travels of Mrs Sarah Murray, 1800 and 1803.

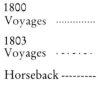

1800
Voyages ....

1803
Voyages · · - - · · ·

Horseback --------

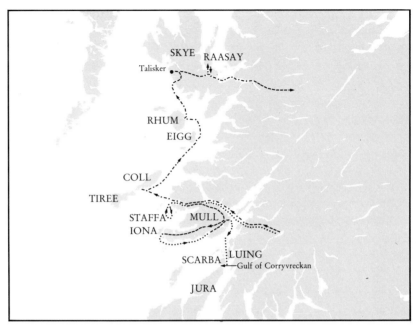

slowly, as well he might, for the poor beast was obliged to put one leg as much as two foot deep amongst the stones and there let it remain till he could drag another leg from equal depth, and so on, dragging his legs out and safely replacing them amongst the broken rocks. In ascending I was obliged to lie on the horse's neck, and in descending almost on his tail, but for all that, though with trembling, I could not help gazing at the huge masses of rock piled up like folio books one upon another, all the way up the mountain, hanging over my head.[128]

The difficulties of making one's way on foot across the wild, trackless expanses of the Isles can only be appreciated by those who have attempted it. This is why, in the period of which I am writing, before paved roads made possible riding with shod horses (and later, in carriages) most journeys were made, whenever possible, by water. Richer tourists took passage in a decked cutter, but Mrs Sarah Murray, like John Knox before her, frequently made crossings in small, open boats. On one crossing by ferry from Ach-na-craig on Mull, she found herself the only passenger in the tiny ferry boat with two seamen who spoke very little English.

182

As soon as we got out of the shelter of the bay [she writes], the sea was rough, and the wind rather high and unfavourable, which put the two seamen in a bustle with the sails. At that time I was not so conversant with nautical business as I have since been; so that the seamen's bustle with the ropes and sails threw me also into a fuss, and I questioned my companions first one, and then the other, with earnestness, if we were in danger of going to the bottom: Oh! yes, was the answer repeatedly given by both men.[129]

Wisely, Mrs Murray decided that it was simply a misunderstanding.

No sooner had the boat settled down, than an incident that other ladies might have taken as even more threatening occurred:

As soon as the sails were hoisted and in order, and the boat set in her proper trim, the boatmen took their stations one on each side of me, and began to examine the parcels I seemed to take the most care of. A bag containing stones lay at my feet, which, without ceremony, one of the sailors placed on his knee, untied it, and took out of it a stone, which he looked at, and laughed. I told him it came from Staffa. His laughter increased; and he made me understand I had been at very useless trouble in conveying stones from such a distance, when I might have gotten plenty of the like on Mull. My left hand companion perceiving my little mahogany box. . .and perhaps never having before seen so neat a piece of workmanship, took a fancy to take it in his hand, and viewed it with admiration. Beside its usual contents*, it included some precious nephritic stones [supposedly efficacious for kidney disease], which added to its common weight, and gave rise to an idea in the sailor's mind that nothing but gold could make it so heavy. After balancing my box for some seconds in his hand, he said, 'is monies?' I laughed in my turn, and took out of my pocket the key of the box, and presented each of them with a small tumbler of wine out of it. Their surprise was extreme: the construction of the box, the bottles, the knife and fork, spoons, and other knick-knacks it contained, seemed matters of as much curiosity to them, as Staffa and its prisms had been to me.

Some of my English friends have commended my presence of mind (as they call it), on this occasion; for, say they, had you not opened your box, and shewn its contents, the sailors might have

---

*Mrs Murray elsewhere lists the contents, which included 'hartshorn and lavender drops, and a cure for bruises' as well as wine and biscuits for eating on her travels.

Ben More, Mull, from Ulva House. Mrs Murray's overland journey across the rough and trackless wilds of Mull caused her considerable discomfort. Aquatint by William Daniell.

given you a watery grave, in order to secure to themselves the imaginary treasure.

By the Lowlanders of Scotland the Highlanders are accused of a strong inclination to take what they have no right to; but such opinions are very erroneous and unjust. Previous to the Union [of the Scottish and English Parliaments in 1707] and the year 1745, they might perhaps have sometimes deviated from the rule of right in respect of cattle; but in these days, they may be trusted as far as a fallible being ought to be. No greater proof of their fidelity, and my confidence in it, can I adduce, than that on all occasions I have entrusted myself to their sole care without having had the least fear for my own safety, or a doubt arising of their integrity, even amongst the lowest class of Highlanders. I consider myself in the hands of men whose fathers had honour and honesty sufficient to guard them against perfidy, when the temptation of thirty-thousand pounds on the head of an unfortunate wanderer [Bonnie Prince Charlie] was in vain held out as a reward for his discovery.[130]

Whatever Mrs Murray's confidence in her escorts might be, the fact is that sea crossings were – and still are, even today – extremely hazardous in bad weather.

184

Here, for example, is Mrs Murray accompanied by her guide, Angus Cameron, attempting to get from Bunessan, on the Ross of Mull, to Eigg. She was travelling in a boat used to transport cattle, a flat-bottomed vessel which pitched crazily in heavy seas. The weather was fine when they set off, but soon deteriorated. The west side of Mull is studded with rocks and virtually devoid of safe anchorages. Headed by contrary winds, with rising seas, the boat was forced to seek shelter on Coll, driven right off course. Mrs Murray describes their predicament:

We passed point after point, but no harbour appeared. The boatmen began to talk loud in Gaelic, and damn in English, for there is no such oath in the Gaelic language; the night was fast approaching, and my spirits were far below par, when on a sudden I heard the joyful sound, Here it is, here it is! The wind was high, and we steered into the Loch full sail. The wind was directly for us, but the tide contrary, which made the sea run high, and roar amongst the rocks. The sea was dashing, the sails rattling, the sailors hallowing and shouting. . .

Just at that moment a small fishing vessel came down the Loch; I had her hailed alongside us, with the intention for her to pilot us to the anchoring place. There was only one savage-looking man in the boat, and a little girl. The fisherman talked loud in order to direct the sailors, who were swearing, because they could not hear what he said by reason of the noise of sea and wind. The cockle-shell danced backwards and forwards around us, struggling with the waves to get to us, and at last the old man caught hold of a rope thrown to him, by which his boat was drawn close alongside of us; and notwithstanding the boat was going full sail, I made no hesitation, but hoisted myself over the side of the larger boat, and slipped down into the small one, which was strewn with the refuse of herrings, and half filled with water. Mr. Campbell [a fellow passenger] followed me, and off we paddled towards the rocks on shore. We had not been out of the large boat three minutes, before she struck upon a rock. The sensations of my heart at that moment were manifold; my own safety raised an instantaneous ejaculation of gratitude; the next moment I started at the danger the faithful Angus Cameron was in, and the loss of my baggage; happily however, the boat was quickly extricated from the rock, and soon after, to my great satisfaction, safely anchored. As soon as the fishing boat reached the shore, Mr. Campbell and I scrambled over a ridge of slippery rocks, the sea having recently left them, and gained the grass fields leading to

185

Coll's mansion, where we were received, although I was a
stranger, with all imaginable attention and hospitality by Colonel
M'Lean and his amiable daughter and family.[131]

Only those who know Loch Breacacha will appreciate the danger.
In an easterly, the onshore wind tends to drive any vessel on to the
numerous rocks, of which the most dangerous is Bogha Dearg,
which is in the fairway. The foolhardiness of two adults swinging
themselves into the tiny, ramshackle, fishing boat, in a rough sea, is
terrifying.

Eventually, but not without incident, she got to Eigg, her intended destination. After her fright on Coll, she was not unnatural-
ly a little anxious, but the 'good-hearted boat lads' cheered her up:

> 'Indeed,' said one of them, 'she [the boat] goes far easier and
> pleasanter than a coach; for my part, I never was in a coach but
> once in my life, and that was from Edinburgh to Glasgow, and
> was *sea sick* all the way.'[132]

After visiting both Eigg and Rhum, she sailed to Skye, under the
protection of a minister, Mr Maclean. Again, they travelled in a small,
open boat. Here is how she describes this voyage:

> On the 5th of August we left Rum for Skye, and a charming clear
> morning we had, sailing in sight of the sovereign of hills called
> Culin [Cuillin], and the jagged top of Bla-Bhein (pronounced
> Blaw vein), with the rest of the Strath mountains, till we came
> under the bold cliffs near the mouth of Loch Einort, where Mr.
> M'Lean's maritime skill was somewhat put to the test, for we
> experienced several great squalls, which made me shrink from the
> blast from Culin's towering crags, and seat myself at the bottom
> of the boat to be out of the way of the gib sail. Angus Cameron
> exclaimed, 'Oh madam, look at the great *pillar!*' Pillars had no
> share at that moment in my attention, but when the squall was
> past, I opened my eyes and beheld in Angus's pillar one of the
> most singular formed rocks I ever saw, standing singly in the sea
> at some distance from the shore. I had on my head at that time a
> very large beaver hat, such as were worn in the year 1778. I had
> kept it by way of curiousity, till I produced it for my seafaring
> campaign in 1802, to shade me from the sun beams, and keep off
> rain. This large hat was tied down with a ribbon on the outside,
> forming altogether an antique and droll appearance; and to my
> surprise, when I looked at the singular rock, I viewed the shape of
> my own head on the top of it. I had passed to the north of that

rock when I first perceived it, and in that direction saw a huge
mass, in form like a lady dressed in a monstrous sized hoop and
petticoat; such as are worn at the court of St. James's, having a
very large hole quite through the middle of the hoop. I suppose it
is a strayed sister of M'Leods maidens [sea stacks standing at the
mouth of Loch Bracadale]. I was very sorry I did not attend to
Angus's exclamation, when I might have had a nearer view of this
curiously shaped rock.[133]

Mrs Murray's sense of the absurd is refreshing compared with the
solemnity of most travellers!

After landing on Skye she found that they could only procure one
mount for the long trail to Talisker. Undeterred, she set off with the
Reverend Mr Maclean and honest Angus Cameron, her guide:

It is not often [she writes] in the Hebrides that females ride
double, but when they do so, it is on the bare rump of the horse;
but as I was not accustomed to such a pillion, my journey, from
the hut near Loch Einort to Talisker, was laughable enough.
Fortunately the day was fair, so I accomplished the distance of 9
or 10 miles without much fatigue, although it took above seven
hours to go it. The road from the head of Loch Einort to Talisker
is extremely bad, up and down rough precipices; and what added
to our distress, there was no such thing as obliging the horse to go
on the road, because having no shoes on, he would scramble to
every patch of green to save his feet, and avoid the stones in the
track. I almost strangled Mr. M'Lean by holding his coat so
tightly, in order to keep myself on behind him, and Angus
walked at the tail of the horse to catch me, in case I slipped off,
which happened every now and then, so that it was a continual
petition on my part, 'Oh! Angus help me; and, Oh! Mr. M'Lean,
stop and take me up, for I am tired with walking.'[134]

Mrs Murray's greatest adventure, however, was a trip in a small
rowing boat right into the famous Corryvreckan. She was accompanied on this expedition by two gentlemen: Mr Macdougall of Luing,
to whom she had a letter of introduction, and a nameless Mr——,
about whom she is exceedingly, and uncharacteristically, scathing.
His appearance, she comments, 'denoted a rather weakly frame,
although his face was ruby colour'. The contrast between the two
gentlemen adds piquancy to her tale.

Mr—— and our heroine had travelled southwards through the
swift running tide race at Fladda to Mr Macdougall's estate on

Luing. That gentleman, though a complete stranger, and in the midst of supervising the haymaking (a time, as Mrs Murray observes, of great importance in the uncertain climate), nevertheless instantly agreed to assist her. Mr Macdougall, she writes,

> most friendlily said he would with pleasure attend me; and I have now the greater satisfaction in having it in my power to acknowledge my gratitude to him, for his goodness and service to me on that occasion; as, had he not done so, I verily believe I should have found a grave in Vreaikain's Coire [i.e. Corryvreckan]. Coire in the Gaelic language signifies a hollow, and Vreaikain a person's name; but I could not learn who Vreaikain might have been, nor why the Coire in the Gulf between Scarba and Jura is called by his name.
>
> Mrs. M'Dugall [Mrs Murray continues] had the goodness to order a basket of provisions for our dinner, and I re-entered the boat, adding to our party Mr. M'Dugall, and a young gentleman who was on a visit at Loing [Luing].[135]

Still borne by the swift tide, they soon reached Scarba's forbidding cliffs. They rowed close inshore, to keep out of the tide race, until they were well within the Gulf of Corryvreckan. Finding a creek, the passengers landed with difficulty and began to make their way across the broken ridges along the cliffs. Mrs Murray's guardian, Mr——, 'had the utmost difficulty to poise himself on the edges and points of rock' and offered the poor lady, hampered by her long skirts, no assistance.

At last they found a viewing spot on the precipitous cliffs immediately above the fiercest of the maelstrom. Mrs Murray would have preferred 'to witness and view the rage of Coire Vreakain,' from the 1474-foot-high summit of Scarba. But the overland route was too daunting:

> . . .to gain that eminence is impracticable for any but shepherds and young Highlanders, who are able to encounter a walk of perhaps more than twenty miles there and back again, amongst rocks, over hills, and through extensive bogs, and heath, up to their chins. . .What adds to the difficulty of a journey through Scarba is the labour of carrying a day's provisions; a necessary not to be without. It is a pity they cannot tame goats sufficiently to carry small panniers on their backs for such scrambling expeditions, where a man has enough to do to surmount the impediments in his laborious fatiguing walk, without the incumbrance of a satchel.[136]

Mrs Murray lamented that the weather was disappointingly calm – the Corryvreckan is at its most fearsome when gale force winds are opposed to the ferocious tidal race. But she was not disappointed by the spectacle. Even in calm conditions the waters pile up creating a backwards-rearing overfall, a standing wave up to twelve feet high and hundreds of yards long. This wall of water, like the rim of a cauldron, surrounds the turbulence, creating the impression of a huge whirlpool:

The object for which I was likely to forfeit my life is grand, and, perhaps, unique; and what is not ungrateful to a feminine mind, I do not think one woman, except myself, has ever seen the Coire of Vreaikain's raging; many have heard its roaring at Craignish castle, at the distance of twenty miles, but I was at the scene of the action. I can but ill describe its appearance; its effect is beyond description. When the tide had been flowing about two hours, small billows rose and burst over the Coire; but at mid flood tide I saw, particularly if any wind met the tide, the sea begin to rise a great way below the Coire, and then gradually swell to vast billows rolling on, some white and foaming, others glassy and smooth, still getting higher and higher, till they came to the grand whirlpool, where they burst with an amazing noise, forming hundreds of small whirls in the surf around, and for a quarter of a mile in a direct line, in the current of the tide. Thus I beheld, for an hour, a succession of rising and breaking billows, some low, others, if a gust of wind met the coming wave, to a vast height; and the noise in breaking was proportionally tremendous. . .

After we had sat between three and four hours admiring the grand scene beneath us, we retraced our steps from one ledge of rock to another, till we gained the creek in which our boat was moored. Our wisdom failed us, when our impatience led us to quit our solid firm seat before the tide slackened; had we waited on the rocks for that event, we should have got out of the gulf with ease and smooth water; whereas the contrary happened, for in a very short time the seamen had no use of their oars, and we began to go backwards instead of forwards. It was absolutely necessary, in order to keep out of the strong current, that we should row as close to the cliffs as possible; the men strained every nerve to get the boat round the projecting points or rocks, till they were nearly exhausted. The confusion was not a little, and all tongues, but mine, were clattering pell-mell in the Gaelic language, with which I was unacquainted, consequently it was to me like the confusion at the Tower of Babel.

189

When nothing could be done with the oars, the sailors fastened one rope to the head, and another to the stern of the boat, and leaping on the jagged rocks, began to tow it. Sometimes they were able to be alongside of us for a few moments, then forced (by pointed or perpendicular rocks) to lengthen the rope, and skip over chasms, or from point to point of rocks, to get to eminences at a great height above us. Then smack went the head of the boat (driven by the sea) against the rocks, which obliged the seamen to leap to the rope at the stern to pull her off; and then scramble back again to their towering stations. Thus we slowly advanced, alternately dashing against rocks, and being pulled from them, till we. . . got out of the influence of the tide.

Nothing could equal the dexterity, the perseverance, and activity of the four seamen; the danger, sometimes, was very great, both to themselves, and to those in the boat, because had they slipped, or made a false step, when leaping the chasms, and from one point of rock to another, they must have been drowned, or have broken their bones. Their assistance to us would thereby have been lost, and the boat carried by the tide to the vortex of the Coire; the like catastrophe must have happened had the rope by which the boat was towed, either given way or broke.

I know not why, but I certainly was not frightened; no doubt I did not see the extent of our danger. I knew Mr. M'Dugall had been to the East or West Indies, and I therefore concluded he was somewhat versed in nautical business. I observed he gave orders, though I did not understand them, with composure; and his countenance, I thought, indicated no signs of danger. So I sat quietly watching the issue of the struggle. . .

Highlanders clambering along a rocky shore, by John Francis Campbell of Islay. It was along such a shore that Mrs Murray's boatmen attempted to tow the small boat against the tide, by 'skipping over chasms, or from point to point of rocks'.

One person in the boat shewed far greater signs of fear than I did; for poor Mr.——, wrapped in his tartan cloke, as soon as the confusion began, slipped off his seat to the bottom of the boat, and silently watched for the moment that (as he probably imagined) was to whirl him to a better world; and so great was his internal agitation, that his face was the colour of crimson, with drops of perspiration as big as peas, running down it.[137]

That evening, entertained by the hospitable Macdougall's, Mrs Murray had many laughs at the expense of Mr——, and at the absurdities of her own escapades.

We must, in the words of a contemporary review,

now take our leave of this agreeable tourist, with thanks for the entertainment afforded us by her singular and valuable performance. Her descriptions appear to us to be generally accurate and just; though we think she rather over-rates the difficulties and dangers which it was necessary to encounter, before a perfect view of the country could be obtained.[138]

Are the strictures of this armchair critic justified? Here is the warning given by that bible of West Coast yachtsmen, the reliable Clyde Cruising Club *Sailing Directions* (1981), on the passage through the Corryvreckan. In calm weather and at slack water, 'an interesting passage can be made through the gulf', it advises, but adds this caution:

It should not be attempted with an unreliable engine, all hatches should be closed, and an adult would be well advised to have a lifeline attached if he has to go on deck.[139]

Mrs Sarah Murray remarried, in about her sixtieth year, a Mr George Aust. A third edition of her popular *Beauties of Scotland* appeared in 1810, not long before her death at the age of 67. In her wake, the fashion for viewing the spectacular romantic scenery of the Hebrides became a craze.

'Dr Prosody in peril at Corry-vreckan'. For Mrs Murray, who made the passage through the Gulf, it was 'the object for which I was likely to forfeit my life'. Illustration from William Coombe's *Dr Prosody* (1821), a parody of Dr Johnson's *Journey to the Western Islands*.

13

CALEDONIA STERN AND WILD

Sir Walter Scott

SCAVAIG AND CORUISK: perhaps the most spectacularly wild and beautiful scene on the whole of the Hebrides's thousands of miles of magnificent coastal scenery.

But how can you convey to others a scene so grand, on such an immense scale? William Daniell, in his engravings and aquatints, begins to give some inkling of the savage majesty of the scene, set amidst the Black Cuillin of Skye. William Turner, who visited the lochs in the 1830s, conveys in his impressionistic watercolour sketch something of the atmospheric intensity of experiencing Coruisk on a wild day. Both artists were drawn to Scavaig and Coruisk by the writings of the arch Romantic of 'Caledonia stern and wild' – Walter Scott, the 'Wizard of the North'.

Scott sailed in to Loch Scavaig in the August of 1814, aboard the cutter *Pharos*. They approached from the Sea of the Hebrides along Skye's spectacular western coasts, and the novelist-poet found the scenery almost overwhelming:

> About 11 o'clock [he wrote in his journal] we opened Loch Slavig [Scavaig]. We were now under the western termination of the high ridge of mountains called Cuillen, or Quillen, or Coolin, whose weather-beaten and serrated peaks we had admired at a distance from Dunvegan. . .They appeared to consist of precipitous sheets of naked rock, down which the torrents were leaping in a hundred lines of foam. The tops of the ridge, apparently inaccessible to human foot, were rent and split into the most tremendous pinnacles. Towards the base of these bare and precipitous crags, the ground, enriched by soil washed down from them, is comparatively verdant and productive.
>
> When we passed within the small isle of Soa [Soay], we entered Loch Slavig, under the shoulder of one of these grisly mountains, and observed that the opposite side of the loch was of a milder character, the mountain being softened down into steep green declivities. From the bottom of the bay advanced a headland of high rocks, which divided its depth into two recesses. Here it had

been intimated to us that we would find some romantic scenery. . .

We. . .embarked in our boat. In rowing round the headland, we were surprised at the infinite number of sea-fowl, then busy apparently with a shoal of fish.

Arrived at the depth of the bay, we found that the discharge from [a] second lake forms a sort of waterfall, or rather a rapid stream, which rushes down to the sea with great fury and precipitation. Round this place were assembled hundreds of trouts and salmon, struggling to get up into the fresh water: with a net we might have had twenty salmon at a haul; and a sailor, with no better hook than a crooked pin, caught a dish of trouts in our absence. Advancing up this huddling and riotous brook, we found ourselves in a most extraordinary scene; we lost sight of the sea almost immediately after we had climbed over a low ridge of crags, and were surrounded by mountains of naked rock, of the boldest and most precipitous character. The ground on which we walked was the margin of a lake, which seemed to have sustained the constant ravage of torrents from these rude neighbours. The shores consisted of huge strata of native granite, here and there intermixed with bogs, and heaps of gravel and sand piled in the empty water-courses. Vegetation there was little or none; and the mountains rose so perpendicularly from the water edge, that Borrowdale, or even Glencoe, is a jest to them. We proceeded a mile and a half up this deep, dark, solitary lake, which was about two miles long, half a mile broad, and is, as we learned, of extreme depth. The murky vapours which enveloped the mountain ridges, obliged us by assembling a thousand varied shapes, changing their shapes, changing their drapery into all sorts of forms, and sometimes clearing off all together. It is true, the mist made us pay the penalty by some heavy and downright showers, from the frequency of which a Highland boy, whom we brought from the farm, told us the lake was popularly called the Water-kettle. The proper name is Loch Corriskin [Coruisk], from the deep *corrie*, or hollow, in the mountains of Cuillen, which affords the basin for this wonderful sheet of water. It is as exquisite a savage scene as Loch Katrine [in the Trossachs] is a scene of romantic beauty.

After having penetrated so far as distinctly to observe the termination of the lake under an immense precipice, which arises abruptly from the water, we returned, and often stopped to admire the ravages which storms must have made in these recesses, where all human witnesses were driven to places of more

Sir Walter Scott.
Portrait by Edwin
Landseer, 1824.

shelter and security. Stones, or rather large masses and fragments of rocks of a composite kind, perfectly different from the strata of the lake, were scattered upon the bare rocky beach, in the strangest and most precarious situations, as if abandoned by the torrents. . .

The opposite side of the lake seemed quite pathless and inaccessible, as a huge mountain, one of the detached ridges of the Cuillen hills, sinks in a profound and perpendicular precipice down to the water. On the left-hand side, which we traversed, rose a higher and equally inaccessible mountain, the top of which strongly resembled the shivered crater of an exhausted volcano. I never saw a spot in which there was less appearance of vegetation of any kind. The eye rested on nothing but barren and naked crags. . .Upon the whole, though I have never seen many scenes of more extensive desolation, I have never witnessed any in which it pressed more deeply upon the eye and the heart than at Loch Corriskin; at the same time that its grandure elevated and redeemed it from the wild and dreary character of utter bareness.[140]

Contrast Scott's description with Dr Johnson's reactions. The Highlands, Dr Johnson wrote,

exhibit very little variety; being almost wholly covered with dark heath, and even that seems to be checked in its growth. What is not heath is nakedness, a little diversified by now and then a stream rushing down the steep. An eye accustomed to flowery pastures and waving harvests is astonished and repelled by this wide extent of hopeless sterility. The appearance is that of matter incapable of form or usefulness, dismissed by nature from her care and disinherited of her favours, left in its original elemental state, or quickened only with one sullen power of useless vegetation.

It will very readily occur, that this uniformity of barrenness can afford very little amusement to the traveller; that it is easy to sit at home and conceive rocks and heath, and waterfalls; and that these journeys are useless labours, which neither impregnate the imagination, nor enlarge the understanding.[141]

Scott, taught by the Lakeland poets Wordsworth and Coleridge – both a few years his elder – took the opposite view. Such scenes *could* impregnate the imagination and enlarge the understanding.

The impression made by the scenery of the Highlands and Islands on the imagination of Scott was immense. He taught his fellow countrymen to see things in a new way:

Breathes there a man, with soul so dead,
Who never to himself hath said,
  This is my own, my native land!
Whose heart hath ne'er within him burn'd,
As home his footsteps he hath turn'd
  From wandering on a foreign strand!
. . .

O Caledonia! stern and wild,
Meet nurse for a poetic child!
Land of brown heath and shaggy wood,
Land of the mountain and the flood,
Land of my sires! what mortal hand
Can e'er untie the filial band
That knits me to thy rugged strand!

Robert Stevenson,
Scott's host
aboard the cutter
Pharos. For 150
years the
Stevenson family
designed, built
and maintained
the lighthouses
that did much to
lessen the dangers
of sailing in
Hebridean waters.
Plaster replica of
bust by Samuel
Joseph.

He peopled the wild scenes with medieval glories, or haunting Jacobite strains:

Old tales I heard of woe or mirth,
Of lovers' slights, of ladies' charms,
Of witches' spells, of warriors' arms;
Of patriot battles, won of old
By Wallace wight and Bruce the bold;
Of later fields of feud and fight,
When, pouring from their Highland height,
The Scottish clans, in headlong sway,
Had swept the scarlet ranks away.[142]

The least happy result of Scott's voyage to the Hebrides is his long poem, *The Lord of the Isles*. Long projected, long delayed, it poured forth from his pen in the three months following his return from the Western Isles. It is a romantic love story enacted between characters as flat as bit-piece actors in a poor historical movie. This feeble romance is swamped by the background events: the flight of Bruce, Scotland's national hero, after his defeat, to the Hebrides; the rallying of support; and the final hard-fought victory at Bannockburn against the English invader in 1314. This great theme Scott derived from Barbour's powerful epic, *The Bruce*, which was composed not long after the heroic events it describes. The sweep of history was far more in accord with Scott's real talent and predelictions.

Scott's real strength was not as a Romantic poet, whether as a lyricist or a writer of epics, however Homeric his attempted theme.

He was, however, destined to become Britain's first great historical novelist.

For all the time he was labouring to give birth to his unsuccessful *Lord of the Isles*, Edinburgh, and indeed the whole of the English-speaking world, was abuzz with praise for his first novel, *Waverley*, published anonymously during his voyage to the Hebrides.

The book, the tale of a young English officer's involvement with the Jacobite cause in the '45, took the literary world by storm. Scott, teasingly, gave no hint of the authorship save to his most intimate friends, but listened impassively to the speculation. The novel made – in the words of Lord Cockburn, the eminent Scottish judge and a member, like Scott, of Edinburgh's elite – 'an instant and universal impression'. He continues:

> The unexpected newness of the thing, the profusion of original characters, the Scotch language, Scotch scenery, Scotch men and women, the simplicity of the writing, and the graphic force of the descriptions, all struck us with an electric shock of delight. . .If the concealment of the authorship of the novels was intended to make mystery heighten their effect, it completely succeeded. The speculations and conjectures, and nods and winks, and predictions and assertions were endless, and occupied every company, and almost every two men who met in the street.

Conjecture included almost every eminent man in literary Scotland. Scott himself joined in the fun, as Lord Cockburn observed:

> the suppression of the name was laughed at as a good joke not merely by his select friends in his presence, but by himself. The change of line, at his age [Scott was 43], was a striking proof of intellectual powers and richness. But the truth is, that these novels were rather the outpourings of old thoughts than new inventions.[143]

Not only in Scotland was *Waverley* a best seller. Whole families listened spellbound to evening readings in parlours and drawing-rooms the length and breadth of the British Isles. Second, third and fourth editions were rushed from the presses to meet popular demand. Scott, who originally had hidden his identity due to misgivings about the venture, found himself rich and – when his authorship at last became public knowledge – even more famous than he had been as a poet.

Waverley is one of the most important books ever written about the Highlands and Islands. Although it is set on the mainland rather than in the Hebrides, it was to shape the perception of the clan society and values for much of the nineteenth century. Scott was writing about the not-yet-distant past: the '45 had occurred within the lifetime of his older readers. But he was writing about the passing of an age. On one level, *Waverley* is a rattling good adventure story. Once you have got past the slow-moving early chapters, covering the dreamy youth of young Edward Waverley, the pace quickens as the handsome Captain of the Dragoons becomes, more by accident than design, enmeshed in treason. He finally joins the Jacobite cause, captivated by the princely bearing and charm of Prince Charles Edward, and fascinated by the vitality and glamour of the Highland chieftain, Fergus Mac-Ivor, and the imperious beauty of Flora Mac-Ivor, his sister, the most ardent of Jacobites. Only at the end does tender, pretty little Rose Bradwardine, the daughter of a Lowland laird, capture his heart, as he turns disillusioned from the cause which has brought defeat and wretchedness to Scotland. It is a story that moves from the Highlands – from wild glens, deep lochs, robbers' caves, ancient castles, feasts accompanied by pipers, the wild excitement of the chase – to the glittering society of Edinburgh with a Stuart prince returned to his own, and from thence to battlefields with plunging horses, swords slashing, redcoats riding, while the wild Highlanders charge with their claymores raised aloft, their battle cries shrieked above the skirl of the pipes and the thunder of enemy guns.

On another, more signficant level, *Waverley* is an imaginative analysis of this traumatic experience. Here, abridged, is part of Scott's observations, which he adds as a postscript to his novel:

> There is no European nation, which, within the course of half a century, or little more, has undergone so complete a change as this kingdom of Scotland. The effects of the insurrection of 1745,—the destruction of the patriarchal power of the Highland chiefs,—the abolition of the heritable jurisdictions of the Lowland nobility and barons,—the total eradication of the Jacobite party. . .commenced this innovation. The gradual influx of wealth, and the extension of commerce, have since united to render the present people of Scotland a class of beings entirely different from their grandfathers. . .This race has now almost entirely vanished from the land, and with it, doubtless, much absurd political prejudice—but also, many living examples of

singular and disinterested attachment to the principles of loyalty which they received from their fathers, and of old Scottish faith, hospitality, worth, and honour.

It was my accidental lot, though not born a Highlander (which may be an apology for much bad Gaelic), to reside, during my childhood and youth, among persons of the above description;—and now, for the purpose of preserving some idea of the ancient manners of which I have witnessed the almost total extinction, I have embodied in imaginary scenes, and ascribed to fictious characters, a part of the incidents which I then received from those who were actors in them. Indeed, the most romantic parts of this narrative are precisely those which have a foundation in fact.[144]

Powerful as Scott's descriptions of Scottish scenery were, almost more telling was his portrayal of Highland society, and in particular, of that epitome of the Highland chief, Fergus Mac-Ivor. It was this that above all caught the imagination of his first readers.

Young Waverley is initially almost overwhelmed by the sheer magnetism of Mac-Ivor. There is a nobility about his bearing, a dash in the flaunted plaid and the scarlet and white chequered tartan trews, a martial air to the bonnet, with its single eagle's feather. He is, by any standards, a superbly handsome man, with his dark curls and male good looks, his animal athleticism and his machismo. Scott sums him up thus:

An air of openness and affability increased the favourable impression derived from this handsome and dignified exterior. Yet a skilful physiognomist would have been less satisfied with the countenance on the second than on the first view. The eyebrow and upper lip bespoke something of the habit of peremptory command and decisive superiority. Even his courtesy, though open, frank, and unconstrained, seemed to indicate a sense of personal importance; and, upon any check or accidental excitation, a sudden, though transient lour of the eye, showed a hasty, haughty, and vindictive temper, not less to be dreaded because it seemed much under its owner's command. . .

It was not, however, upon their first meeting that Edward [Waverley] had an opportunity of making these less favourable remarks. . .[145]

Indeed, Edward is at first swept along by the romantic excitement of the way of life of a Highland chieftain, the proud descendant of Ian nam Chaistel (Ian of the Castle). Mac-Ivor is the eleventh chief of

The Pass of Ballybrough, with Fergus Mac-Ivor and his guest, Edward Waverley. The young Englishman was initially overawed by the medieval splendours of the hunt through the rugged domains of Mac-Ivor. Illustration from an early edition of *Waverley*.

199

his line, the Mac-Ivors of Glennaquoich. There is the great castle itself, in the wild, rugged country, a fastness of antiquity and apparently virtually impregnable. There is his numerous retinue, or 'tail' – 'Ah!' exclaims Evan Dhu, Mac-Ivor's foster brother, to Waverley just before Mac-Ivor makes his first appearance,

> 'If you Saxon *Duinhe-wassel* [English gentleman] saw but the Chief with his tail on!'
> 'With his tail on!' echoed Edward, in some surprise.
> 'Yes—that is, with all his usual followers, when he visits those of the same rank. There is,' he continued, stopping and drawing himself proudly up, while he counted upon his fingers the several officers of his chief's retinue—'there is his *haunch-man*, or right-hand man; then his *bàrd*, or poet; then his *bladier*, or orator, to make harangues to the great folks whom he visits; then his *gilly-more*, or armour-bearer, to carry his sword and target, and his gun; then his *gilly-casfliuch*, who carries him on his back through the sikes and brooks; then his *gilly-comstrian*, to lead his horse by the bridle in steep and difficult paths; then his *gilly-trushharnish*, to carry his knapsack; and the piper and the piper's man, and it may be a dozen young lads besides, that have no business, but are just boys of the belt, to follow the laird, and do his honour's bidding.'
> 'And does your Chief regularly maintain all these men?' demanded Waverley.
> 'All these!' replied Evan, 'ay, and many a fair head beside that would not ken where to lay itself, but for the mickle barn at Glennaquoich.'[146]

Some of Scott's most brilliant writing comes in the great set pieces: the feasting in the castle, with recitations from the bard, the wild evocative music of the pipes, the thronging clansmen, the elegant wines, smuggled from France for the dinners at the high table, and the free-flowing whisky for the ravenous followers; the mounting tension of a deer hunt across the moors in the company of the assembled chieftains – and the under-currents of fanatical Jacobitism which mix with the chase (for under cover of the hunt, the chiefs are planning the uprising).

But, as the book progresses, the darker side of Mac-Ivor's character, so tragically flawed, becomes clearer to the young man. To the last, Fergus Mac-Ivor remains unswervingly loyal to the white cockade – the badge of the Stuart cause. To the Prince he gives that absolute dedication he expects and receives from his own

The execution of Fergus Mac-Ivor and Evan Dhu at Carlisle Castle. Illustration from an early edition of *Waverley*.

clansmen. But he is revealed as an unscrupulous schemer, Machiavellian in his methods, an egoist motivated by ambition, pride, and the hope of reward in the title of Earl of Glennaquoich. As the enterprise begins to disintegrate, his irritability and over-weening sense of personal dignity lead to cooler relations with young Waverley, whom he had hoped to marry to his sister, the proud, fanatically loyal Flora.

Mac-Ivor's end is noble. Captured by the English, he faces his trial with dignified courage. When the sentence is pronounced on him and his foster brother, Evan Dhu (the bonds between foster brothers were deeper than those of blood), the English court is given a display of Highland clan values which is profoundly disturbing and potent.

Fergus Mac-Ivor goes to his death with dignity, and a proud 'God save King *James!*' on his lips. His sister, the lovely Flora, as proud and even more pure and single-hearted in her fanatical devotion to the Stuart cause, departs for a French convent. And Edward leaves Carlisle, heavy hearted and sobered.

Waverley launched Scott on a new career as a novelist. But it also projected the Highlands into the consciousness and imagination of the British reading public in a way that no previous book had done: not Martin Martin's quaint, rambling *Description of the Western Isles*; not Johnson's pontifications in his *Journey*, nor Boswell's egocentric – *Journal*; not Pennant's informative, well-written *Voyage*, a standard work which accompanied every traveller for several generations.

Scott brilliantly succeeded in re-creating imaginatively and evoca-tively Scotland's scenery, Scotland's history, and Scotland's peoples

201

– and in giving Scotland her voice. But how far did he also falsify these?

Every author, be he a creative writer or a seemingly objective historian, must have his own perspectives and perceptions, must select and shape his material. So some distortion is inevitable; there can only be, at best, as truthful a statement as the author can arrive at, within the limitations of his own personality and understandings, the sources available to him, and the received truths of his generation.

Scott's achievements were great. Of that there can be no doubt. But, partly because he was a bestseller – Britain's first bestselling novelist – and shaped the perceptions of the public for generations (his influence lingers still), his perceptions, dangerously simplified, undoubtedly distorted the public view of the Highlands and Islands, and of Scotland.

As a poet – his first ambition – his work is largely forgotten, while Burns, his slightly older contemporary, still has international acclaim. Like so many of his fellow countrymen in the folk tradition, both Lowland and Highland, Burns was a singer of songs: an extemporizer, a song repairer, a song collector and a song maker in the great oral tradition. His songs have a trueness of tone and sureness of touch, a marriage of words and melody where the simplicity of the language conceals a mastery of his craft:

> O, my luve's like a red, red rose,
>   That's newly sprung in June.
> O, my luve's like a melodie
>   That's sweetly play'd in tune.[147]

Scott seldom achieved this gem-like beauty. Nor could he compete with that other strain in Burns – the bawdy humour, the ranting drinking songs, the couthy, down-to-earth wisdom of the vernacular poems like 'To a Mouse', and the splendid satires, such as 'Tam O' Shanter' and 'Holy Willie's Prayer'. Burns' poetic use of the Ayrshire dialect – his mother tongue – is masterly. Scott, as a poet, perhaps wisely did not attempt imitation. He belonged to the Edinburgh elite, who spoke, or attempted to speak, standard English, and to excise 'Scotticisms' from their speech and, even more important, from their writing.

Yet Scott as a novelist did use the vernacular. His critics complained that his novels would be 'improved by being translated into

English'. The same journal (the *Quarterly*) spoke disparagingly of his use of the 'dark dialect of Anglified Erse' (Gaelic) spoken by characters like Ewan Maccombich. But his public loved the dialect speakers. Much of Scott's liveliest dialogue, and most telling portrayal of character through dialogue, comes through the use of a slightly literary but nonetheless vigorous Scots. But it is largely confined to the speech of the lower orders, or an older generation. This gives his English-speaking heroes a rather wooden speech, while his servants and peasants are rumbustious but quaint in their dialect. His difficulties are even greater when dealing with the Gaelic speakers. Scott's problems with the use of the vernacular have not been fully resolved to this day. But I tend to believe that Scott's use of literary southern English for the speech of his gentrified characters, and the vernacular to mark out lower classes, was a disservice to Scottish writing, and an anachronism in some of his historical novels. It allowed the public to believe that his Gaelic characters, for example – and by extension, all Highlanders – were comic yokels, except for the chiefs who were the monarchs of their glens.

Fergus Mac-Ivor, the Highland chief under whose banner young Edward Waverley served, is an archetype of the species. Scott found a rich inspiration for Mac-Ivor of Glennaquoich in Alastair Ranaldson Macdonell of Glengarry. Glengarry's family seat was at Glenquoich – the coincidence of the names is obvious. Glengarry and Scott were exactly of an age: both had been born in 1771. Glengarry was obsessed with a never-never land of a legendary past. He wore nothing but the full Highland dress, and Raeburn's portrait of him shows a man proud, sensitive of his honour, extravagantly dressed in kilt, plaid, sporran and bonnet. He went everywhere with the traditional 'tail' of henchmen, bard, piper and gillies. He insisted on Gaelic being spoken. Actually, his chieftainship was purely theatrical, and in no way a paternalistic chieftainship in the old tradition. His extravagant style of living put a severe strain on his purse. His rent roll was a mere £5,090 a year, and his debts by the time of his death, in 1828, amounted to an astronomical £80,000. (The *annual* wage for a farm servant on his estate was about £10.) His debts mounted partly because he was extremely litigious. He deeply resented the Caledonian Canal, which was being cut through his estates, had a running battle in the courts with the government over the construction, and constantly harrassed the workmen, physically destroying their supplies of timber and threatening their lives. Telford, the great engineer in charge of the canal, regarded him as one of the most rapacious of the Highland landlords with whom he had to deal.

In 1815 – the year after *Waverley* was published (and no doubt partly as a result of the spectacular success of that romanticizing of Glengarry in the shape of Mac-Ivor) – Alastair Ranaldson founded a 'pure Highland Society in support of the Dress, Language, Music and Characteristics of our illustrious and ancient race in the Highlands and Isles of Scotland, with their genuine descendants wherever they may be'. He persuaded gentlemen to attend Highland feasts, where pipers played and bards recited, on the model of the feasts in *Waverley*. Their escapist play-acting extended to stag hunting, Highland balls, and Highland games of gruesome barbarity, where limbs were torn off cattle for the spectators' delight.

Ironically, Glengarry died in 1828, in an ill-judged leap from the wreck of a steamer in the Caledonian Canal — one of the steamers he had so much resented as they passed within sight of his mansion, threatening the 'entire domestic retirement and seclusion from the inroad of strangers and the public which he always deemed of the utmost value'. His passing was unmourned by his clan – most of them had already left. But a sumptuous feast was held by the Highland Society, which, however, did not long survive Glengarry.

This, then, was the man on whom Scott modelled Mac-Ivor. 'A treasure', Scott dubbed him. But Glengarry in life, and Mac-Ivor in fiction – were they not a dangerous falsification, a romantic myth that distorted the real economic and social truths about the conditions of the Highlands and Islands?

Let Scott have the last word. More perceptive than his readers, he observed:

> In too many instances the Highlands have been drained, not of their superfluity of population, but of the whole mass of the inhabitants, dispossessed by an unrelenting avarice, which will be one day, found to have been as short-sighted as it is unjust and selfish. Meantime, the Highlands may become the fairy ground for romance and poetry, or the subject of experiment for the professors of speculation, political and economical. But if the hour of need should come—and it may not, perhaps, be far distant—the pibroch may sound through the deserted region, but the summons will remain unanswered.[148]

14

THE DEVIL'S ENGINE

Henry Bell's *Comet*

WHEN THE *COMET* – the world's first steam-powered sea-going vessel – appeared in the Highlands and Islands, the inhabitants fled. The uncanny stranger with smoke and sparks belching from her funnel was surely the work of the Devil. A certain grim satisfaction was felt when, on 15 December 1820, the *Comet* foundered in a snowstorm on the point of Craignish, swept onto the jagged rocks by the fierce tidal race of the Dorus Mor. At the wheel was Henry Bell, the inventor. No lives were lost, but the boat split in two, and the after end was swept away toward the dreaded Corryvreckan.

It is more than probable that at least one of the passengers on this ill-fated voyage had laid out six shillings and sixpence to purchase Lumsden's *The Steam Boat Companion and Stranger's Guide to the Western Islands and Highlands of Scotland*, which had been published that very year. The possessor of this pocket guide would have been able to read a brief introduction to the fascinating region which this new invention, steam, opened to the tourist of modest means; furthermore, as he steamed through the maze of islands and penetrated the deep sea lochs, the *Companion* offered him a guide to the 'particular incidents of LOCAL HISTORY, ANTIQUITIES, AND PICTURESQUE SCENERY, ALONG WITH INTERESTING MINERALOGICAL AND GEOLOGICAL PHENOMENA'. So, with the pages of this edifying volume to assist us, let us board the *Comet* for her last voyage.

Despite the fact that the *Comet* made her maiden voyage on the Clyde eight years earlier (in 1812), and has been plying the west-coast route to Fort William for eighteen months, the barbaric regions of the Highlands and Islands – 'the northern realms of ancient Caledon' in Scott's words – are still regarded with some apprehension. Lumsden's *Steam Boat Companion's* first task, therefore, is to calm our fears about the dangers of the voyage from hostile natives, or the perils of the newfangled steam navigation:

Before the publication of Pennant's Tour [reads the reassuring

Henry Bell,
builder of the first
sea-going steam-
boat. Portrait by
James Tannock.

Introduction to the work], our southern neighbours regarded the north of Scotland as the land of barbarism and misrule; and looked upon a visit to the Scottish lakes, and Highland districts, as little short of a journey to the source of the Nile; and considered a perambulation through our country of Alpine wonders, as an undertaking not less hazardous than that of penetrating the savage wilds of Africa.

But, of late years, the case is altered. Pennant showed that the north of Scotland was no such terrific region, but contained objects of unusual grandure, capable of fascinating the most indifferent observer, and rousing his profound admiration; and we now find. . .the very general use of steam vessels on our rivers and seas, particularly on the Clyde, have greatly diminished, if not wholly obviated, those obstacles which formerly rendered Scottish tours so irksome and laborious. Those easy and pleasant modes of travelling invite strangers from all countries to explore the innumerable beauties which the mountainous regions of the north disclose; and they rush towards them with a degree of enthusiastic ardour, no less commendable than it is rational.

The picturesque scenery of the Highlands and Western Islands; the sublime prospects of Loch Lomond and the Trossachs, with many other places, have been attempted to be delineated by the painter, the poet, and the tourist; but

'Who can paint like Nature?'

for neither the pencil nor the pen can do them justice. To such, however, as are desirous of visiting those countries, this publication has been projected as a guide; and, it is hoped, will go far to supply what has hitherto been an important *desideratum* to travellers.[149]

The *Steam Boat Companion* then helpfully gives us a potted history of the exciting invention – the steamboat – which was opening up the ways to the Hebrides. It points out that as long ago as 1733 there were proposals being submitted by Scots to 'impel [vessels] by wheels, or paddles', but the proposal was considered 'chimerical'. Half a century later the 'enterprising and patriotic Mr. Millar of Dalswinton, in Dumfriesshire' constructed a model boat with a steam engine in 1776. A decade later, a larger vessel was built under his direction in Grangemouth, and

several experiments were made on the Forth and Clyde Canal, in the presence of Sir Thomas Dundas, and several other gentlemen connected in the management of the canal, which gave entire satisfaction; but from the agitation of water which the action of the wheels produced, and the consequent risk of injuring the banks, this vessel was not considered as eligible for canal navigation.[150]

A visiting American, Mr Fulton, observing the new invention, borrowed and developed the idea on the other side of the Atlantic (even then a common fate of British inventions). But it was Henry Bell who, 'with much labour and expense, invented several material improvements in the machinery' and thus succeeded in developing the world's first sea-going passenger-carrying steamship:

In 1800, Mr. Bell produced a large model of a steam vessel, 27 feet long, which he presented to the late Lord Melville, then the head of the Board of Admiralty; but being overlooked by his Lordship, and his colleagues, was eagerly adopted by the American government, and speedily put into successful practice upon the great rivers and lakes of that country.

In the present age, when discoveries in science, and improvements in the arts, meet with general encouragement, it is surprising, and to be regretted, that nothing has been done towards procuring Mr. Bell a permanent remuneration for the great advantages which this extensive community, as well as the whole kingdom, derive from his indefatigable exertions;—a consideration which becomes the more imperious, when we reflect on the unwearied toil, and the anxiety of mind, as well as the loss of health and property, which he has experienced in the completion of so important a national discovery.[151]

The passengers on this last voyage of the *Comet* would have had

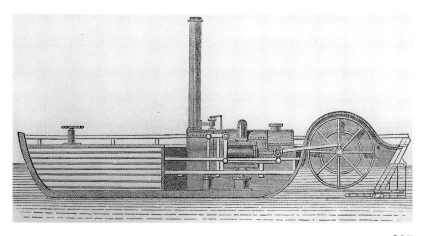

The *Charlotte Dundas*, the first practical steamboat. The boat was used experimentally on the Forth and Clyde Canal, but never ventured into the open sea.

many opportunities to reflect on the inventor's unwearied toil. Henry Bell often sailed on his pride and joy, the *Comet*. Although by now well into his fifties, he was still full of an infectious enthusiasm for his invention. 'Man, Mr. Bell,' remarked a Helensburgh acquaintance, Danney MacLeod the tailor, 'ye're a desperate clever chiel, that boat o' yours is just a perfect world's wonder.' To which the ardent-minded Bell is said to have replied, 'Danney, tak' my word for it this is only the beginning of the uses that steam engines will be put to in the way o' conveyin' passengers; if you leeve lang ye'll see them fleein' and bizzin' about on land, wi' croods o' passengers at their tail, lively as—' (and here his eye lit on the tailor's little goose-necked smoothing iron) '—as a spittle loupin' alang a tailor's het goose.'

When on board Bell is said to have busied himself with all the affairs of the little vessel, though he also liked to buttonhole his passengers in order to expound on the marvels of his invention. He had a vision of steam engines drawing a string of carriages across the land; the first steam locomotive on a public railway had been greeted with gasps of amazement in this very year of 1820. Bell, when excited by his hobbies and plans, was a persuasive and unwearying talker, and would hold forth into the small hours. Whatever his failures, setbacks and disappointments, he was eternally optimistic. Many there were who doubted whether the newfangled invention was more than a passing whim of fashion. The enormous weight of coal which was required to stoke the boilers, the instabilities of the small vessel which, when she was rolling in a heavy swell, caused one paddle to labour below water like a millwheel in a flood, while the paddle on the opposite side thrashed the air – these problems seemed to make the paddle steamer a loser. Clearly, steam power could not be applied except in cotton mills, on solid ground. Yet Bell, as he supervised the stoking of the boiler, or took the helm in turbulent seas, never ceased to say, 'Aye, but they will yet traverse the ocean!' And the stout, fresh-complexioned, genial gentleman's determination to make his *Comet* succeed was reassuring.

Not that the *Comet* was a financial success. Far from it. Bell might appear to be 'a shrewd pawky Scot', and as far as mechanisms and engineering went, he was canny and quick to seize the salient points. But he was a child with money, and often seemed not to have two coins to rub together. Fortunately his wife was a good businesswoman. She it was who ran the hotel (later known as the Queen's

Hotel) in Helensburgh, at which it was possible to enjoy the health-giving sea waters in Mrs Bell's Baths. She saw that steamboats offered a quick and easy connection from Helensburgh to Glasgow. Helensburgh was already a fashionable watering place and summer resort for Glaswegian merchants, but the roads were poor, and the River Leven difficult to pass. No doubt it was Mrs Bell who financed the building of the *Comet*. Perhaps even the apt name, which commemorates a comet seen at the time, was her suggestion.

The *Comet* was small. She was a mere 33 feet long, and built along the same lines as the hundreds of modest fishing packets that plied the west coast and the Clyde. She had a beam of 11 feet (including her paddlewheels) and drew 5 feet 7 inches. Into this small hull had to be crowded the awkward, heavy addition of a boiler and engine together with the mechanism necessary to turn the giant paddles. The whole construction was highly experimental. The hull and paddles were built by the Glasgow yard of Messrs John Wood and Co. The boiler, mounted on brickwork, was supplied by David Napier, later to achieve great fame in steam locomotion, and cost £52. The engine, by John Robertson, incorporated important advances developed by another Scot, James Watt; it had a nominal horsepower of only 4hp (most outboard motors for small sailing cruisers, far lighter than the *Comet*, have 4hp). The engine cost £160. When the *Comet* had been launched in 1812 she had had four radial paddles – two paddles on each side. These, which resembled the arms of a windmill rather than paddlewheels, gave endless trouble. Eventually the paddles were replaced with two large paddlewheels, one on each side amidships. These, in calm waters, could propel the *Comet* along at a handsome six knots when she was lightly laden. But, on the belt and braces argument, Bell also incorporated sail into his design. A slender funnel, 12 inches in diameter and 25 feet high, could double as a mast and carry a square sail, and a staysail could be set on the forestay from the bowsprit to the top of the funnel.

Small wonder this strange vessel caused consternation when she appeared. From the top of her unsightly 'mast', smoke and sparks belched out, while her thrashing paddlewheels churned up the sea and the throbbing of her engine resounded in noisy contrast to the silent progress of the old sailing ships. Many believed that this was the Devil incarnate.

Henry Bell's
Comet I steaming
up Loch Linnhe.
Contemporary
lithograph.

The *Comet* had made her maiden voyage on the Clyde in 1812. Within a few years many 'puffers' were plying on the Clyde, larger and more comfortable than the world's first commercial steamboat. Bell was never a man to accept defeat; he was the trailblazer, and if he had pioneered steam navigation on the relatively sheltered waters of the Clyde, he could do it on the more exposed west-coast routes.

Accordingly, and no doubt with Mrs Bell's help again, the *Comet* had in 1818 been given a complete overhaul. It was a drastic refit. She was cut in half and extended by six feet. A larger engine was put in. Even so, the accommodation was hardly spacious. With the longer voyages proposed – 170 miles to Fort William – she had to carry a heavy burden of coal to feed that hungry boiler. So, although first-class passengers had a small saloon under the deck house, affording good views of the by now renowned romantic Highland scenery, the second-class passengers had to make do with the cramped benches in the tiny cabin forward. Here the headroom was so low that, even when sitting, the taller passengers had to stoop.

In addition, of course, there was a captain and a crew of seven, one of whom was a salaried piper. Passengers often enjoyed dancing on the deck – it was one way of keeping warm. Gentlemen would, naturally, be accompanied by a personal servant, who would serve a picnic meal in the saloon. At night the *Comet* moored. Gentlemen would perhaps avail themselves of an introduction to one of the noblemen whose landed properties lined the route (Lumsden's *Steam Boat Companion* thoughtfully provides the owners' names, so that the well-connected could make contact). Those of more modest means would have to put up with the doubtful comforts of a local hostelry, while the poor, including the evicted clansmen driven from their glens to seek work in Glasgow, would wrap themselves in their plaids and sleep in the stuffy cabin or in the heather.

What had made the west-coast route a possibility was the opening, at long last, of the Crinan Canal. For the *Comet*, rounding the Mull of Kintyre was not feasible. In 1818 she began to work the west-coast route, plying between Glasgow and Fort William – a round trip of 340 miles – each week. 'The ease and rapidity with which the traveller may be conveyed,' remarks the *Steam Boat Companion*, was 'astonishing':

> While the Canal is passable, the *Comet* Steam Boat plies from Glasgow to Fort William, every Thursday, occupying two days going, and two days returning.[152]

Before the invention of steam such a trip would have taken at least a fortnight.

The first day's voyage was from Glasgow down the Firth of Clyde, through the beautiful Kyles of Bute, to the eastern end of the Crinan Canal. The night was spent in the Canal, and the voyage resumed the next day.

The reassuring *Steam Boat Companion* gives little hint to the trusting tourist of the navigational problems as the little *Comet* heads for Fort William:

> Gliding out of Loch Crinan in a northerly direction, to the right is seen Loch Craignish, in which are several small green islands, and at the head of it, Barbreck House, General Campbell. On the left are also many islands, betwixt one of which and the point of Craignish, four miles from the canal, the Steam Boat passes, the space being named the Dorristmore [Dorus Mor], the great door. During the flood and ebb of the tide, particularly in springs, the current here is very rapid, being often so strong as to render it impossible for a vessel to stem it. All along this coast, up to Fort William, the tide is more or less powerful, according to situation, occasioned by the multiplicity of islands, with its vicinity to the Atlantic.
>
> In fine weather the prospect around, from this point, is very grand. To the south, the rugged coast of Knapland [Knapdale]. . .to the west of which is seen, dim in the distance, a part of Islay, and nearer the bleak shores of Jura, with its fine conical

The route of Henry Bell's *Comet*.

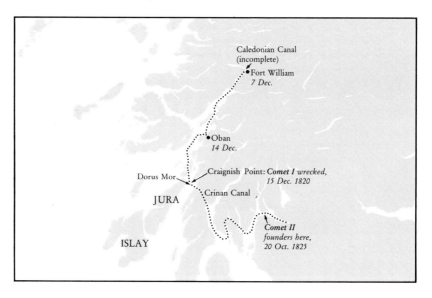

mountains, called the Paps, above 2000 feet high. Jura is divided
from the island of Scarba, placed at its northern extremity, by the
Gulf of Corryvreckan, a tremendous whirlpool, like that of
Maelstrom, on the coast of Norway; a prince of which country,
named Rackan, is said to have perished in this Gulf, and hence its
name.[153]

This passage, through the Dorus Mor and out past Fladda, is one of
the most exhilarating on the west coast. The tiny *Comet*, like
today's yacht, would head northwards on the rising flood tide, to be
swept through the Dorus Mor and on up the Sound of Luing to
shoot out past the islet of Fladda, then without its present
whitewashed lighthouse, into the Firth of Lorn: a ten-mile passage
that can often be accomplished in a small boat in under an hour's
sailing. For this is one of the most formidable tidal races in Europe,
renowned for its violence, turbulance, speed, complexity and extent. Only if you can work the tides is it a safe route.

The *Steam Boat Companion* continues in a garrulous fashion to
point out landmarks and note the names of proprietors, geological
formations, caves, and other points of interest, until at length we
arrive at our destination, Fort William:

From the fort a delightful prospect of mountain grandure is to be contemplated; and if the stranger is to be captivated with nature in her boldest form, it is here that his eye will have full enjoyment; for the scenery all around is of a character, for richness and extent, hardly to be met with anywhere else. . .

The garrison of Fort William is situated near the confluence of the river Lochy with the sea, where there is a considerable salmon-fishing. Two miles from it, upon the bank of a river, stands the ruin of Inverlochy Castle, one of the ancient fortresses of the Highlands; and from its situation amidst the fierce and turbulent clans, was often the posture of misrule and blood; and latterly, in 1746, it was witness of more barbarity and massacre, indiscriminately exercised on the innocent and helpless, than had ever before disgraced any period of the mountains. A short way above this castle is a ferry across the river, and a road that leads along the border of an extensive moss, to the sea-lock of the Caledonian Canal at Corpach.

The Caledonian Canal extends from this place to the eastern sea, but is not yet completed. The intention is to cut off the long navigation through the Pentland Firth and the Western Isles. It is wholly carried out at the expense of the Government; and though it appears a chimercial undertaking, has benefited the working community, but not so as to prevent emigration from the Highlands; under which impression it was originally projected. A considerable part of the course is through a natural chain of fresh water lakes, which form the greater proportion of the distance; and during this season, it is understood that steam vessels are to be provided for navigating this canal, and the lakes connected with it; so that travellers will then go from Glasgow to Inverness, by this track, in less than three days.[154]

Less than three days! Proof indeed of the power of steam. But the passenger on the *Comet* could have had little idea of the impact of the new technology. Within a generation, steamboats were plying the length and breadth of the Islands, bringing them forcibly into the nineteenth century. Yet the vast majority of boats were still powered by wind even in the late nineteenth century.

Under normal circumstances, the *Comet's* voyage ended at Fort William on Friday evening (if all had gone according to plan). She had accomplished the 170-mile trip in under three days. The return journey began on the Saturday, if possible. The Sabbath, naturally, was a day of rest. But if all went well, she should be back in her berth in Glasgow by Tuesday evening, ready for her next trip on the Thursday. That, at any rate, was the timetable. . .

In the winter of 1820, however, the timetable was not so easily adhered to. The weather was poor and daylight hours too short to allow the long hours of steaming through the dangerous waters. She sailed northwards from Glasgow, via the Crinan Canal, in late November, with a crew of seven all told, and a salaried piper. On reaching Fort William on the 4 December, she discharged her passengers and goods. It had been a worrying journey, for she had bumped a half-tide rock, and sprung a slight leak.

The return journey began on 7 December. At Sallachan the vessel met with another mishap of such a serious nature as necessitated her being docked, or more probably beached, on the 12th, and a large team of men were employed for two days repairing the damage the craft had sustained. Matters having been made as right as possible, the homeward run was resumed on the 14th. It is certain the little steamer was at Oban in a somewhat crippled state on the 15th, because the captain's cash book on that date shows an expenditure of ten shillings for one night's pumping of the vessel at that port; that would be the evening of the 14th.

Leaving Oban on the 15th she limped southwards. It was a wild day, with head winds and flurries of snow, sleet and rain. She reached the Dorus Mor as the tide was turning against her. It was already dark, and a blizzard made visibility very poor. There are still no buoys or leading lights to mark the way, and in the hurly-burly of spray and snow even a sharp lookout could not discern land until they were almost on it. I suspect that they had been driven to attempt the Dorus Mor using one of the back eddies to wash them round the point against a turning tide. At any rate, they rammed Craignish Point, a jagged jaw of toothed rocks which juts out into the fairway. The *Comet* parted amidships – at the point where she had been lengthened eighteen months earlier. The bow end was stuck firm on the rocks, but the after end was wrenched away by wind and the now rising flood tide, and was last seen swept along crazily in the direction of the dreaded Corryvreckan.

Fortunately, Henry Bell (who had been at the helm or besides the helmsman), together with his passengers and crew, managed to scramble ashore on the bleak rocks.

The bill paid for whisky supplied to the parties engaged in the salvage work from the 15th, when she struck, to the 25th, when they abandoned all hope of saving anything further, amounted to nearly £6. Whisky was then about nine shillings (45p) a gallon – so the salvors consumed over thirteen gallons. 'Verily a good fill', said a commentator, 'of the barley bree at the breaking up of the historic craft.' Soon after the salvors abandoned the ship on Christmas Day, the forward part too slid into deep water and disappeared for ever.

Among the items salved was the engine. This was to be incorporated, to some extent, in a second steamer of the same name. Bell had been shattered by the loss, and seriously damaged financially. But he was irrepressible. He was the moving spirit in commissioning the new *Comet* of 94 tons (the first *Comet* was a mere 28) built by James Lang of the Dockyard, Dumbarton, in 1821. This had one engine of 25 horsepower and a copper boiler weighing nine tons. Like her namesake, the new *Comet* plied the west-coast route, and with the opening of the Caldonian Canal, she sailed all the way from Glasgow to Inverness, via the Crinan and Caledonian Canals, on a regular timetable.

By now Bell was, although only in his late fifties, growing infirm. He was not well off; later the river Clyde trustees gave him a pension of £100 a year – a modest recognition of the Clyde's immense debt. But he received many tributes. Among these was this naive versifying in the *Steam-Boat Traveller's Remembrancer*, written by the versatile William Harriston, 'weaver, soldier, fisherman and poet'. This poetical guidebook was the forerunner of many more in a similar vein. On passing Helensburgh, Harriston informs his gentle reader that

> There lives Henry Bell, so much fam'd
> For exerting mechanical skill,

The Cloch Lighthouse on the Clyde, near where the *Comet II* foundered. Engraving by Joseph Swan from *The Beauties of the Clyde* (c. 1854).

Who the first of our Steam-vessels fram'd
Thus he merits the nation's good will.

Far advanc'd in old age is the sire
Of the Steam-boats in Scotland, yet he
Retains a great share of the fire
Of activity, humour and glee.

Though infirm, yet he holds on the paths
Of Business; and here I may tell,
His House has some elegant Baths,
A commodious Inn and Hotel.

Disappointment's discouraging pangs
He often has suffer'd in part,
But Despair with its terrible fangs
Never yet found its way to his heart.[155]

That was written in 1824. But a fate even worse than verse awaited Bell.

On Tuesday, 18 October 1825, the steamship *Comet*, with Captain McInnes as master, sailed from Inverness for Glasgow via the Caledonian and Crinan Canals. She left Inverness at six in the morning, and took a day to make her way through the Great Glen, arriving at Fort William the same evening. At ten o'clock on Wednesday she resumed her journey, and arrived late the same evening at Crinan, where she lay until six o'clock the following morning. She then got under way, but did not reach Lochgilphead, at the eastern end of the Canal, until ten in the morning – too late to leave the sea lock, as the tide was then too low to float her out. This delay was to cost her dear. 'What awful destinies were involved in that fatal delay', reminisced an old man later.

By six in the evening, the tide was high enough to float her out. At the urgent request of some English gentlemen, who were passengers on board the steamer, the captain somewhat reluctantly touched at Rothesay, on the island of Bute, and allowed them to disembark there. The cause of his reluctance was that the wind blew freshly, and by calling in at Rothesay he would have to make up a lot of leeway.

The vessel, after leaving Rothesay, shaped a straight course up the Clyde. The night was cold, and some of the passengers 'endeavoured to get up a comfortable animal heat by dancing on the deck' to the accompaniment of the pipes. About midnight the great

Colonel Alastair Macdonnell of Glengarry, the inspiration for Scott's Fergus Mac-Ivor. In reality Macdonnell's interest was more in the outward appearances of chieftainship than in its traditional responsibilities. Portrait by Henry Raeburn, c. 1812.

The First Steamboat on the Clyde, John Knox's well-known painting of Henry Bell's *Comet I*, looking down the Clyde towards Dumbarton.

219

Inverlochy Castle, near Fort William, the destination of the *Comet's* west-coast cruises. Painting by Horatio McCulloch, 1857.

Landseer's famous painting, *The Monarch of the Glen*, epitomizes both the romantic wildness and the sporting opportunities that the Victorians valued in the Highlands. Landseer painted the *Monarch* in Glen Quoich, seat of Macdonnell of Glengarry.

220

majority of the travellers went below into the cabins. In the early part of the night there was moonlight, but soon after twelve-thirty the moon dipped below the horizon. Even so, by the light of the stars, the hills on both sides of the Firth were clearly visible.

Between one and two o'clock the *Comet* was off Kempoch Point, Gourock, and everything was apparently in order. But the master had neglected to order the display of lights, and a jib sail had been set to take advantage of the breeze. There should have been a lookout, but he may have dozed off. Suddenly those on deck were startled by a crazy, 'A steamboat ahead; help a-port!' The on-coming vessel was hidden by the sail. Almost immediately the *Comet* was struck, first on the bow, and then on the port paddle-box.

The vessels drifted asunder, their occupants being filled with 'utmost consternation'. There was an ear-piercing cry of despair from the crowd on the deck of the *Comet*, for they found their vessel was sinking. Within a few minutes of the collision she went bow foremost down in seventeen fathoms of water, about 165 yards from the shore.

The steamer with which the *Comet* had collided was the *Ayr*, a vessel of considerable power, bound for Ayr and having as master Captain McClelland. The *Ayr* could not be faulted on her navigation. She had displayed a light (the regulations requiring port and starboard lamps and a masthead light were a thing of the future). She had had a lookout, who however had failed to spot the unlit *Comet*, or hear her engines above the powerful pulse of the *Ayr's* own. But what happened next was a disgrace. The crew of the *Ayr* were stupified, and made no attempt to pick up the swimmers in the dark sea. Two sailors, however, on leave from their ship the *Harmony*, who were passengers aboard the *Ayr*, set about trying to launch a boat from the *Ayr*. But, while the boats had been lowered until they almost touched water, the engines of the *Ayr* began to play, and the men and boat were nearly lost. The captain had discovered that his vessel, too, had sustained some damage, and feared that, like the *Comet*, he might go down. He abandoned the wretched passengers of the *Comet* to their fate, turned his own ship, and headed back to Greenock full steam ahead, crossing the very spot where the *Comet* had been engulfed, and where still a few desperate wretches clung to bits of timber in the chill and dark waters, crying pitifully for rescue. Seventy were lost, and only twelve managed to escape.

$\boxed{1}\boxed{5}$

THE CRUISE OF THE *BETSEY*

Hugh Miller

IN THE SUMMER OF 1844 you might have seen a small yacht, with racing lines but now decidedly elderly, ploughing her way across the seas to Eigg. At her wheel was John Swanson, Free Kirk minister of the Small Isles (Eigg, Rhum, Muck and Canna). Besides him, wrapped in a shepherd's plaid, was one of the most influential writers in Scotland: Hugh Miller. The son of a seaman, he braced his bulky frame against the cabin coach-top to haul up the top sail, or handle the sheets.

Miller was an enigma: dynamic, yet subject to fits of deep melancholy; a journeyman mason, yet a brilliant writer; a deeply conservative evangelical of passionate convictions, yet admired by Charles Darwin for his stunningly beautiful yet deeply scholarly essays on the geology of the fossil-bearing old red sandstones of Scotland; a man of the people, of working-class origins and radical sympathies, who disapproved nevertheless of Chartism and strikes; a Lowlander with a Gaelic mother.

Miller had joined the Free Church yacht, the *Betsy*, a few days earlier. It was midnight on a short July night, and he had arrived in Tobermory on Mull from Glasgow in the steamship, the *Toward Castle*. He scanned the harbour.

An exceeding small boat shot out from the side of a yacht of rather diminutive proportions, but tautly rigged for her size, and bearing an outrigger astern. The water this evening was full of phosphoric matter, and it gleamed and sparkled around the little boat like a northern aurora around a dark cloudlet. There was just light enough to show that the oars were plied by a sailor-like man in a Guernsey frock, and that another sailor-like man—the skipper, mayhap, attired in a cap and pea-jacket, stood in the stern. The man in the Guernsey frock was John Stewart, sole mate and half the crew of the Free Church yacht *Betsey*; and the skipper-like man in the pea-jacket was my friend the minister of the Protestants of Small Isles. In five minutes more I was sitting . . .beside the little iron stove in the cabin of the *Betsey*; and the minister, divested of his cap and jacket, but still looking the veritable skipper to admiration, was busied in making us a rather late tea.

The cabin,—my home for the greater part of the three following weeks, and that of my friend for the greater part of the previous twelvemonth,—I found to be an apartment about twice the size of a common bed, and just lofty enough under the beams to permit a man of five feet eleven to stand erect in his nightcap. A large table, lashed to the floor, furnished with tiers of drawers of all sorts and sizes, and bearing a writing desk bound to it a-top, occupied the middle space, leaving just room enough for a person to pass between its edges and the narrow coffin-like beds in the sides, and space enough at its fore-end for two seats in front of the stove. A jealously-barred skylight opened above; and there depended from it this evening a close lanthorn-looking lamp, sufficiently valuable, no doubt, in foul weather, but dreary and dim on the occasions when all one really wishes from it was light. The peculiar furniture of the place gave evidence of the mixed nature of my friend's employment. A well thumbed chart of the Western Isles lay across an equally well thumbed volume of Henry's 'Commentary'. There was a Polyglot [a Bible in many languages] and a spyglass in one corner, and a copy of Calvin's 'Institutes', with the latest edition of 'The Coaster's Sailing Directions', in another; while in an adjoining state-room, nearly large enough to accommodate an arm-chair, if the chair could have but contrived to get into it, I caught a glimpse of my friend's printing-press and his case of types, canopied overhead by the blue ancient [ensign] of the vessel, bearing in stately six-inch letters of white bunting, the legend, 'FREE CHURCH YACHT'.

A door opened which communicated with the forecastle; and John Stewart, stooping very much to accommodate himself to the low-roofed passage, thrust in a plate of fresh herrings, splendidly toasted, to give substantiality and relish to our tea. The little rude forecastle, a considerably smaller apartment than the cabin, was all a-glow with the bright fire in the coppers, itself invisible: we could see the chain-cable dangling from the hatchway to the floor, and John Stewart's companion, a powerful-looking, hand-some young man, with a broad bare breast, and in his shirt sleeves, squatted full in front of the blaze, like the household goblin described by Milton, or the 'Christmas Present' of Dickens. . .

We tumbled in, each to his narrow bed,—comfortable enough . . .though not over soft; and slept so soundly. . .[156]

223

Hugh Miller, stonemason, evangelical, and one of the greatest geologists of his age.

Thus began a voyage which Miller, through the pages of the *Witness* – the influential twice-weekly newspaper which he edited – shared with his readers. It still makes excellent reading, for Miller was a gifted writer, and moreover he wrote for many who had never sailed in a small vessel, who perhaps had never even seen the sea, and had certainly not visited the Hebrides. Miller, with all the advantages of a lad who had grown up by the sea, the son and grandson of seafarers, was able to communicate what it was like to venture out in an 'exceedingly small yacht', through fair weather and foul, in circumstances when the boat was often in peril and once came near to foundering.

Yet Miller's intention was not merely to enjoy a memorable holiday, nor simply to write for the delectation of his readers.

Miller and Swanson were but two of the participants in the 1843 Disruption – the dramatic split of the Presbyterian Church of Scotland which resulted in no less than 474 ministers – over a third

224

The cruise of Hugh Miller and the *Betsey*, 1844.

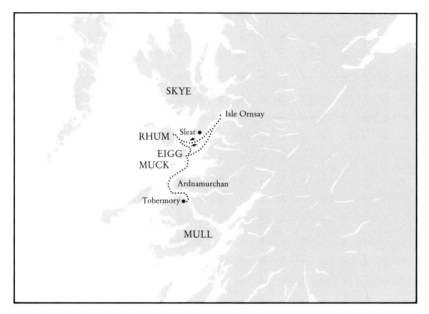

of the ministry of the Church – seceding. Why this came about, and how it affected the Hebrides profoundly, I will allow to emerge, as Miller does, as we follow the two men on their cruise in the Free Church Yacht, the *Betsey*.

'We weighed anchor', Miller records of their departure from Tobermory the following day,

> about two o'clock, and beat gallantly out of the Sound, in the face of an intermittent baffling wind and a heavy swell from the sea. I would have fain have approached nearer the precipices of Ardnamurchan, to trace along their inaccessible fronts the strange reticulations of trap [i.e. basalt formations] figured by Macculloch; but prudence and the skipper forbad or trusting even the docile little *Betsey* on one of the most formidable lee shores in Scotland, in winds so light and variable, and with the swell so high. We could hear the deep roar of the surf for miles, and see its undulating strip of white flickering under stack and cliff. The scenery here seems rich in legendary association. At one tack we bore into Bloody Bay, on the Mull coast,—the scene of a naval battle between two island chiefs; at another, we approached, on the mainland, a cave inaccessible save from the sea, long the haunt of a ruthless Highland pirate. Ere we rounded the headland of

225

Ardnamurchan, the slant light of evening was gleaming athwart the green acclivities of Mull, barring them with long horizontal lines of shadow, when the trap terraces rise step beyond step, in the characteristic stair-like arrangement to which the rock owes its name; and the sun set as we were bearing down in one long tack on the Small Isles.

We passed the Isle of Muck, with its one low hill; saw the pyramidal mountains of Rum looming tall in the offing; and then, running along the Isle of Eigg, with its colossal Scuir [Sgurr] rising between us and the sky, as if it were a piece of Babylonian wall, or the great wall of China, only vastly larger, set down on the ridge of a mountain, we entered the channel which separates the isle from one of its dependencies, Eilean Chathastail, and cast anchor in the tideway. . . We were now at home,—the only home which the proprietor of the island permits to the islanders' minister; and, after getting warm and comfortable over the stove and a cup of tea, we did what all sensible men do in their own homes when nights wear late,—got into bed.[157]

Miller and Swanson spent the next and many another glorious day rambling over this fascinating island, armed with geologist's hammers. Miller was intrigued to discover that the gigantic Sgurr of Eigg – that colossal bulwark of igneous rock, a 'veritable Giant's Causeway. . .columnar from end to end' – rested on the fossilized remains of a 'prostrate forest'. Here was a riddle peculiarly puzzling to the investigative ex-mason. Miller was already an authority on sedimentary rocks; his masterly volume, *The Old Red Sandstone*, was a leading work on the subject. But the presence of fossils in such ancient stones was to give rise to very serious, and, in Miller's case, overwhelming, doubts about the credibility of a literal interpretation of the creation story in Genesis. Miller's contemporary, Charles Darwin, was similarly disturbed by the enigmatic evidence of fossils, and was already giving tentative form to the theory of evolution, though he did not publish his *Origin of Species* until 1859. By that time Miller had died by his own hand, at the age of 54. His doubts had torn him apart. His health was failing – he suffered from the painful quarrier's disease, silicosis, contracted as a stone mason. Weakened, the brilliant editor of the influential *Witness* fell prey to a depressive illness. His fundamentalist religious convictions and his scientific interests could not be reconciled, and his disappointments in the outcomes of the Disruption of the Church of Scotland led to further instabilities.

226

But all this lay ahead, as the two men explored the island. Hugh Miller writes exultantly of the massive Sgurr – the ravines and cliffs, the basalt walls and rich fossils, the vitrified ramparts and shattered columns. Finally, the two men sat, side by side, atop the Sgurr, gazing on the island which had once been Swanson's home and parish.

It was now evening, and rarely have I witnessed a finer. The sun had declined half-way down the western sky, and for many yards the shadow of the gigantic Scuir lay dark beneath us along the descending slopes. All the rest of the island, spread out at our feet as in a map, was basking in yellow sunshine; and with its one dark shadow thrown from its one mountain-elevated wall of rock, it seemed some immense fantastical dial, with its gnomon [pointer on a sundial] rising tall in the midst. Far below, perched on the apex of the shadow, and half lost in the line of the penumbra, we could see two indistinct specks of black, with a dim halo around each,—specks that elongated as we arose, and contracted as we sat, and went gliding along the line as we walked. The shadows of two gnats disporting on the edge of an ordinary gnomon would have seemed vastly more important, in proportion, on the figured plane of the dial, than these, our ghostly representatives, did here. The sea, spangled in the wake of the sun with quick glancing light, stretched out its blue plain around us; and we could see included in the wide prospect, on the one hand, at once the hill chains of Morven and Kintail, with the many intervening lochs and bold jutting headlands that give variety to the mainland; and, on the other, the variously-complexioned Hebrides, from the Isle of Skye to Uist and Barra, and from Uist and Barra to Tiree and Mull. The contiguous Small Isles, Muck and Rum, lay moored immediately beside us, like vessels of the same convoy that in some secure roadstead drop anchor within hail of each other. . .I took one last look of the scene ere we commenced our descent. There,—in the middle of the ample parish glebe, that looked richer and greener in the light of the declining sun than at any former period of the day,—rose the snug parish manse; and yonder,—in the open island channel, with a strip of dark rocks fringing the land within, and another dark strip fringing the barren Eilean outside,—lay the *Betsey*, looking wonderfully diminutive, but evidently a little thing of high spirit, taut-masted, with a smart rake aft, and a spruce outrigger astern, and flaunting her triangular flag of blue in the sun. I pointed first to the manse, and then to the yacht. The minister shook his head.

''Tis a time of strange changes,' he said: 'I thought to have lived and died in that house, and found a quiet grave in the burying ground yonder beside the ruin; but my path was clear though a rugged one; and from almost the moment that it opened up to me, I saw what I had to expect. It has been said that I might have lain here in this out-of-the-way corner, and suffered the Church question to run its course, without quitting my hold on the Establishment.

'It is easy [he explained to Miller] securing one's own safety, in even the worst of times, if one look no higher. . .But the principles of the Evangelical party were my principles; and it would have been consistent with neither honour nor religion to have hung back in the day of battle, and suffered the men with whom in heart I was at one to pay the whole forfeit of our common quarrel. So I attended the Convocation [of the dissenting ministers], and pledged myself to stand or fall with my brethren. On my return I called my people together, and told how the case stood, and that in May next I bade fair to be dependent for a home on the proprietor of Eigg. And so they petitioned the proprietor that he might give me leave to build a house among them,—exactly the same sort of favour granted to the Roman Catholics of the island [Eigg was traditionally Catholic]. But month after month passed, and they got no reply to their petition; and I was left in suspense, not knowing whether I was to have a home among them or no. . .[Eventually] I suggested to them the scheme of the *Betsey*, as the only scheme through which I could keep up unbroken my connection with my people. So the trial is now over; and here we are, and yonder is the *Betsey*.'[158]

Let no one deny the courage of the 474 ministers – more than one third of the ministry – who walked out of the General Assembly of the Church of Scotland in the 1843 Disruption. They sacrificed their manses, their glebe (the smallholding on which they depended for food) and their stipends. They were left with almost no income, and many, like Swanson, had wives and families to support. Stern were the tenets of their faith: the *Institutes* of Calvin, the faith of John Knox, the Presbyterian system of church government (so threatened by the imposition by England's Parliament of patronage by landlords). They preached hell fire and the sanctity of the Scottish sabbath. But they stood too for the freedom of their congregations in the face of exploiting landlords and negligent establishment ministers. Men like Swanson evoked the strongest

loyalty from their congregations, who followed the minister from the stone-built kirks provided by landlords into ramshackle hovels or even the open air. 'Rarely,' writes Miller of Swanson's congregation on Eigg,

> Rarely have I seen human countenances so eloquently vocal with veneration and love. The gospel message, which my friend had had been the first effectually to bring home to their hearts, the palpable fact of his sacrifice for the sake of the high principles which he has taught,—his own kindly disposition,—the many services which he has rendered them, for not only has he been minister, but also the sole medical man, of the Small Isles, and the benefit of his practice they have enjoyed, in every instance, without fee or reward,—his new life of hardship and danger, maintained for their sakes amid sinking health and great privation,—their frequent fears for his safety when stormy nights close over the sea,—and they have seen his little vessel driven from her anchorage, just as evening has fallen,—all these circumstances that have concurred in giving him a strong hold on their affections.[159]

The anchorage at Eigg is cruelly exposed, and so the *Betsey* often took shelter at Isleornsay, on the Sleat peninsula of Skye. Here kind folk had offered shelter to Mrs Swanson (a fluent Gaelic

A Free Church minister preaching from the sea. After the Disruption of 1843, the dissenting ministers were evicted from their churches, and many had no alternative but to preach in the open air. Illustration from the Rev Thomas Brown's *Annals of the Disruption 1843* (1877).

229

speaker) and the Swansons' two small children. Here too Miller heard his friend preach in English, to a mixed assembly of Scots and Gaelic-speaking seamen and fishermen:

> The anchoring ground at Isle Ornsay was crowded with coasting vessels and fishing boats; and when the Sabbath came round, no inconsiderable portion of my friend's congregation was composed of sailors and fishermen. His text was appropriate,— 'He bringeth them into their desired haven'; and as his sea-craft and his theology were alike excellent, there were no incongruities in his allegory, and no defects in his mode of applying it, and the seamen were hugely delighted. John Stewart, though less a master of English than of many other things, told me he was able to follow the minister from beginning to end,—a thing he had never done before at an English preaching. The sea portion of the sermon, he said, was very plain: it was about the helm, and the sails, and the anchor, and the chart, and the pilot,—about rocks, winds, current, and safe harbourage; and by attending to this simpler part of it, he was led into the parts that were less simple, and so succeeded in comprehending the whole.[160]

Swanson, indeed, seems to have had a gift for powerful but simple analogies. John Stewart, and other Eigg islanders, were able to recall for Miller a sermon preached by their minister some twelve months earlier, at the time of the Disruption. In times of peril and alarm, said the minister, your ancestors had two essentially different places of refuge. Either the islanders could retreat to the 'deep unwholesome cave, shut up from the light of heaven', or they could seek security on the great Sgurr of Eigg, 'the tall rock summit, with its impregnable fort, on which the sun shone and the wind blew'. There was little need to elaborate the analogy. Every islander knew the terrible tale of how the MacLeods had descended on Eigg, how the islanders had taken refuge in a great cave, and the horrible death almost all had suffered when a huge, smoky bonfire was lit by their enemies in the narrow mouth of the cave. To follow their minister into the wilderness of the Disruption was analogous to mounting to the highest point of their island home:

> Much hardship might no doubt be encountered. . .when the sky was black with tempest, and rains beat or snows descended; but it was found associated with no story of real loss or disaster,—it had kept safe all who had committed themselves to it. . .[161]

That the hardships were real, the dangers considerable, are amply

230

demonstrated in Miller's pages. Here we can follow the *Betsey* on a voyage to Rhum, where dwelt many of Swanson's parishioners:

The gale, thickened with rain, came down, shrieking like a maniac, from off the peaked hills of Rum, striking away the tops of the long ridgy billows that had risen in the calm to indicate its approach, and then carrying them in sheets of spray aslant the furrowed surface, like snow-drift hurried across a frozen field. But the *Betsey*, with her storm-jib set, and her mainsail reefed to the cross, kept her weather bow bravely to the blast, and gained on it with every tack. She had been the pleasure yacht, in her day, of a man of fortune, who had used, in running south with her at times as far as Lisbon, to encounter the swell of the Bay of Biscay; and she still kept true to her old character, with but this drawback, that she had now got somewhat crazy in her fastenings, and made rather more water in a heavy sea than her one little pump could conveniently keep under. As the fitful gust struck her headlong, as if it had been some invisible missile hurled at us from off the hill-tops, she stooped her head lower and lower, till at length the lee chain-plate rustled sharp through the foam; but, like a staunch Free Churchwoman, the lowlier she bent, the more steadfastly did she hold her head. The strength of the opposition served but to speed her on all the more surely. At five o'clock in the morning we cast anchor in Loch Scresort,—the only harbour of Rum in which a vessel can moor,—within two hundred yards of the shore.

It was ten o'clock ere the more fatigued aboard could muster resolution enough to quit their beds a second time; and then it behoved the minister to prepare for his Sabbath labours ashore. . .Bad as the morning was, however, we could see the people wending their way, in threes and fours, through the dark moor, to the place of worship,—a black turf hovel, like the meeting-house in Eigg. The appearance of the *Betsey* in the loch had been the gathering signal; and the Free Church islanders—three fourths of the entire population—had all come out to meet their minister.

On going ashore, we found the place nearly filled. My friend preached two long energetic discourses, and then returned to the yacht, a 'worn and weary man'. The studies of the previous day, and the fatigues of the previous night, added to his pulpit duties, had so fairly prostrated his strength, that the sternest teetotaller in the kingdom would scarce have forbidden him a glass of our fifty-year-old Madeira. But even the fifty-year-old Madeira

231

proved no specific in the case. He was suffering under excruciating headache, and had to stretch himself in his bed, with eyes shut but sleepless, waiting till the fit should pass,—every pulse that beat in his temples a throb of pain.[162]

Miller's vivid writing brings so much to life that it is difficult not to follow the *Betsey* throughout that memorable summer cruise. Whether he is describing the delicate beauty of 'medusae' (jellyfish) or the geology of the mountains of Rhum, the vageries of tides in the Kyle Rhea or the abject poverty of a crippled old woman, Miller is an involved but deeply perceptive observer. His power of vivid description, his detailed and accurate delineation of colour and form, texture and mood, captures so much. Yet this might well have never been penned had the *Betsey* been less fortunate in their last voyage, from Eigg to Isleornsay (from whence Miller planned to catch the southbound steamer and thus return to the Clyde).

It was the morning of Wednesday, 25 June when the *Betsey* set out, with, Miller notes, a 'smart breeze from the north-west'. He noted that the sky was 'tolerably clear', but the highest mountains were wreathed in cloud:

When every other patch of vapour in the landscape was in motion, scudding shorewards from the Atlantic before the still-increasing gale, there rested along the Scuir of Eigg and the tall opposite ridge of the island, and along the steep peaks of Rum, clouds that seemed as if anchored, each on its own mountain-summit, and over which the gale failed to exert any propelling power. They were stationary in the middle of the rushing current, when all else was speeding before it. . .[In fact] instead of being stationary, they are ever-forming and ever-dissipating—clouds that form a few yards in advance of the condensing hill, and that dissipate a few yards after they quit it.

The weather continued to worsen. Miller, seated in the little cabin, became aware of a new kind of noise:

There was the usual combination of sounds beneath and around me,—the mixture of guggle, clunk, and splash,—of low, continuous rush, and bluff, loud blow, which forms in such circumstances the voyager's concert. I soon became aware, however, of yet another species of sound which I did not like half so well,—a sound as of the washing of a shallow current over a rough surface; and, on the minister's coming below, I asked him, tolerably well prepared for his answer, what it might mean. 'It means,' he said, 'that we have sprung a leak, and a rather bad one'. . .

There are, I am convinced, few deaths less painful than some of those untimely and violent ones at which we are most disposed to shudder. We wrought so hard at pail and pump,—the occasion, too, was one of so much excitement, and tended so thoroughly to awaken our energies,—that I was conscious, during the whole time, of an exhilaration of spirits rather pleasurable than otherwise. My fancy was active, and active, strange as the fact may seem, chiefly with ludicrous objects. . .When matters were at the worst with us, we got under the lee of the point of Sleat. The promontory interposed between us and the roll of the sea; the wind gradually took off; and having seen the water gaining fast and steadily on us for considerably more than an hour, we, in turn, began to gain on the water. It came ebbing out of drawers and beds, and sunk downwards along panels and table-legs,—a second retiring deluge; and we entered Isle Ornsay with the cabin floor all visible, and less than two feet of water in the hold. On the following morning, taking leave of my friend the minister, I set off, on my return homewards, by the Skye steamer, and reached Edinburgh on the evening of Saturday.[163]

Thus ends Miller's account in the *Witness*, essays later collected together as *The Cruise of the Bestey* and published in 1856.

To this day, the Free Church is a dominant influence in the more northerly of the Hebridean isles. Some parts of the Hebrides never experienced the Reformation of the sixteenth century. Where clan chiefs, such as the Macdonalds of Clanranald (the owners of South Uist and the Small Isles, and the neighbouring mainland) remained within the Catholic church, their clansmen did so too. Thus, almost all the islanders from the Outer Hebrides south of Benbecula, through South Uist to Barra and Vatersay, are Catholic. Many of their traditions date back to the Celtic church, to the days of the seventh-century missionary saint of the isles, St Columba. These isles were untouched by extreme Calvinism.

Where, however, the people had followed their chiefs into the Presbyterian church created by John Knox, it was a different story. This is not the place to outline Scotland's complex religious history. The Hebrideans were too far from the centre to be deeply involved in the persecutions and enthusiasms of Covenanters, Dissenters, Episcoplians, Auld and New Lichts, and so on. Old beliefs, some older not only than the Reformation but also than Christianity, still

233

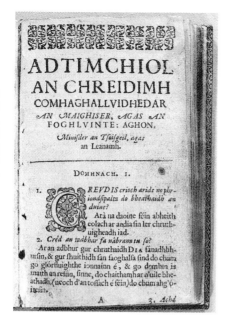

The title page of Calvin's Catechism, translated into Gaelic by John Carswell and published in 1631.

moulded the islanders' religious beliefs and rituals. The influence of the chief was paramount, however, and in general each clan followed the directions of the chief. Thus it was that Eigg, a Clanranald holding, gradually became Protestant as the descendants of Old Clanranald espoused the official church of the Hanovers. This was further confirmed when Reginald George, spendthrift crony of the Prince Regent, sold Eigg to clear his debts, to a minister's son, Dr McPhearson, in 1827. The established church was the landlord's property, its minister his nominee. Such was the law imposed by England. So long as the minister acquiesced with the dictatorial powers of the proprietor, so long as he neither criticized the laird's morals, nor his right to evict his hapless tenants and cottars, he had nothing to fear. Neither laxity in the minister's personal life, nor neglect of his clerical duties, endangered his position and his glebe. But as the rift between the lairds and their tenants widened, so too did the gap between the ministers and their flocks.

In 1805 Skye had been swept by a religious revival. The evangelical fervour which had set ablaze so much of Britain – creating, for example, the Methodist revival in England and Wales – caught like a flame in dry stubble. In that year, on the island of Skye, an illiterate preacher, John Farquarson, had converted a blind fiddler, Donald Munro. Munro's powerful preaching caught the imagination of the people. Spiritually, economically, politically and materially they were frustrated at every turn. Hungrily they accepted the new Puritanism offering salvation. The Islands were

234

swept with an orgy of renunciation. The old ways – the song and dancing, the games and sports, the fiddle music and the bagpipes, the pipe of tobacco and the dram of whisky – all were ruthlessly condemned as the work of the Devil. A huge bonfire was made at Loch Snizort, in Skye, onto which the people tossed their fiddles and bagpipes, and whatever cherished objects they had which did not accord with the stern precepts of the preachers.

The 'moderate' party in the established church had little sympathy with these extremes. Evangelicals, fired by the revival, were different. But the ministers of the newly freed kirk were to become as despotic about codes of behaviour as the landlords were in economic terms. Alexander Carmichael, the great nineteenth-century folklorist, recounts how an old man told him that, long ago, under the heavy condemnation of his minister, he had burned his violin, a beautiful instrument made by a pupil of Stradivarius. Thereafter 'he never laughed again'. The incident took place on Eigg, and the minister concerned must have been Swanson. (Carmichael collected most of his material in the 1860s and 1870s).

The most lasting loss was of the oral literature. Though the islanders lived in abject poverty, they cherished a literary heritage of the very highest order. It was (in Carmichael's words) 'the product of far-away thinking, come down on the long stream of time'. He adds:

> Some of the hymns may have been composed within the cloistered cells of Derry and Iona, and some of the incantations among the cromlachs of Stonehenge and the standing stones of Callernis [Callanish]. The poems were composed by the learned, but they have not come down through the learned, but through the unlearned—not through the lettered few, but through the unlettered many—through crofters and cottars, the herdsmen and shepherds, of the Highlands and Islands.[164]

These poems, hymns and stories were handed down from generation to generation by word of mouth. Few chains can be more easily broken. The impoverishment and dissipation of this marvellous heritage in the mid-nineteenth century (when Carmichael was travelling in the Hebrides far and wide, noting every poem or song he heard) was due, so he believed, to many factors: to the Reformation; to the Jacobite risings of 1715 and 1745, and the harsh repression of those events; to the evictions; to the Disruption; to the introduction of schools which imposed the English language on the children; and to what he calls 'the spirit of the age'. He comments:

> Converts in religion, in politics, or in aught else, are apt to be intemperate in speech and rash in action. The Reformation movement condemned the beliefs and cults tolerated by the Celtic Church and the Latin Church. Nor did sculpture and architecture escape their intemperate zeal. The risings harried and harassed the people, while the evictions impoverished, dispirited and scattered them over the world. Ignorant school-teaching and clerical narrowness have been painfully detrimental to the expressive language, wholesome literature, manly sports and interesting amusements of the Highland people. [165]

One of the institutions most sternly condemned by the Free Church ministers was the ceilidh. While almost every daylight hour through the long light summers was filled with labour, the long winter nights were enlivened by the ceilidh. The ceilidh (pronounced *kay-lee*) is a unique Highland institution: the spontaneous gathering of friends and neighbours around the central peat fire for an evening's entertainment. Traditional stories and tales are recited, poems and ballads rehearsed, songs with their haunting ancient melodies sung, conundrums put, proverbs quoted.

Sternly, the more extreme of the Free Kirk ministers repressed the innocent conviviality of the ceilidh. Metrical psalms, sung in a curious harsh rendering of the fine old Scottish tunes, took the place of secular songs and the ancient piety of the Isles. Austerity reigned. The kine were not milked on the Sabbath, and the joyless disciplines of Calvinism banished the communal singing at work and play. Memories died as the older generation passed away, irreplaceable. Thus was lost much of the Islands' legacy of song, hymns, tales and riddles, though fortunately in the Catholic isles the more tolerant attitude of the priests allowed the ceilidh to survive and flourish.

The bigotry and austerity of the Free Church ministry was to cause Miller no little dismay in the years to come. His paper, *The Witness*, had sounded like a clarion call for the shining spiritual aspirations of the newly freed kirk. While, like most reformers, he had a dynamism and crusading zeal that drove him into passionate arguments, he had a breadth and humanity that some reformers lack. It is a lack that is all too apparent in the dominance that Free Kirk ministers exercised over the souls, minds and bodies of their congregations.

Thus in the mid-nineteenth century religion yet further isolated the Hebrides from mainland Britain. Neither the unreformed Catholicism of the southerly isles of the Outer Hebrides (and some related parts of the mainland), nor the austere, fundamentalist Calvinism of the northerly isles off the west coast, were mainstream religious traditions in Britain. Add to this the language barrier, the increasing poverty of the Islanders, the cultural divide between the still feudal Islands and the newly industrialized cities of Britain, and the gulf becomes wider.

Other forces, however, counteracted this. Poverty and enforced clearances drove thousands of Islanders away, either temporarily or permanently. The dispossessed crowded to Glasgow's slums, and other major cities, where they wrestled with a strange language, strange customs, and the tuberculosis, cholera and other endemic diseases of the grim, overcrowded tenements. They served in Britain's navies and the Highland regiments. They colonized overseas possessions. Nostalgically, they dreamed of home, sang the old songs, and saved their meagre wages to visit again the isles of their birth, travelling on the new steamships that brought the Islands so much closer.

Close enough for a British monarch to visit. . .

James Guthrie's painting of a Highland funeral captures the sombre mood inspired by the Free Church in the Highlands and Islands.

237

16

A BHAN RIGH: THE FAIR QUEEN

Queen Victoria

FOR THE FIRST TIME for over three centuries a reigning monarch was to visit the Hebrides. Her gracious majesty, Queen Victoria, was in the tenth year of her reign. She was accompanied by her consort, Prince Albert, and the two eldest of their five offspring. She was not yet 30. It was high summer, the August of 1847.

Some trepidation was no doubt felt in official circles. Although a century had passed since the risings of the '45, and neither the Bonnie Prince nor his brother Henry, the Cardinal, had left any legitimate issue, the remote Gaelic-speaking Isles were still something of a mystery. It was a time of unrest. Potato blight had brought starvation to that other Celtic possession, Ireland, and was rumoured to be spreading to the Hebrides. The Tory government had fallen, split by the repeal of the Corn Laws, a measure necessitated by the crisis in Ireland. The Royal Squadron was therefore quite a sizeable force, designed to impress but also, if the need should arise, to protect.

In the event, no protection was necessary. The Queen received a rapturous welcome. She did not actually set foot on any Hebridean island, and her gaze was carefully protected from the poverty and sufferings of her subjects. The visit was to live in her memory, though she never again, in her long reign, ventured to the Hebrides, and was mystified and astonished when, by the 1880s, the protests of the local populace against evictions reached such a pitch that police forces and the Marines had to be called in to maintain order. That the conditions of these, her subjects, should be little better than that of slaves – bought and sold with the huge estates, evicted by the burning of thatches over the heads of little children, the aged and decrepit –was not credible. After all, were not their chiefs valued members of her court?

The last reigning monarch to visit this remote corner of the kingdom had been James V of Scotland, who in 1540 had circum-navigated his kingdom. So the voyage of Queen Victoria in 1847 was an event of note, at least for the long-neglected Hebrideans.

Her Majesty had set out from Osborne Pier, on the Isle of Wight, on the evening of Wednesday, 11 August 1847. After a royal progress around Land's End, and through the Sea that separated her Majesty's possessions, with England and Wales on the starboard and Ireland on the port, Her Majesty sailed into Scottish waters. An ecstatic welcome awaited her on the Clyde. The pages of both local and national newspapers were filled with details of her crowded programme.

A few days later the fleet headed down the Clyde once more; the *Illustrated London News* waxed eloquent:

> Wednesday [18 August]
> To-day, the Squadron started from Rothsay at eight o'clock, and, passing through the Kyles of Bute round Lamont Point and up Loch Fine, entered Loch Gilp. The scenery of the Kyles is soft and beautiful, the land rising gently from the water's edge, clothed with brushwood, and the distant landscape closed in by fine ranges of green hills. . .
> The Royal Visit to Inverary Castle was the great event of Wednesday. The preparations were in magnificent style. . .
> The Queen was evidently highly gratified with her reception; her Majesty wore a blue and white striped silk dress, broadly fringed; a black damask silk *visite* [light cape], with a deep flounce, bracelets, and primrose gloves; a white chip bonnet, trimmed with straw-coloured crape, and white marabout feath-ers, with dark green velvet flowers inside; and she carried a green parasol. . .[166]

After a sumptuous luncheon at the castle, the royal party embarked in the *Fairy* and steamed away down Loch Fyne to Ardrishaig, the village at the eastern end of the Crinan Canal. On the canal banks excited crowds cheered the young queen. Passing under a 'tasteful arch of flowers, topped by the national heather, a nicely formed crown, and V.R. in flowers', Her Majesty embarked in the *Sunbeam*, the horse-drawn canal boat. It had one spacious cabin, 20 foot by 12 foot, with a smaller private cabin (12 foot by 6), both with plate-glass windows and crimson and gold draperies and furnishings. Should Her Majesty wish to go on deck a canopy measuring 18 foot by 10 foot provided shelter from the sun and the rain.

The Queen noted in her journal,

> We entered a most magnificently decorated barge, drawn by three horses, ridden by postillions in scarlet. We glided along very smoothly, and the views of the hills—the range of Cruachan—were very fine indeed; but the eleven locks we had to go through—(a very curious process, first passing several by rising, and then others by going down)—were tedious, and instead of the passage lasting one hour and a half, it lasted upward two hours and a half, therefore it was nearly eight o'clock before we reached Loch Crinan.[167]

Here, according to the *Illustrated London News*,

> A great concourse of people were assembled. . .where the canal falls into the Loch, in order to witness the landing from the barge, and the embarkation on the Royal yacht, which was lying on the calm water of the land-locked Loch Crinan. The crags around the landing place are very romantic; and the situation is altogether unique in its features. . .
>
> As the barge was rowed to the yacht, the sun was setting behind the hill of Jura, and thus allowed the Royal Party to see one of those magnificent colourings of the landscape which last but only a few minutes, when his beams are falling almost level on the still waters of the land-locked western loch. After sunset, the fleet of steamers anchored in Crinan.
>
> During the evening, fires were lighted on the hills around Crinan, and on many of the mountain tops between that and Oban. On the estates of Mr. Mathieson alone fifteen of these fires were kindled, and the effect on the water was truly splendid.[168]

The royal squadron off Ailsa Craig. From the *Illustrated London News*.

'It is a very fine spot', the Queen noted that night in her journal. 'We dined, and went on deck; and the blaze of the numerous bonfires—the half moon, the stars, and the extreme stillness of the night—had a charming effect.'

The Royal Squadron, wrote the *Illustrated London News'* reporter,

> passed the night at Crinan—the western extremity of the Canal—a wild naked spot, whence the eye wanders over the waste of rock and water—the intricate labyrinth of bay and creek and island and isthmus which give its distinguishing features to this curiously indented part of the Scottish coast.[169]

The following day's journey was, enthused another reporter from the *Illustrated London News*, 'the strangest intermingling of stern and beautiful scenery, famed in song and story, and rich in stirring historical memories':

> The Royal Yacht left Loch Crinan, at seven a.m. The morning was fair and clear, permitting a beautiful view of the islands that stud and mountains that surround the Loch. The yacht, followed by the *Scourge*, passed out of the northern corner of Jura, keeping wisely the celebrated gulf of Corryvreckan, the Maelstrom of the west, and Scarba island to the left, proceeding up the Sound of Luing into Loch Linnhe, passing next Seil Island and Easedale on the right.
>
> From the hills above the village of Easedale a Royal salute was fired; and passing the entrance of Loch Feochan on the right, and Gylen Castle on the left the yacht entered the narrow channel between Kerrera Island and the mainland, and ran into Oban Bay, which is almost land-locked, and completely sheltered by the island.

The passage of the royal party through the Crinan Canal on board the *Sunbeam*. From the *Illustrated London News*.

Queen Victoria, Prince Albert and their elder children. This portrait by F.X. Winterhalter was painted in 1846, the year before Victoria's Hebridean trip.

From Oban the fleet sailed northwards, up the Sound of Mull, a long deep arm of the sea, fringed with wild and desolate mountains. Here lies a ledge of rocks on which Maclean of Duart left his wife to be drowned by the rising ride, when she was rescued by her brother's galley, which happened to be passing just at the critical moment. . .

The Royal tourists now commanded, at the entrance to the Sound, 'one of the finest of our Scottish views':

The farm-houses had all their little flags fluttering away in the breeze; there, too, was the lighthouse [on Lady Rock], and clusters of picturesque cottages: all Lismore was green and cheerful. Morven was on the right, frowning in a darker colour and a sterner form; and here were the curious ruins of Duart Castle—once the seat of the Macleans—on the left, in Mull.

The Royal yacht was placed under the pilotage of Captain McKillop, of the *Dolphin*; and, from her frequent crossing and re-crossing of the channel, so as to command the best points of view, it was evident that the Queen and her party were greatly delighted with a passage which Sir Walter Scott describes as so tempting 'in fine weather'.[170]

The voyage of Queen Victoria, 1847.

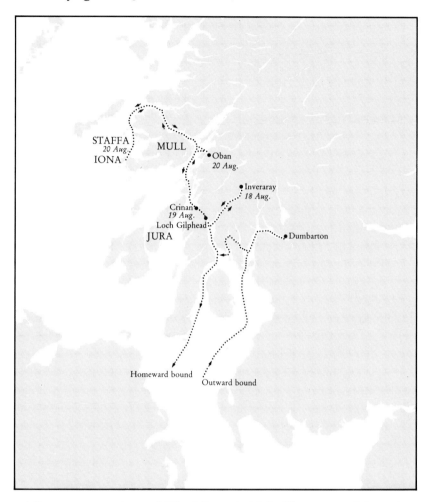

The correspondent of *The Times* (which, like most of the other national papers, covered the trip) describes the 'wild and wonderful coast' in these flowing terms:

On either shore, as the fleet steered up the Sound of Mull, far off to the south and east stretched the mountains of Appin and Lochabar, flanked by Ben Cruiachan at the one extremity, and Ben Nevis on the other. On the west lay the stately Ben More, and eastward Morven—the country where Fingal fought and Ossian sang; or where, to use more guarded language, Macphearson said they did so. The sea, which was as smooth as glass,

243

reflected on its surface every feature of the adjacent heights, and at short intervals, on either side, the ruins of ancient strongholds rise on the sea-side, their grim and solitary aspect calling back the mind to times of violence now past.

Doward [Duart] Castle, once the stronghold of Maclean of Doward, appeared on the left, and on the right the ancient fortresses of Ardtonish and Mingarry. The former belonged in remote periods to the Lords of the Isles, and the latter to the MacIans of Ardnamurchan. In one or both of them James IV. and V. resided when visiting the Highlands to compel the submission of the refractory chiefs; nor have these wild shores and deserted promentaries been since visited by the soverign, until yesterday her Majesty surveyed them from the deck of the *Victoria and Albert*. The changes which have been wrought on that coast in the interval are striking enough, for few can help recognizing the distinction between the peaceful objects of Queen Victoria and the mission of her predecessors; or, observing, that lands which, in the 16th century, must have produced a numerous, hardy, and adventurous race of mountaineers, now support little else than black-faced sheep, and are entirely devoted to pasture.[171]

(Is the irony of this passage conscious? Only a few years later – in 1851 – chieftains like the Duke of Sutherland were to find themselves unable to raise the troops of Highlanders which so much reflected to their credit in times of war. When the recruiting officers, desperate for young men to come forward to fight for Queen and country against the Russian foe in the faraway Crimea, demanded why there were no volunteers, the few remaining clansmen responded, 'Baaa! Baaa!'. Where once there had been thriving crofts and large families, now only the roofless shells stood open to the winds, and the 'four-footed clansmen' grazed in the deserted glens. But let us return to 1847, and the *Times*. . .)

As the Royal Squadron cleared out of the Sound of Mull, and round the northern extremity of that island, a noble prospect lay before it, the steep and barren headlands of Ardnamurchan stretching away into the Atlantic on the right, on the left the precipitous cliffs of the Mull coast, and far away and embosomed in the ocean, the fantastic and varied forms of the adjacent islands. The horizon toward the north was a good deal obscured by haze, but, notwithstanding, Skye was distinctly visible.

Having steamed round the point of Calluch [Caliach Point, on Mull]. . .the fleet at length stopped off the lonely island of Staffa,

and her Majesty in her barge was rowed to the furthest extremity of the great cave. The construction and appearance of this wonderful natural temple have been so often described that it is unnecessary to attempt giving an account of it here, yet the circumstances of yesterday's visit to the cave were so striking and novel as to impress most powerfully the minds of those who witnessed the scene. The deserted and solitary aspect of the island was brought out with a strange and startling effect by the presence of so many steamers; and as her Majesty's barge with the Royal standard floated into the cave, the crew dipping their oars with the greatest precision, nothing could be more animated and grand than the appearance which the vast basaltic entrance, so solemn in its proportions, presented.[172]

A regatta of the Royal Northern Yacht Club. Victoria's Hebridean cruise was to inspire many to follow in her wake. Aquatint by E. Duncan.

The Queen herself was awed, but also felt she conferred a special dignity on the renowned natural edifice: 'It was,' the young Queen noted, 'the first time the British standard with the Queen of Great Britain, and her husband and children, had ever entered Fingal's cave.'

The young couple were never to return to the Western Isles. Perhaps the gales and the rain were too much. Prince Albert, though not yet 30, already suffered rheumatic pains. The drier climate at their beloved Balmoral – they had purchased the estate in 1844 – suited his health better.

But though the Queen did not return to the Hebrides, her tour had given the royal seal of approval to pleasure cruises in Hebridean seas, and the increasingly fashionable and gentlemanly pursuit of yachting. Scottish waters afforded the thrill of danger and of sailing in magnificent and romantic scenery for which the yachtsmen of the period yearned.

Many of these yachtsmen were members of the Royal Northern Yacht Club. This club, one of the earliest in Britain, had been founded in 1824, and won the patronage of William IV, the Sailor King, in 1830, and of his successor Queen Victoria. Based on the Clyde, it provided a meeting place for gentlemen of wealth to display their talents at an annual regatta and in other events. In 1856 it was joined by the Clyde Model Yacht Club for 'model' yachts (under eight tons). Later it too was to receive royal patronage and change its name to the Royal Clyde Yacht Club. By 1873, the three Clyde-based clubs – the Royal Northern, the Royal Clyde, and the Mudhook Club (founded 1873) – had joined ranks to sponsor the famous 'Clyde Week'.

Although the Clyde-based clubs were principally engaged in racing and social activities, the more adventurous members ventured forth and cruised in the Hebrides. Magnificent schooners too, like Lord Brassey's *Sunbeam*, regularly conveyed rich, leisured and titled gentlemen to the Hebrides:

> The *Sunbeam* [wrote Hector Rose Mackenzie] is quite a floating palace fitted up in the most luxurious manner. Her many saloons and sleeping cabins are marvels of elegance and comfort, while the taste of Lady Brassey is displayed in the numberless pictures and curios which adorn the walls and tables in the different appartments. On deck, as below, everything is the perfection of neatness and tidiness. The crew numbers twenty-seven, and the yacht carries six boats.[174]

While the gentlemen in smaller craft actually participated in the sailing of their boats (though frequently they engaged a small crew), the wealthiest – and some were, like the multi-millionaire Brasseys, exceedingly rich – were denied this outlet for their physical energies. Instead, they devoted themselves to the pursiuit, with rod, line and gun, of anything that moved across the hills or swam in the sea: the

whale, the seal and the salmon; puffins, cormorants, the endangered sea eagle, swans, geese; the rare phalarope and the great northern diver; ducks of all kinds; grouse, partridge and other game birds; the blackcock and capercaillie and, of course, the stags and smaller land mammals.

Small wonder property values soared as the titled and their emulators sought to follow the royal example. But there was a problem: the 'question of the irrepressible crofter' as a *Times* correspondent, Alexander Shand, put it in 1883.

> Most of the properties in the Western Isles and perhaps on a few of the sea lochs on the mainland. . .may be said to be more or less swamped in squatters. These properties must necessarily hang on the market. The poor-rates at the best of times are out of all proportion to those on the mainland parishes; while in the worse seasons the purchasers will have the privilege of accumulating hopeless arrears of rent and feeding a population of starving paupers, who may abuse him for a tyrant when the pressure has gone by.[175]

While some visitors to the Islands describe in patronizing terms the quaintness of the natives' simple dwellings and way of life, many

Deerstalking on Jura by Gourlay Steell (1819-94). The painting gives little inkling of the human misery inflicted by landowners in order that they and their friends might enjoy their sport unhindered by a resentful tenantry.

247

found them irritating beyond words. Typical of these is James Wilson, who was able to spend six weeks touring the Islands in 1848 on a government fisheries vessel, in considerable comfort and at no personal expense. With the energy and self-righteousness of the well-fed, leisured, upper middle classes of Victorian England, he decried the sloth of the Hebridean population:

> Their indolence and inactivity, except in fits and starts, cannot be denied, and their dark, moist, dirty dwellings, with the unseemly byre as a hall of entrance, are surely their own free choice rather than nature's doom. . .The most distressful feature of the poverty of these people is its demoralising influence. The flocks of sheep farmers are yearly thinned by the reckless hand of want, goaded on by approaching famine, and uncontrolled by the now nearly dissevered chains of feudal affection.[176]

As far as possible, attention was averted from the unpalatable sight of these distressing scenes. Unfortunately, as the century wore on this became increasingly difficult. The tiresome natives would intrude on the activities of the sportsmen. One such irritated sportsman, Charles Peel, Fellow of the Royal Geographical Society and of the Zoological Society, complained

> It is not conducive to sport to be followed by a gang of men and ordered out of the country, nor is it pleasant to be cursed in Gaelic by a crowd of irate old women, even if you do not understand every word they say. They accused us of shooting their horses and sheep, shouted to put up geese when we were stalking, cut up the canvas and broke the seats of our folding-boat, and tried in every possible way to spoil our sport. They were especially insolent and troublesome in Benbecula and Barra. Taking them as a whole, the crofters are an ignorant lot of creatures and the less said about them the better.[177]

Whatever was the British empire coming to, if it could not even deal with these ignorant peasants on the northwest fringe of the mother country?

Queen Victoria was to ask this distressing question not a few times as her ministers had to inform her, more than once, that it had been necessary to draft in extra police forces from Glasgow, or dispatch Marines or warships to the troubled Hebrides.

The Haven of Our Peace

The Royal Commission

O Thou who pervadest the heights,
Imprint on us Thy gracious blessing,
Carry us over the surface of the sea,
Carry us to the haven of our peace.[178]

BY ONE OF THOSE strange ironies of fate, the Marines dispatched to Skye in 1882 to quell the uprisings in the crofting communities landed at Uig. Uig is only a mile or two from the beach where Flora MacDonald and her strange 'Irish serving wench, Mistress Betty Burk' had landed in 1746, nearly one hundred and fifty years earlier, and slipped through the patrols of Hanoverian redcoats. Now again there was a military presence in the Hebrides. The Marines marched, drenched by November rain and buffeted by gales, across Skye by much the same route as the fugitive prince had taken. But they were come to quell not a revolt of a bygone royal house but disturbances among the common people, driven to extremity by the oppression of landlords.

It would take another volume larger than this to outline the many causes of unrest in the Islands. The Islanders were in ferment, and the imprisonment of their leaders, god-fearing men like John Macpherson and John MacLeod, did little to quell the so-called insurrection. The result was a long overdue Royal Commission, headed by Lord Napier, instructed to inquire into 'the condition of the crofters and cottars in the Highlands and Islands of Scotland'.

From May to August 1883, the Commission plied the seas, set on visiting all the centres of population in the Hebrides. They were delayed when their vessel, the H.M.S. *Lively*, sank in the Orkneys, though no lives were lost. As autumn storms came on, they turned to the Highlands on the mainland, travelling far and wide, on horseback and on foot, for the roads were abominable. They held public meetings and private interviews. They took testimony from 775 people, a few great and powerful, but many simple people,

249

Lord Napier, head of the Royal Commission into the condition of the crofters in the Highlands and Islands. Portrait by George Frederick Watts, 1866.

crofters and cottars, most of them Gaelic speakers whose words had to be translated. Some of the witnesses risked their livelihood to give testimony, for they had been threatened with eviction by the landlord's factors.

The evidence fills many hundreds of pages, and is a most important source book for conditions in the Highlands and Islands in the nineteenth century. It has some of the drama of a court room, as the distinguished gentlemen of the Commission, frock coated, well fed, with silver sideburns and soft white hands, cross-examined the witnesses. These came in shyly, in their Sunday-best homespun tweeds, ruddy faces washed and gleaming, beards trimmed, freshly laundered neck ties, polished boots on feet that were oftener bare. As the strangeness of the interview wore off, tongues loosened, and in the gentle sing-song of the Gaelic they told of ancient woes and present hardships, of burning injustices that were insupportable from their own chieftains, and doubly insupportable from the moneyed incomers who had bought the clan lands for a fortune. The Gaelic genius for narrative was given full play, with vivid retellings of forced evictions and the exploitation of the clearances. Hands scarred with toil at the *cas chrome* – the ancient spade of the isles – and the oar, now pounded the table to emphasize an argument, or gesticulated to drive home a point.

The tale they told was a bitter one. The clearances had all but destroyed their way of life. Nostalgically they recalled the old days, when crofting communities were bonded by ties of clan to the chiefs

Marines landing at Uig, Skye. They had been dispatched to quell the uprisings in the crofting communities against the tyranny of the landlords. From the *Illustrated London News*, 1884.

who were the fathers of their people. Then the communally held lands were farmed by the bailie (the crofting hamlet), with arable land allocated by the village elders according to the ancient run-rig system of tenure, and the grazing lands belonged to the whole community, whose members had time-honoured rights to graze certain quotas of beasts:

> Donald McQueen, catechist, said, 'I do not know exactly how old I am, but my age is more than ninety years at any rate. . .I remember that when I was young, it was the custom for the people to have sheep, horses, and cattle upon the hill, and to live in shielings.'
>
> The Chairman: 'From your recollection, do you think that the people in those days were better off and happier than they are now?'
>
> Answer: 'Is it not likely that they would be better off and more contented when they had cattle, sheep, and horses of their own in plenty, which they have not today?'[179]

In olden times, one of the witnesses at Tarbert in Harris recalled, when one of the MacLeods came home with his young wife the people were delighted to see him. Twenty young women went out and danced a reel before the present laird on his marriage. 'Before the year was out, these twenty women were weeping and wailing for their houses, which were unroofed, and their fires quenched. One hundred and fifty families were so treated at that time by order of the estate, and were scattered abroad.'

John Mac-pherson, one of the crofters' leaders, addressing a meeting in Skye. From the *Illustrated London News*, 1884.

The voyages of the Royal Commission, 1883.

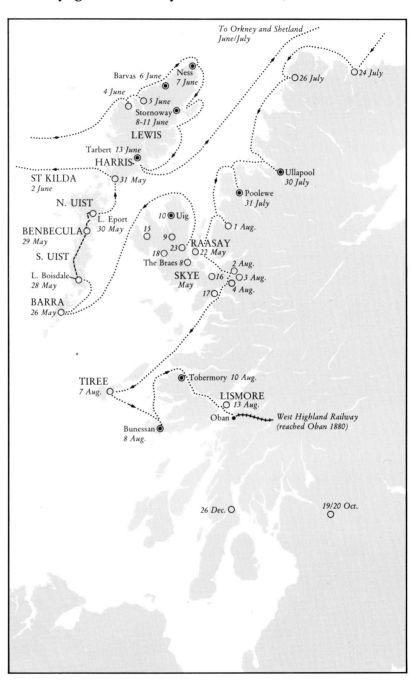

Places where
evidence was
taken ○

By sea ⋯⋯⋯⋯

Overland ‑‑‑‑‑‑‑‑

8 to 23 May:
Skye and Raasay

26 May to 13
July: Outer
Hebrides and St
Kilda

July: Orkney and
Shetland

24 July to 6
Aug.: Cape
Wrath to Arisaig

7 to 13 Aug.:
Inner Hebrides

4 Oct. to 24
Oct.: Caithness,
Sutherland, Ross,
Glasgow,
Edinburgh

To Orkney and Shetland
June/July

○ 24 July

○ 26 July

Barvas 6 June Ness
7 June
4 June
○ 5 June
Stornoway
8-11 June

LEWIS

Ullapool
30 July

Tarbert 13 June
HARRIS

Poolewe
31 July

ST KILDA
2 June   ○ 31 May

N. UIST

○ 1 Aug.

L. Eport
30 May   10 ◉ Uig

BENBECULA
29 May   15   9
○   ○   RAASAY
18○   23○ ◉ 22 May
S. UIST   The Braes 8○
2 Aug.

L. Boisdale   SKYE ○ 16 ○ 3 Aug.
28 May   May   ◉ 4 Aug.
17○
BARRA
26 May ○

TIREE
7 Aug. ○   ◉ Tobermory 10 Aug.

LISMORE
○ 13 Aug.
Oban West Highland Railway
(reached Oban 1880)

Bunessan ◉
8 Aug.

26 Dec. ○   19/20 Oct.
○

252

Many felt the cruel comparison between their loyal service to their laird, or to the crown, and the bitter fate which had befallen them, driven from their clan lands, their homesteads, fields and landmarks, harried, evicted, crowded onto unprofitable land:

Alex. Mackaskill, cottar and boatman, Isle of Soa, said, 'My great grandfather served with the army. My grandfather was forced to go to the army, and his bones are bleaching in a West India island. My father was in the militia. . .and now I am on a rocky island that is not fit to be inhabited. . .At first the agreement was that we were to have four milk goats, a cow, and ten sheep. The farmer by degrees reduced the number of our cows. He did not reduce the rent a farthing. There are twenty-three families on the island. The crofts are on bogs and rocks. . .'
    John McCrae, 35, cottar and fisherman, Soa, said, 'I agree. . .I could not put down potatoes or oats this year, because the ground was so soft. . .My present house is built on the seashore, and the tide rises to it every stormy night that comes. I have to watch and put out all my furniture, such as it is. A sister of mine. . .died as a consequence. . .The ground is so soft. . .I have had to pave a way with stones for my cow to get up the hill. . .
    'I just manage to keep soul and body together. I was forty years roaming at sea, and my reason for staying on the island was just to keep my aged parents out of the poorhouse.'[180]

At Locheport, in North Uist, the crofters told how 'repeated evictions from other districts were the cause of many townships being overcrowded'. Once they had lived 'in ease and plenty', but now their fertile lands had been taken over by the big landowners, and were given over to sheep rearing, with the crofters hemmed into a miserable infertile strip of land. The hardships to which they were exposed, the interpreter told the Commission,

were beyond description. The houses were knocked down about their ears, and they got no compensation for anything on the ground. They got no assistance in building their new houses. It was towards the end of the year, in winter, that they were building their temporary houses.
    The severities of the winter, living in rude turf huts, and without fuel, except what they had to carry twelve miles, told on the health of many. The inferiority of the soil they now lived on, and its unsuitableness for human existence, was indescribable. . .The ground was of such a nature that it could scarcely be improved, and the soil was so much reduced by continual

253

cropping that it was almost useless. The place too was over-crowded, there being thirty crofts, on which forty families lived, where formerly there were only three.

The common pasture. . .was extremely bad, so much so, that in winter those of the people who had cattle, had to keep constant watch, else they would stick in the bogs. Human beings could not travel over portions of their crofts in winter. The people were at present in poverty, and suffering privations. . .

It was the same story wherever the Commissioners took evidence. A crofter from Milovaig said:

We have very miserable dwellings, and never get aid to build better. They are thatched with straw, and our crofts do not produce the amount of straw necessary for fodder and thatch for our houses, and we are prohibited from cutting rushes and pulling heather. The condition of our dwelling-houses in rainy weather is most deplorable. Above our beds comes down pattering rain, rendered dirty and black by soot in the ceiling above. . .

Dr Fraser of Edinbane in Skye was asked:

'Are you aware of any cases of disease which can be distinctly traced to the habits and food of the people?'
Answer: 'I have seen a good deal of scrofulous disease [tubercular glands], a good deal of lung disease, and a large proportion of eye disease, due to the houses, feeding, and want of clothing. I think the diet of the people much too limited, even in a good year—potatoes, fish, and meal.'[181]

Many crofters had been evicted to make way for deer forest for the sport of the landlords:

'There were four townships cleared thirteen years ago to make room for the deer, and a large number of those evicted were brought down to our village. . .We cannot keep strange sheep off our grazings, because our herd is not allowed to keep a dog.'
Another witness: 'In our township we are very much troubled by deer. I had a dog to protect my crop, but a game keeper, named Robert McGregor, came down to my lot and shot it in the presence of my wife and myself. I complained to the [Procurator] Fiscal about it.'
'Did he prosecute the case?'
'The answer I got from the Fiscal was that the factor was saying we had no right to keep a dog. Nothing was done in the case. We have been making complaints for years about the deer. When we

complained to the factor, he said that if we were not satisfied we could throw our place up. . .'

'What do you do when deer come on your arable land?'

'We have to watch them at night.'

'Did anyone ever kill a deer that came on his arable land?'

'We dare not.'

'What would happen to you if you did?'

'We would be evicted.'

Evicted. That was the grim word that struck terror in the hearts of the crofters and cottars.

John Macfie, 74, crofter, Harlosh [near Dunvegan, Skye], said, 'The people began to fall in arrears when the kelp industry ceased. In 1840 there were seventeen families removed from Feorlick by Mr Gibbon, the tacksman. . .They were placed, some by the sea and some on peat land which had never been cultivated. Some of them did not get a place on earth on which to put a foot. I myself saw them living under a sail, spread on three poles, below the high-water mark. One of the crofters—Donald Campbell—was warned by the ground officer for giving refuge to a poor man who had no house. The ground officer came and pulled down the house, and took a pail of water and threw it on the fire. . .The wife went out of her senses. . .I never saw one who was so mad. When Campbell was put out of his house, not a tenant was allowed to give him shelter. He had nine of a family, and they had to remain on the hillside on a wet night.'[182]

A Highland deerstalker, one of the few natives not considered a nuisance by the sportsmen of Victorian England. Photograph from the Hill Adamson Collection.

In their Report, Lord Napier and his fellow Commissioners analysed the causes of unrest, in particular the inequities of land tenure, the insecurity of the crofter and cottar, the callous injustices of the system, and the threats to a traditional way of life. The Commission's conclusions, though diplomatically couched, were remarkably sympathetic to the crofters. In an age which considered the rights of property to be sacrosanct, and government intervention unwarranted, the Commissioners argued cautiously for far-reaching changes in land tenure, a more interventionist approach from central government, and the building of roads, piers, schools, and, on the mainland, railways. The condition of the Highlanders and Islanders, said the Commissioners, was 'precarious and dangerous'. Unrest would continue unless radical changes were made.

The Report of the Royal Commission led in due course to legislation which laid the foundations for today's crofting communities. It was a remarkable, if belated, triumph for human rights and parliamentary democracy.

This is not to say that all the problems of the Highlands and Islands were solved by the Crofting Acts. Many remain to this day. Some perhaps are insoluble, and that wished-for haven of peace may be unobtainable. But the 1884 Royal Commission Report marked a turning point in the fortunes of the Island communities; the worst storms were over, and the cruellest of the clearances were ended. There still remains the insidious depopulation and breakup of communities brought about by poverty and unemployment, but no longer does the factor burn thatches over the heads of crofting families.

The Highland clearances have much in common with events in the Third World today: the pauperization of peasant communities; the treatment of a racial minority as sub-human; the destruction of old systems of communal land tenure; the dislocation of family and tribal life; the callous disregard of cultural traditions.

Alexander Carmichael, the great collector of Gaelic poetry and songs who compiled the appendix of the Royal Commission's report.

It was only after long delays, and as a result of serious unrest in the Highlands and Islands, and campaigns in the press, that the Napier Commission had been appointed in 1883 by Gladstone's government. It was, in its time, a bold step: a Royal Commission charged to investigate the malpractices of the landowners – members of the British ruling classes – and the injustices of the economic and social system. The findings were unpalatable; but they were published. Legislation followed, and it was legislation that protected the poor against the greed of the great. But there was no retributive justice, nor court proceedings against exploitative proprietors.

The Report of the Royal Commission, with its massive evidence and extensive press coverage, laid bare the Hebrides to the gaze of the nation as never before. Now, surely, they were mapped and researched, explored and exposed, reported and documented. But can the life of such communities be captured on paper in words of English?

One of the most interesting parts of the Report is Appendix A, written by a local excise man, Alexander Carmichael of Lismore. As we have seen in these pages, in time he was to become one of the greatest early collectors of oral literature, particularly of the folk poetry, of the Hebrides. (John Campbell of Islay, with whom he collaborated, was the foremost collector of folk tales.)

256

In his appendix to the Report, Carmichael describes in careful and loving detail the customs and traditions of a people whose way of life was based on ancient communal systems of land tenure and agriculture, communities sustained by custom and folklore and tradition, a people 'peaceable and gentle, and eminently well-mannered and polite', a people poor in worldly goods, but with a cultural heritage of remarkable beauty, not in stone or the visual arts, not in books nor in precious stones, but in spirit, in the spoken word, and in music.

And, at the request of Lord Napier, he offered the evidence. In few official reports does one expect to find a love song with so exquisite an opening image as one of the poems Carmichael quotes:

Mar chirein nan stuagh uaine, ta mo ghoal. . .

To the white crest of the green wave, I liken my love. . .[183]

Here was a society in which all labour was accompanied by songs, hymns and runes, many of great antiquity and beauty, combining magic and folklore elements with a faith both simple yet profound which dated back to St Columba in the sixth century. Here, for example, is a parting blessing that used to be sung by the old people in South Uist when sending their cattle away to the pasture in the morning:

Siubhal beinne, suibhal baile. . .

Travel ye moorland, travel ye townland,

The protection of God and of Columba,
Encompass your going and coming;
And about you be the milkmaid of the smooth white palms,
Bridget of the clustering hair, golden brown![184]

Song supported and ritualized the communal traditions, flexible but sustaining, which governed every aspect of life.

Winter was the hardest time of the year, but life was enlivened by the social gatherings – the ceilidhs – when songs were sung, tales told, jokes shared, riddles posed, experience passed on, traditions strengthened, and the life of the community renewed.

With the spring came new life, symbolized in the coming of the migratory birds. 'The people of St Kilda', Carmichael tells us, 'used to sing a joyous song on the arrival of their birds.' The song begins

Bui 'cheas dha 'n Ti. . .

Planting potatoes in Skye with the cashrom, the primitive hand plough. This photograph was taken in Skye in the late nineteenth century.

Thanks be to the Being, the Gannets have come,
Yes! and the Great Auk along with them.
Dark haired girl!—a cow in the fold!
Brown cow! brown cow! brown cow, beloved ho!
Brown cow! my love! the milker of milk to thee!
Ho ro! my fair skinned girl—a cow in the fold,
And the birds have come!—glad sight, I see.[185]

In the summer, leaving the men to tend the crops, the women and girls travelled up into the bracing mountains with their herds, where their cattle grazed the sweet grass of the summer shielings:

Grianan-aluinn aona chrainn...

A lovely summer shieling of one tree
Behind the wind, in front of the sun,
Where we could see the world all,
But where no man could see us.[186]

Here the milk turned into butter and cheeses, to be taken back for consumption in the winter. Now, mourned Carmichael, gazing from such a shieling, 'The smoke of the whole people...ascends through the chimney of a single shepherd.'

258

Was this society doomed? Would the dispersal of the people empty the land?

Cha till, cha till, cha till mi tuille!
I return, I return, I return never more![187]

Could so frail a flame as an oral culture, an ancient way of life based on tradition and custom, survive the black night of the clearances, to glow again in the dawn?

Carmichael tells how each night of old, the good wife smoored the fire – banking up the pear, covering it with turf, so that the ashes would smoulder through the night, ready for the morning. And with this action went a prayer:

Tha mi smaladh an teine. . .

I smoor the fire
As it is smoored by the Son of Mary.
Blest be the house, blest be the fire,
And blessed be the people all.
Who are those on the floor? Peter and Paul.
Upon whom devolves the watching this night?
Upon fair gentle Mary and her Son.
The mouth of God said, the angel of God tells.
An angel in the door of every house,
To shield and protect us all,
Till bright day-light comes in the morning.[188]

Some kindly spirits watched over the Island communities, burned the flames never so low. For, remarkably, the Island way of life today – a century later – still survives: remote, mysterious, curiously resilient. The Gaelic is still spoken, song comes naturally, man is still pitted against wind and rain, cruel sea and harsh land.

Yes, bread comes in sliced white loaves from the mainland. Television carries familiar images of city life into the living rooms of the remotest crofts. Battered cars rust by white beaches or are toppled over cliffs into the wild sea.

But the twentieth century suffers a sea change when it reaches the Isles. The pace changes. 'In Spanish,' said one visitor to an Islander, 'they have a word they use when they do not want to do something immediately – *manyana*, they say, tomorrow. Is there such a word in the Gaelic?' 'Nay, we dinna ha' sich a worrd,' replied the Islander, 'I am thinking, we dinna feel that degrree of urrgency.'

In an area where unemployment is higher than anywhere else in

Scotland, Island crofting communities have organized themselves into cooperatives to purchase goods and sell produce; their success owes not a little to communal traditions that date back a thousand years or more. On the hills in early summer men and boys gather to round up their flocks for shearing, hardy sheepdogs at their heels. Whole neighbourhoods turn out to cut the peat for winter fuel – backbreaking labour. And the peats for the community's old folk are freely given. The village children round up the kine. Cows lumber gently across the machair returning home for milking time. The cooperative's tractor crosses the white beaches to collect storm-blown seaware to enrich the village in-fields. Here potatoes and tiny fields of barley grow in patchwork plots recalling the run-rig system of agriculture. Reapers swing the scythe and keep rhythm to melodies generations old.

The old black house, with its massive stone walls, slit windows and heavy thatch, is now a byre, and the crofter stands proudly by his modern home. 'I was born in that black house,' he tells you. A woman stands in the door of her croft, changes from the Gaelic to English to greet you as you pass. 'It's a fine day, only a wee bit o' fine drissle, I am thinking.'

The Islanders' powerful modern trawlers, bought with substantial loans from the Highlands and Islands Development Board, ride at anchor in a remote and seemingly isolated anchorage, where once the birlinn of the chief moored. These seafarers are direct descendants of the Vikings who once ruled the Hebrides, of the Gaels who sailed their galleys along the western seaboard of Europe. The skipper trawls his nets in the fishing grounds off Norway and Iceland, the Faroes, Rockall and St Kilda as his forefathers did. Of such voyages might the clan bards like Alexander MacDonald have sung.

The fisherman comes home from the sea, the garage mechanic is back from Glasgow, the 'lad o' pairts', now a university professor, is returned from Edinburgh or Dunedin in New Zealand or Nova Scotia – and spontaneously, they gather for a ceilidh. The fiddle is bowed, Highland fashion, feet tap, the glass is raised, someone begins to dance. As the night draws on, they turn to tales of days gone by, and music flows. A woman takes up a folk song, a melody her grandmother knew. She sings, sweet and true, traditional words, but may add her own, adapting, extemporizing, within the time-honoured idiom, just as she uses recipes handed down from

260

The interior of a crofter's house, c. 1889.

her grandmother. Other voices join in the chorus. The past is reinterpreted in the present, old verities restated in modern form. Two and a half centuries separate us from the Hebridean adventure of the Stuart prince. In 1745 the Hebrides were the most remote, inaccessible part of the British Isles. Now, undeniably, the Hebrides have been discovered.

Yet in another sense they remain inaccessible and enigmatic. For two centuries the Hebrides were explored and exploited, romanticized and sentimentalized, depopulated and neglected. Protected by their Gaelic language and culture, their history and their traditions, the Islanders resisted absorption by the Sassenachs, the Lowland Scots and the English. They remain an island people, a people set apart. Ultimately perhaps they defy discovery.

References and Bibliography

Readers wishing to know more about individual voyagers should consult the *Dictionary of National Biography*.

Most of the books I consulted in writing this book were first editions, to be found in major national libraries. Happily, in recent years, facsimile editions and reprints have begun to appear, and these are indicated below, together with other books of interest.

CHAPTER 1: Antient Customs: the Hebrides before the '45

1　Martin Martin, *A Description of the Western Highlands of Scotland* (London, 1703, 2nd [enlarged] edition 1716). Facsimile reprint of 1716 edition (Edinburgh: James Thin, 1976).

2　Samuel Johnson, *A Journey to the Western Islands of Scotland* (London: T. Cadell, 1775).

3-10　Martin, op. cit.
　　See also:
　　Kenneth Macauley, *The History of St Kilda* (1764). Facsimile reprint (Edinburgh: James Thin, 1976). A Presbyterian minister's visit to the remote islands forming the St Kilda group.

CHAPTER 2: Over the Sea to Skye

　　Bishop Forbes, *The Lyon in Mourning, or a collection of speeches letters journals etc. relative to the affairs of Prince Charles Edward Stuart by the Rev Robert Forbes, AM Bishop of Ross and Caithness* (1746-1775; Ms in National Library of Scotland) (Edinburgh, 1895). Reprint (Edinburgh: Scottish Academic Press, 3 vols., 1975).

11-13　Donald MacLeod, as reported by Forbes, op. cit.

14, 15　Alexander MacDonald (Alasdair MacMhaighstir Alasdair), as reported by Forbes, op. cit.

16-19　Flora MacDonald, as reported by Forbes, op. cit.

20　Donald MacLeod, as reported by Forbes, op. cit.

See also:
John S. Gibson, *Ships of the '45: the rescue of the Young Pretender* (London: 1967). Illustrated.

CHAPTER 3: The Birlinn of Clanranald

21　Forbes, op. cit.

22　Martin, op. cit.

23　Alaisdair MacMhaighstir Alasdair (Alexander MacDonald), *Birlinn Chlann-Raghnaill*. Trans. Hugh MacDiarmid, *Complete Poems 1920-1976*, ed. Michael Grieve and W.R. Aitken (London: Martin Brian and O'Keeffe, 1978).
　　See also:
　　A. and A. MacDonald (eds.), *The Poems of Alexander MacDonald* (Inverness: 1924). The most complete collection of MacDonald's poems, with Gaelic text and translation.

　　J.L. Campbell, *Canna, the Story of a Hebridean Island* (Oxford: Oxford University Press, 1985). Illustrated. Alexander MacDonald was baillie of Canna. Dr Campbell, one of the foremost authorities on the Hebrides, sets the story of Canna in a wide historical context. A work of love and scholarship.

CHAPTER 4: The Charting of the Seas

24　Murdoch Mackenzie, Charts (1775-76), and *A Nautical Description* (1776).

25　Quoted by G. Chalmers in *Caledonia* (London: 1807), Vol. II, p. 60, from letter dated at Newcastle, 29 December 1745.

26　Murdoch Mackenzie, *A Treatise on Maratim Surveying* (1774).

27　John Clerk of Eldin, *Justification of Mr Murdoch M'Kenzie's Nautical Survey of the Orkney Islands and Hebrides, in answer to accusations of Dr Anderson* (Edinburgh: 1785).

28　*West Coast of Scotland Pilot* (London: Admiralty, 1974).

29　Mackenzie, *A Nautical Description*.

See also (for the nautically minded):
John McLintock, *West Coast Cruising* (London & Glasgow: Blackie & Son, 1938). Illustrated.

Craig Mair, *A Star for Seamen: The Stevenson Family of Engineers* (Frome & London: Butler & Tanner, 1978). Illustrated. The story of the building of the lighthouses around Scotland's coasts, beginning in the mid-eighteenth century.

Clyde Cruising Club, *Sailing Directions* (Glasgow: Clyde Cruising Club Publications, SV Carrick, Clyde Street, Glasgow G1 4LN): Vol. I, The Clyde (1985); Vol. II, Mull of Kintyre to Ardnamurchan (1981); Vol. III, Ardnamurchan to Cape Wrath (1984); Vol. IV, The Outer Hebrides (1979). Illustrated with plans of anchorages. Vol. II includes plans by the present author.

CHAPTER 5: A Voyage to the Hebrides

30-43   Thomas Pennant, *A Tour of Scotland and a Voyage to the Hebrides; MDCCXII [1772]* (London: Benj. White, 1773, 1790). Vol. I, *A Tour of Scotland*, has been reprinted (Edinburgh: James Thin, 1979). Illustrated. Vol. II, *The Voyage to the Hebrides*, has not been reprinted.

CHAPTER 6: That Cathedral of the Seas

44   Joseph Banks, article in the *Scots Magazine* (1772).

45   Joseph Banks, as quoted by Pennant, op. cit.

46, 47   James MacPhearson, introduction to 2nd edition, *Fingal, an Epic Poem* (1760).

48   James MacPhearson, *Fingal, an Epic Poem* (1752), Book IV.

49   Walter Scott, review in the *Edinburgh Review* of the *Report of the Committee of the West Highland Society of Scotland into the nature and authenticity of the poems of Ossian* (Edinburgh: 1805).
See also:
David Jenkins and Mark Vicocchi, *Mendelssohn in Scotland* (London:

Elm Tree Books, 1978). Based on Mendelssohn's own journals, letters and sketches, and including his visit to Fingal's Cave.

CHAPTER 7: A-roving in the Hebrides

50   Johnson, op. cit.

51   James Boswell, *The Journal of a Tour of the Hebrides, with Samuel Johnson, LL.D.* (London: Charles Dilly, 1785).

52   Johnson, op. cit.

53   Boswell, op. cit.

54   Johnson, op. cit.

55   Boswell, op. cit.

56-8   Johnson, op. cit.

59   Boswell, op. cit.

60, 61   Johnson, op. cit.

62, 63   Boswell, op. cit.

64   Johnson, op. cit.

65   Boswell, op. cit. (extended quotation)

66   Johnson, op. cit.

67   Boswell, op. cit.

68   Johnson, op. cit.

69   Boswell, op. cit.

70   Johnson, op. cit.

71   Boswell, op. cit.

72   Johnson, op. cit.
Johnson's *Journey* and Boswell's *Journal* are available in numerous modern editions, often bound together in a single volume.

CHAPTER 8: The Sailing of the White-sailed Ships

73, 74   Boswell, op. cit.

75   Oath prescribed by the Disarming Act, 1746.

76   *Report of the Commissioners of Inquiry into the Condition of the Crofters and Cottars in the Highlands and Islands of Scotland* (the Napier Commission) (London: 1884).

77-81   Alexander MacKenzie, *The History of the Highland Clearances* (Inverness: 1883).

82   Anon., attributed to John Galt, c. 1820.
See also:
John Prebble, *The Highland Clearances* (London: Secker & Warburg, 1963; Harmondsworth: Penguin in association with Secker &

Warburg, 1969, 1982). Illustrated. The best modern account of the clearances.

CHAPTER 9: The Silver Darlings
83-94   John Knox, *Tour of the Highlands of Scotland and the Hebride Isles, A Report to the British Society for Extending the Fisheries, 1786* (London: 1786). Facsimile reprint (Edinburgh: James Thin, 1970).

CHAPTER 10: The Wandering Shepherd
95   From the Gaelic of Angus MacMhuirich, as quoted in J. Prebble, op. cit. See also Samuel Maclean, 'The Poetry of the Clearances', in *Transactions of the Gaelic Society*, Vol. XXXVII.
96-109   James Hogg, Letters printed in the *Scots Magazine*, 1805. Reprinted as *Highland Tours*, ed. William F. Laughlin (Hawick: Byways Books, 1981).
110   Sir Alexander Geikie, *Scotish Reminiscences* (Glasgow: 1904).

CHAPTER 11: The Solitary Reaper
111   William Wordsworth, 'The Solitary Reaper', in *Poems in Two Volumes* (1807).
112   Sarah Murray, *A Companion and Useful Guide to the Beauties of Scotland*, 2nd (enlarged) edition (London: 1804).
113   Alexander Carmichael, *Carmina Gadelica* (Edinburgh: Oliver & Boyd, 1900-1954): Vols. I & II, 1900, 2nd edition 1928, ed. Mrs E.C.C. Watson (Carmichael's daughter); Vols. III, IV, 1940, 1941, ed. Prof. James Carmichael Watson; Vol. V, 1954, ed. Prof. Angus Matheson; Vol. VI, notes. Reprint (Edinburgh: Scottish Academic Press, Vol. 1 1984, Vol. II 1984. Vol. III 1940, Vol. IV 1978, Vol. V 1986, Vol. VI 1971). The earliest authoritative collection of many Gaelic texts, with sensitive translations and copious notes. Only two volumes were published in Carmichael's lifetime. A short collection of hymns, charms and prayers from *Carmina Gadelica* is

available in paperback under the title *The Sun Dances: prayers and blessings from the Gaelic* (London: Christian Community Press; Edinburgh, Floris Books, 1977).
114   Anon., trans. Deórsa Caimbeul Hay, *Fuáran Sleibh* (Glasgow: William Maclellan, 1947), as quoted in Derick Thomson, *An Introduction to Gaelic Poetry* (London: Victor Gollancz, 1977).
115   Aonaghus Iain MacDhomhnuill, in Donald A. Fergusson (ed.), *From the Farthest Hebrides* (Toronto: Macmillan of Canada, 1978). Illustrated. A delightful and elegant book with words and music gathered from Hebridean settlers in Canada and elsewhere.
116   Alexander Carmichael, introduction to *Carmina Gadelica*, Vols. I & II (1900).
117, 118   Fergusson, op. cit.
119, 120   Anon., in J.L. Campbell and F. Collinson (eds.), *Hebridean Folksongs*, 3 vols. (Oxford: Oxford University Press, 1969, 1977, 1981). This collection of words and music is by an outstanding pair of scholars. The songs were collected in this century, mainly from people living in the Outer Hebrides.
121, 122   Anon., in Margaret Fay Shaw, *Folksongs and Folklore of South Uist* (London: Routledge & Kegan Paul, 1955; Oxford: Oxford University Press, 1977). Illustrated. Gaelic folktales, proverbs and songs (words and music) with translations, collected in the 1930s by Margaret Fay Shaw, a young music student who subsequently became the wife of Dr J.L. Campbell (see above).
123, 124   Rachel MacDonald, in Fergusson, op. cit.
125, 126   Anon., in Carmichael, op. cit.
See also:
Francis Collinson, *The Traditional and National Music of Scotland* (London, 1966). Records from Tangent Records, 176a Holland Road, London W14 8AH.

Derick Thomson, *An Introduction to Gaelic Poetry* (London: Victor Gollancz, 1974, reprint 1977). Prof. Thomson, a Gaelic speaker and poet, provides a sympathetic and readable introduction for English readers to the rich and varied oral and written literature of the Isles.

I.F. Grant, *Hebridean Folk Ways* (London: Routledge & Kegan Paul, 1961, reprints 1975, 1977). Illustrated. An interesting, well-documented account of the Hebridean way of life.

Further information: Folklore Institute of Scotland.

CHAPTER 12: The Beauties of Scotland

127-137   Murray, op. cit. Mrs Murray's *Companion* has been reprinted in paperback, ed. William F. Laughlin (Hawick: Byways Press, 1982). Modernized spelling. Illustrated.
138   *Monthly Review* (London), 1804.
139   Clyde Cruising Club, *Sailing Directions, Mull of Kintyre to Ardnamurchan* (Glasgow: 1981).

CHAPTER 13: Caledonia Stern and Wild

140   Walter Scott, Journal, quoted in notes to *The Lord of the Isles* (1814). Subsequently printed in J.G. Lockhart, *Memoirs of the Life of Sir Walter Scott, Bart.* (1837-38). Scott's journal of his circumnavigation of Scotland has been reprinted in paperback, ed. William F. Laughlin, under the title *Northern Lights* (Hawick: Byways Books, 1982). Illustrated.
141   Johnson, op. cit.
142   Walter Scott, *The Lay of the Last Minstrel* (1805).
143   Lord Cockburn, *Memorials of his Time* (Edinburgh: 1856).
144-146   Walter Scott, *Waverly, or, 'Tis sixty years since*, 3 vols. (Edinburgh: 1814). Available in numerous modern editions.
147   Robert Burns, 'A Red Red Rose', in *Selection of Songs*, ii (1794).
148   Walter Scott, quoted in Alexander MacKenzie, op. cit.

CHAPTER 14: The Devil's Engine

149-154   Lumsden (pub.). *The Steam Boat Companion and Stranger's Guide to the Western Islands and Highlands of Scotland* (Glasgow: Lumsden, 1820).
155   William Harriston, *The Steam-Boat Traveller's Remembrancer* (1824).

CHAPTER 15: The Cruise of the *Betsey*

156-163   Hugh Miller, *The Cruise of the* Betsey (1856)
164,165   Carmichael, introduction to *Carmina Gadelica*, op. cit.
          See also:
          George Rosie, *Hugh Miller: Outrage and Order: a biography and selected writings* (Edinburgh: Mainstream Pubishing, 1981). Illustrated. A modern biographical essay, introducing short extracts from Hugh Miller's writing.

CHAPTER 16: A Bhan Righ: the Fair Queen

166   *Illustrated London News*, 1847.
167   Queen Victoria, *Leaves from the Journal of our Life in the Highlands* (London: 1868).
168-170   *Illustrated London News*, 1847.
171, 172 *The Times* correspondent, quoted in the *Illustrated London News*, 1847.
173   Queen Victoria, op. cit.
174   Hector Rose Mackenzie, *Electioneering in the Western Isles* (Privately printed, c. 1880).
175   Alexander Shand, in *The Times*, 1883.
176   James Wilson, *A Voyage round the Coasts of Scotland and the Isles* (Edinburgh: Adam & Charles Black, 1842).
177   Charles Peel, *Wild Sport in the Outer Hebrides* (c. 1880).

CHAPTER 17: The Haven of our Peace

178   Anon., in Carmichael, op. cit., Vol. I.
179-182   *Report of the Commissioners of Inquiry into the Condition of the Crofters and Cottars in the Highlands and Islands of Scotland* (the Napier Commission) (London: 1884).
183-188   Appendix A of above.

FURTHER READING

W.H. Murray, *The Islands of Western Scotland: The Inner and Outer Hebrides* (London: Eyre Methuen, 1973). Illustrated. The most reliable introduction for the general reader to the Hebrides, covering the geology, natural history, prehistory and history of the Isles.

J. Fraser Darling and J. Morton, *The Highlands and Islands* (London: Collins, 1947; Fontana New Naturalist, 1964, 1969). Illustrated. A modern classic, introducing the amateur naturalist to the flora and fauna of the Western Isles.

W.C. Mackenzie, *History of the Outer Hebrides*, facsimile reprint of 1903 edition (Edinburgh: James Thin, 1970). The earliest attempt at a serious history of the Hebrides. Anecdotal and rather unreliable.

Popular histories of Scotland concentrate on mainland issues, and touch on the Hebrides only in passing. The most readable recent histories include:

Fitzroy Maclean, *A Concise History of Scotland* (London: Thames & Hudson, 1970, 1974). Illustrated.

Tom Steel, *Scotland's Story: a new perspective* (London: Collins in association with Channel 4, 1985). Illustrated.

For the serious historian:

Gordon Donaldson (general ed.) *The Edinburgh History of Scotland* (Edinburgh: Oliver & Boyd, 1965-75). The most authoritative and scholarly history of Scotland. Vol. I, *Scotland: The Making of the Kingdom* (to 1057), ed. A.M. Duncan; Vol. II, *Scotland: The Later Middle Ages* (1057-1603), ed. Ranald Nicholson; Vol. III, *Scotland: James V to James VIII* (1501-1699), ed. George Donaldson; Vol. IV, *Scotland: 1689 to the Present*, ed. William Ferguson.

Illustration Acknowledgements

The Publishers would like to thank the following for giving their permission to reproduce the illustrations on the pages listed below.

Aberdeen University Library: 178, 258
BBC Hulton Picture Library: 102 (bottom), 108
Elizabeth Bray: 18, 76, 81, 85, 90, 91, 166, 170, 175, 215, back cover
Ian Crofton: frontispiece
John Dewar & Sons Ltd., Scotch Whisky Distillers: 220 (bottom)
Glasgow Art Gallery and Museum, Kelvingrove: front cover, 102 (top), 136 (top), 218-219, 237, 247
Calum MacKenzie: 86, 92, 94 (both), 95
Mansell Collection: 31, 39, 207
Mitchell Library, Glasgow: endpapers, 9, 38, 46, 62, 72, 78, 101 (both), 120, 123, 126, 129, 135, 138, 139, 143, 152, 184, 198, 201, 229, 240, 241, 250 (bottom), 251, 256

National Galleries of Scotland: 20, 22, 32, 33, 52, 93, 121, 136 (bottom), 142, 149, 190, 195, 206, 217, 220 (top), 224, 250 (top), 255
National Library of Scotland: 67, 110, 111, 114, 135 (bottom r and l), 234
National Maritime Museum: 60, 64, 245
National Portrait Gallery: 89, 163, 194
National Trust for Scotland: 25
Patrick Allan-Fraser of Hospitalfield Trust, Arbroath: 51 (photographed by Iain Wight)
Popperfoto: 96
Reproduced by gracious permission of Her Majesty the Queen: 50-51, 242
Royal Commission on the Ancient and Historical Monuments of Scotland: 56
School of Scottish Studies, University of Edinburgh: 261
Science Museum, London: 210
Scottish National Museum of Antiquities: 12
Trinity College Library, Dublin: 49
University Library, Cambridge: 63, 66, 145, 191
Victoria and Albert Museum: 157

Index